"From mashups to fan fiction, the digital age has been a wellspring of creativity that builds on copyrighted works. Drawing on insights from cognitive psychology and creativity studies, Omri Rachum-Twaig articulates a provocative new theory for understanding the rationale for, proper scope of, and remedial framework for copyright law's right to prepare derivative works. Such fundamental rethinking of how society can best promote cumulative creativity deserves serious attention."

–Professor Peter S. Menell
Koret Professor of Law and Director, Berkeley Center for Law & Technology
University of California at Berkeley School of Law

"*Copyright Law and Derivative Works* offers a novel account of the nature, justification and scope of the derivative work right in copyright law in light of insights about the essence of creativity culled from cognitive psychology and genre theory, thus richly evoking the variegated junctures between critical analysis of copyright doctrine, creativity theory, and the relation between extra-legal theory and specifically legal theory and practice. Worthwhile reading for anyone engaged with copyright law, its justification, and its place and role in broader social and theoretical concerns."

–Abraham Drassinower
Professor and Chair in the Legal, Ethical and Cultural Implications of Technological Innovation
University of Toronto Faculty of Law

Copyright Law and Derivative Works

Copyright law regulates creativity. It affects the way people create works of authorship *ex-ante* and affects the status of works of authorship significantly *ex-post*. But does copyright law really understand creativity? Should legal theories alone inform our regulation of the creative process?

This book views copyright law as a law of creativity. It asks whether copyright law understands authorship as other creativity studies fields do. It considers whether copyright law should incorporate non-legal theories, and if so, how it should be adjusted in their light. For this purpose, the book focuses on one of the many rights that copyright law regulates – the right to make a derivative work. A work is considered derivative when it is based on one or more preexisting works. Today, the owner of a work of authorship has the exclusive right to make derivative works based on her original work or to allow others to do so. The book suggests a new way to think about both the right, the tension, and copyright law at large. It proposes relying on non-legal fields like cognitive psychology and genre theories, and offers new legal-theoretical justifications for the right to make derivative works.

As the first book to consider the intersection between copyright law, creativity, and derivative works, this will be a valuable resource for students, scholars, and practitioners interested in intellectual property and copyright law.

Omri Rachum-Twaig is adjunct professor of law at the Faculty of Law, Tel Aviv University, Israel. He teaches and writes about copyright, cyber and information law, artificial intelligence and emerging technologies. He has published on all these matters in leading law reviews and journals, has won several academic awards and prizes, and his work is frequently cited in scholarly work and courts, including the Supreme Court of Israel.

Routledge Research in Intellectual Property

Intellectual Property and Traditional Knowledge in the Global Economy
Translating Geographical Indications for Development
Teshager W. Dagne

The Object of Copyright
A Conceptual History of Originals and Copies in Literature, Art and Design
Stina Teilmann-Lock

Well-Known Trade Marks
A Comparative Study of Japan and the EU
Hiroko Onishi

Contemporary Issues in Pharmaceutical Patent Law
Setting the Framework and Exploring Policy Options
Bryan Mercurio and Daria Kim

Intellectual Property, Finance and Corporate Governance
Janice Denoncourt

Protecting Intellectual Property in the Arabian Peninsula
The GCC States, Jordan and Yemen
David Price and Alhanoof AlDebasi

Biodiversity, Genetic Resources and Intellectual Property
Developments in Access and Benefit Sharing
Charles Lawson and Kamalesh Adhikari

Pharmaceutical Patent Protection and World Trade Law
The Unresolved Problem of Access to Medicines
Jae Sundaram

Patent Pools, Competition Law and Biotechnology
Devdatta Malshe

Copyright Law and Derivative Works
Regulating Creativity
Omri Rachum-Twaig

Copyright Law and Derivative Works

Regulating Creativity

Omri Rachum-Twaig

Routledge
Taylor & Francis Group
LONDON AND NEW YORK

First published 2019
by Routledge
2 Park Square, Milton Park, Abingdon, Oxon OX14 4RN

and by Routledge
52 Vanderbilt Avenue, New York, NY 10017

First issued in paperback 2020

Routledge is an imprint of the Taylor & Francis Group, an informa business

British Library Cataloguing in Publication Data
A catalogue record for this book is available from the British Library

Library of Congress Cataloging-in-Publication Data
A catalog record has been requested for this book

ISBN 13: 978-0-367-58350-7 (pbk)
ISBN 13: 978-1-138-34327-6 (hbk)

Typeset in Galliard
by Taylor & Francis Books

To my dear parents, Tamar and Sami,
To my loved Danielle,
And to our baby girl

Contents

Illustrations

Figure

Table

Acknowledgements

I owe profound gratitude to a significant number of people and institutions who substantially contributed to the writing of this book.

First, I wish to thank the Zvi Meitar Center for Advanced Legal Studies in Tel Aviv University, who granted me a full scholarship for the entire duration of my PhD which was the starting point of this book, and allowed me to dedicate my time for research and even sponsored my research visit to UC Berkeley. In addition, I thank the Edmond J. Safra Center for Ethics in Tel Aviv University that provided an additional one-year scholarship and the S. Horowitz Institute of Intellectual Property in the Memory of Dr. Amnon Goldenberg that provided additional grants for the research.

My thanks and gratitude are owed to a long list of researchers who dedicated significant amounts of time to read early drafts of this research and share their knowledge with me to make this project better. Michael Gluzman and Shulamit Kreitler were kind enough to advise in their fields of expertise – genre theories and cognitive psychology – and my talks with them were priceless. For this I thank them from the bottom of my heart. In addition, I wish to thank Orly Lobel, Shai Lavi, Dotan Oliar, Peter Menell, Pamela Samuelson, Mark Lemley, Paul Goldstein, Arthur Ripstein, Abraham Drassinower, Peter Jazi, Molly Van Houweling, Dan Burk, David Heid, Maytal Gilboa, Dror Mishani and Mark Runco, who contributed their time and expertise, each in her or his field, to improve the various arguments in this book.

Finally, but perhaps most profoundly, I thank those whose assistance was not confined to the academic endeavor rather extended to strong friendship and everyday support. To Asaf Wiener, Ohad Somech and Omer Yehezkel Pelled, who shared their time with me every day throughout this research, had many deep conversations with me on the various arguments of this book and read far too many earlier drafts, but most importantly are dear friends whom I cherish. To my dear parents, Tamar and Sami, who were always there for me in every decision, in my personal and professional lives, and to whom I am most indebted for my achievements. To my beloved wife, Danielle, who supported me in the happy and more difficult times during this research, was always willing to read and listen and mainly for accepting the hours I dedicated for this research, in the university, at home, day, night and during weekends, all with uncompromising love. And last, but definitely not least, to my PhD supervisor, colleague and friend, Michael Birnhack, whose guidance, support, good advice, and ever-insistence on quality and accuracy, extend far beyond the expectations from a PhD supervisor and were the central pillar allowing me to complete this research. Without his support, this book would not have been written.

Sometimes words are not enough to encompass, grasp and express feelings and emotions, and this is the case with my gratitude to and appreciation of all the above mentioned.

Introduction

I. Regulating creativity

Copyright law regulates creativity. It affects the way people create works of authorship *ex-ante* and has significant implications on the status of works of authorship *ex-post*. But does copyright law really understand creativity? Should legal theories alone regulate creativity? This book aims to examine the relationship between the law and creativity, and asks whether copyright law should be adjusted to better accommodate non-legal understandings of the creative process.

A derivative work is one based on a preexisting work. Today, the owner of a work of authorship has the exclusive right to make derivative works based upon the original or to allow others to do so. This means that the owner may prevent other authors from using the original to make their own new works. Thus, in contrast to other copyright doctrines, which are often viewed in light of the tension between users and authors, the derivative works right raises a tension between authors and other authors. This makes the right to make derivative works a good lens through which to examine the relationship between the law and creativity.

This book examines such tension in light of cognitive psychology and genre theories' understanding of creativity and the creative process, in order to review the relationship between copyright law and creativity. It suggests a new way of thinking about the right to make derivative works that could both relieve this tension and harmonize the normative basis for the right with non-legal understandings of the creative process.

II. The role of the derivative work right in regulating creativity

Copyright law is in constant tension with two competing purposes – promoting creativity by incentivizing authors, and granting maximum access to users. Often, users are themselves authors, which creates a more complex tension between first and second authors. This tension is most prominently evident in the right to make derivative works.

Authors' rights to their works are divided into two main types: the material right to economically exploit the work, and the moral right, which protects the personal relationship between the author and her work. Most countries in the world grant authors the material-financial protection of copyright. This grant usually comes in the form of a bundle of specific rights which protect an author's ability to economically exploit their work. In the United States, for example, the Copyright Act grants an author five different rights – the reproduction right, the distribution right, the public performance right, the public display right, and the right to make derivative works.[1] Similar rights exist in many other countries, thanks mainly to the broad application of international treaties.[2]

The right to make derivative works, in its modern sense, grants the owner of an original work the exclusive right to make works based on the original, and thus the right to prevent others from making derivative works.[3] The first work's owner also gains all of the other rights copyright guarantees with respect to the second work.[4] Derivative works can be created in the same medium or a different medium. For example, an adaptation of the book "Harry Potter and the Chamber of Secrets" into a motion picture would constitute a derivative work. J.K. Rowling, the owner of the novel, owns the exclusive right to make such an adaptation, and only she is allowed to make such use or allow others to do so. This, despite the fact that the second work, the film adaptation, is in a different medium to the first work, a novel. Similarly, writing a new book using themes, characters, and locations detailed in the Harry Potter book series but a different plot may also constitute a derivative work.[5] A derivative work can be created within the same medium of the first work (creating a sequel to a book series) but also across different media (as in a motion picture adaptation of a literary work). In both instances, second authors cannot create and use the second works unless they obtain proper consent from the first author or unless specific legal defenses apply. Who owns a derivative work created without the first author's consent remains unclear.[6]

There are two problems with the derivative works right's current formulation. First, it is too narrow in the sense that it is often overshadowed by the reproduction right, and it gets applied and discussed in too few cases. Second, it offers the first author full control over derivative second works, making it much too strong.

The derivative works right applies to a crucial aspect of the creative process and the creative world as a whole. The common saying "standing on the shoulders of giants" refers to the "obvious" notion that no work of authorship is created from nothing. In order to create and innovate one has to rely on previous knowledge and creations.[7] This notion is so obvious that it has become cliché.[8] Moreover, literature on the cognitive process of creation informs us that, as far as the creative process is concerned, using preexisting knowledge relevant to the creative domain is a central and crucial component.

Sociological study of the creative world has also revealed that preexisting expressions form common creative building blocks for authors and audience members alike. Authors use these building blocks as tools to enable their own creativity. In turn, audience members use them as meaning making tools, to help understand and attribute value to creative works. Preexisting expressions thus play a central part in all creative fields, including cultural creativity. Together with technological innovations, they enable the development of new creative patterns and new types of culture. Consider, for example, appropriation art, like musical mash-ups and remixes, the cultures they enrich, and the subcultures they have created.[9]

Using preexisting expressions to make new works also ensures cheap and available creative raw materials. This enables the creative world to grow in an economically efficient way. Additionally, the use of preexisting expressions has a distributive effect, because the wide availability of cheap building blocks ensures that those who could not otherwise afford to participate in the creative world have access to creative raw materials.

The right to make derivative works is essential, and protecting it, at least to a certain extent, is important. However, protection raises its own challenges. The modern right significantly extends the quasi-monopoly that copyright grants the first author. This is true not only with respect to the exploitation of a first work, but also and perhaps mainly with respect to any and all additional works of authorship that flow from a first work. Because every original work potentially serves as the basis for another work, this extensive grant raises a constant tension between first authors' rights to make and control derivative works and second authors' rights to create new works. In this sense, the right to make derivative works is very different from other domains of copyright law, which focus on the tension between authors and users. In fact, it crystalizes the theoretical and practical difficulties of the copyright regime as a whole. These tensions and the optimal ways to deal with them are at the heart of this book.

To understand the essence of the right to make derivative works and the tensions it raises, we must first understand its legislative development and its positive scope. Initially, first authors were only granted the right to prohibit literal or verbatim reproductions of their works. However, this right was gradually extended. During the nineteenth century, it grew to include a right against non-consensual translations and dramatic adaptations. The United States Copyright Act of 1909 further extended first authors' rights to protect their works from other types of non-consensual uses. The right to make derivative works was first introduced as an independently legislated right in the United States in 1976 as part of the new Copyright Act. The act defined derivative works as "work[s] based upon one or more preexisting works."[10]

American courts also gradually expanded the reproduction right to include protections against "partial reproduction" and even material substantially similar to a first work. This judicially effected expansion constituted a *de facto* acknowledgement of the right to make derivative works even before it was even legislated.[11] However, as the right to make derivative works developed, it expanded in comparison to the reproduction right.[12]

The right to make derivative works now exists in various forms in other jurisdictions as well. The English Copyright, Designs and Patents Act from 1988 does not include a broad right to make derivative works. Instead, it grants the author of a first work the right of adaptation, which includes the right to specific uses of works based on the first work. These uses are quite extensive, and are in addition to the author's general exclusive right to make copies or partial copies of the first work. This scheme also functions as a *de facto* grant of an exclusive right to make derivative works.[13] The derivative works right exists in continental Europe as well. For example, in France, authors have the exclusive right to translate, adapt, or transform their first works. Likewise, in Germany, authors have the exclusive right to exploit or publish adaptations or transformations of their works.[14]

In contrast to the reproduction right, which grants the owner of the first work the exclusive right to reproduce the work itself, the modern day derivative works right grants first authors control over any secondary markets that second authors create by changing or adding expression to first works.[15] Consequently, an argument has developed in the literature that, in its modern definition, the right is overbroad and unsupported by the theoretical justifications of copyright law.[16]

By granting first authors rights in second works, the derivative works right also raises questions about the originality requirement. Second authors can enjoy some copyright protection in their derivative works. However, copyright only affords them protection of the specific creative elements which they add to the first works they change.[17] Moreover, before a work can be considered derivative and not a reproduction, a second author must affect a change in the first work. Moreover, not every change necessarily qualifies. For example, Patrick Ogilvy has argued that using a first work in its entirety, changing only its "method of presentation," should be differentiated from embedding a first work in another, new work in a manner that changes the first work substantively.[18]

Scholars such as Nimmer and Goldstein, have in fact argued that a derivative work requires a higher standard of originality in comparison to the lower "modicum of creativity" required from the author of the first work.[19] And indeed, in various circumstances, a derivative work can also constitute an original work of authorship under modern copyright law. Yet, the making of a derivative work itself may infringe on the first author's derivative works right.

This book examines whether the broad right to make derivative works, as described above, is justified both in its scope and in the strength of the remedies it affords the first author. It uses not only legal theory and tools, but also non-legal fields which look at the behavioral and sociological-philosophical aspects of creativity. After extracting the relevant notions to derivative works from the fields of creativity studies (Chapters 1 and 2), reevaluating the normative theoretical aspects the derivative works right (Chapter 3), and examining the relevant case law, it argues that the right to make derivative works is too narrow in scope and too broad with respect to the strength of the remedies it affords the first owner (Chapter 4). It then challenges modern copyright law to fully separate the right to make derivative works and the reproduction right, and to offer a new remedy model which restricts the first author's control over the making of new derivative works (Chapter 5).

Beyond its independent importance to the rights it addresses directly, this discussion also emphasizes the need to reexamine basic doctrines from time to time and ask if and to what extent they fulfill their intended purposes. It may also serve as a case study for the potential contribution of interdisciplinary analysis to copyright and intellectual property law in general.

III. The existing legal debate on the derivative work right

Relatively little existing literature specifically addresses the derivative work right, especially in comparison to other copyright law doctrines. Those discussions focus on the right's theoretical justifications, concerns about its scope in modern legislation, and its hypothetical implications on the creative world. But the definition of the derivative works right's scope is inconsistent in the case law and the literature, perhaps because it is so new and broad.[20] To the extent it has been addressed, scholars agree that, in its modern form, the derivative works right is broader than its theoretical justifications merit, and that it may have a restraining effect on creativity.[21] There are, however, different approaches as to the theoretical and practical grounds of this conclusion.

One of the criticisms levelled focuses on the constant tension between the derivative works right and freedom of speech. The argument is that granting the first owner an exclusive right to control the development of the discourse with respect to the first work unjustifiably and perhaps unconstitutionally restricts freedom of speech.[22] This approach is based on the democratic justification to copyright law, casting it as inseparable from the democratic mechanism. Under this theory, the ultimate goal of copyright protection is to facilitate and enable free public discourse independent of the state, thereby safeguarding available access to information and enabling individuals to participate in the public discourse and create meaning.[23]

Another common criticism is that the broad scope of the derivative work right outstrips copyright law's economic justifications. Under this theory, copyright protection is justified because it incentivizes private investment in the production of original expressions by granting authors the exclusive right to exploit their works. This enables authors to recoup their original investments and potentially make gains.[24] However, it has been argued that granting first authors exclusive control over derivative works provides only marginal additional incentive, and that this limited value is outweighed by the costs associated with prohibiting second authors from making unauthorized derivative works. In essence, these critics are arguing that the exclusive right to exploit the first work is already sufficient incentive and that the inefficient transaction costs imposed by an exclusive right to make derivative works therefore unnecessarily limit the scope of future creativity.[25]

In fact, after reviewing the literature, only two commentators hold the opinion that the broad definition of the derivative work right is justifiable. According to Michael Abramowicz's approach, the broad right to make derivative works is economically justified. While he agrees that a broad derivative work right may lead to a deadweight loss in some circumstances, he argues that granting first authors exclusive rights over the derivative markets of their first works is the only way to prevent rent dissipation in these secondary markets.[26] Pamela Samuelson's approach is to limit interpretation of the derivative work right under American copyright law to the nine examples detailed in the Copyright Act, or their close analogies. According to Samuelson, these are the only cases in which the American case law has afforded protection of the derivative works right, and she argues that under this interpretation, the right's scope cannot be considered as overbroad.[27]

Despite relative homogony in the criticism of the derivative works right's broad scope, there is disagreement as to how that scope should be narrowed. Proposed limitations can be divided into two categories, internal and external. Commentators in favor of internal limitations suggest narrowly interpreting the right based on its current statutory definitions,[28] or redefining the right through legislation.[29] Those who propose external limitations suggest narrowing the right's scope by adjusting its remedy component. They have suggested denying injunctive relief for infringement of the derivative works right in favor of monetary reliefs that take into consideration both the first owner's financial interest and second author's contributions.[30] They have further suggested using other legal doctrines, including the fair use doctrine and freedom of speech, to limit the derivative works right's scope.[31] They have also suggested binding the derivative works right to the infringement of another right included in copyright's bundle of rights[32] by granting property rights to second authors in the unauthorized derivative works they create. The idea being that this might mitigate the high transaction costs involved in attempting to obtain the first owner's approval.[33] A compulsory license mechanism could then enable authors other than the first author to make derivative works.[34]

It is noteworthy that the derivative works right's scope has almost never been examined, at least in Anglo-American literature, under the two main theoretical justifications for copyright – the Lockean labor-desert theory and personality theory. This is not necessarily surprising due to the fact that most of the literature on the derivative works right is American, whereas these two theories are dominant and accepted mostly in England and continental Europe. However, as already noted, the derivative work right exists in these jurisdictions as well. Thus discussing these theories is equally important.

Other concerns raised in the literature include the level of originality and creativity required for a derivative work to be considered an original work on its own;[35] the affect that the development of new technologies has on the right;[36] and the relationship between the derivative works right and particular fields of creativity.[37]

Chapter 3 focuses on the steady stream of literature criticizing the broad right to make derivative works under the economic and democratic approaches to copyright law. While it agrees with most of the extant criticisms, it also challenges some of the arguments presented. With respect to the argument that the scope of the derivative work is too broad, it suggests that the scope of the right's application is not the only component which may conflict with its underlying normative justifications. Rather the scope and strength of the right's remedies also present significant conflict. It also argues that a narrowly interpreted derivative works right does not solve the tension between the right and its normative basis. Such normative justifications actually require a broader scope of application for the right, specifically in comparison to the reproduction right. Such understanding also fits better with non-legal understandings of creativity.

In addition, Chapter 3 suggests a broader normative discussion on the derivative works right, including an analysis of right-based theories such as the Lockean and personality approaches to copyright law. With respect to the doctrinal aspects of the right, Chapters 4 and 5 present a revised definition for the scope of application, which focuses on the additional creativity of the second author and its relation to the preexisting expressions. Second, they propose a new remedies regime for the right to make derivative works that substantially reshapes the right in comparison to existing law and literature.

IV. Non-legal aspects of creativity

Chapters 1 and 2 examine the right to make derivative works in light of notions and research from other fields of knowledge which relate to creativity. Most of the literature examined in this regard does not deal directly with derivative works, although there is some that focuses on creative patterns which may relate directly.[38] However, at least two fields offer insights into the derivative works right. The first is cognitive psychology, which focuses, among other things, on the study of the cognitive aspects of the author during the *creative process.* The second is genre theories, which focuses on the analysis and characterization of *creative products* that belong to the same creative domain.

Cognitive psychology understands the creative process as a versatile and complex field. It views the creative process as a sub-category of the cognitive process of problem-solving. Yet, in contrast to classical problem-solving, its purpose is known but the steps towards a solution are not. Indeed, cognitive psychology has offered various characterizations of the creative process based on empirical studies and theoretical approaches. These characterizations and other notions from the field of cognitive psychology help explain why the scope of the right to make derivative works should be expanded, and why its strength and remedies should be narrowed, as will be elaborated in Chapter 1.

Genre theories can be traced back to classical Greek philosophy and to European literature from the seventeenth to nineteenth centuries. Its basic principles have been applied to other fields such as cinematography, music and the visual arts, and today the modern discourse on genre focuses on these fields too. Classical literature understood genre as a set of explicit formal rules with universal applicability through which discourse could be classified. As of the twentieth century, however, significant changes in the field led to a questioning of the premodern approach and even to doubting the validity of the theory itself. Despite several post-romantic era scholars announcing the dissolution of genre, in the last few decades its use has returned to the academic arena and many commentators presently use genre as a theoretical tool.

The modern approach still sees classification as an inseparable part of understanding genres. However it expands the scope of examination beyond the mere classification by looking to understand the social meaning of discourse and the way in which it affects its participants, its products, and the development of new discourse. Modern genre theories use tools from the field of semiotics, including semantics and syntax, to examine the building blocks of the specific discourse and the form and structure of the discourse's product.

Chapter 2 uses the genre theories literature to show that classifying the products of creative discourse is a significant and central feature of the mere existence of such discourse because the discourse itself is based, to a certain extent, on the comparison of mutual building blocks to the new and existing works of authorship. In addition, it shows that other players in the discourse rely on common building blocks to understand new works as well as to interact with them. In other words, the use of common building blocks is inseparable not only from the creative process, but also from the meaning-making process. The term "common building blocks" refers not only to the abstract ideas which underlie a specific genre, but also to the concrete expressions which participants in the genre are aware of, acknowledge, and use. This notion is relevant to the derivative works right as a legal norm because it explains that the understanding of any work requires treating it, at least to a certain extent, as a derivative work. In this sense a derivative work is not qualitatively different from an original non-derivative work.

V. Research questions

This book seeks to better understand the right to make derivative works. It focusses on two main aspects of this phenomenon – the non-legal aspects of creativity and the right to make derivative works as a legal norm. The main question with respect to creativity's non-legal aspects is the place and significance of reliance on previous knowledge, including previous concrete expressions, in the creative world. Chapter 1 examines the internal creative process of the author, using literature from the field of cognitive psychology. Chapter 2 uses genre theories to examine how participants in the creative discourse, both the authors and the audience, create and understand the creative products. With respect to legal norms, Chapter 3 considers the extent to which the theoretical justifications for the derivative works right are persuasive and whether its broad definition and strong remedies should remain intact. Chapter 4 examines the scope of the derivative works right under current law and asks whether a stable definition exists for such a right. Lastly, Chapter 5 discusses what the scope of the derivative works right ought to be, both with respect to its applicability and its accompanying remedies, in light of the non-legal conclusions and the legal theoretical justifications previously addressed.

1) Non-legal aspects of creativity – what is the significance of using prior knowledge?

In order to critically assess the desirable scope of the derivative works right, the significance of the use of prior knowledge in the creative process must first be examined. This does not mean undertaking a quantitative examination of the number or types of derivative works in the world. The feasibility of that task is questionable. It means assessing the significance of the reliance on prior knowledge, including reliance on protected expressions, to both the creative process generally and to the development of the world of creativity as a whole. This in turn requires examining two aspects of the creative world: the creative process and creative products.

Examining the creative process requires asking how and to what extent authors rely on preexisting works, knowingly or unknowingly, and to what extent parts of such works may influence new works. Chapter 1 reviews cognitive psychology literature that analyses and examines the different stages and sub-processes of the creative process both theoretically and empirically.

Examining creative products requires assessing the extent to which society needs to use prior knowledge in order to understand new works of authorship and how significant to this purpose the inclusion of previous expressions in new works is. Chapter 2 uses genre theories to attempt to explain society's needs in this respect. Society, as it is exposed to various works of authorship, defines creative domains on the basis of substantial similarity between works in those domains. This reinforces the notion that understanding is, at least in part, based on identifying common building blocks and the use of preexisting works.

Addressing these questions is important on various levels. First, it facilitates understanding how significant the reliance on prior knowledge is to the creative world, both to the process of creation and to the meaning-making process. Second, dealing with these questions concretizes and analyzes the previously mentioned cliché, according to which every work is based on the works that came before it. This is important because although the idea of progress does appear in copyright literature, current law does not fully implement it.[39] Third, it clarifies whether the right to make derivative works as a legal norm matches the non-legal understanding of creativity. Although the model presented for redesigning the right is not based on these non-legal notions, they do assist in portraying and explaining it.

2) The legal world – what is the scope of the derivative works right and is it justifiable?

This book's second part examines the extent to which the right to make derivative works matches its underlying normative justifications. For this purpose, it reviews the theoretical justifications for the right's existence, both on their own and in light of the notions from the first part of the book. As part of this examination, it is important to ask whether the main justifications to copyright law – the utilitarian approach, which includes economic analysis; the Lockean approach; the corrective justice approach; and the personality approach – also justify the derivative works right. As previously noted, the existing literature on derivative works focuses mainly on the economic and democratic justifications for its existence. Therefore, this part only offers one new criticism of the one economic analysis that justifies the current derivative works right in its entirety. However, with respect to the personality, corrective justice, and Lockean approaches, it offers full and extensive examinations of the derivative work right that do not exist in current literature, it revisits these questions, and offers new analysis.

After reviewing the normative justification for the derivative works right and its positive expression in case law, this part examines how the right could and should be adapted in order to remain within its normative grounds. One aspect addressed is the desired scope of the rights applicability to various uses of first works. The focus here is mainly on the interrelation between the right to make derivative works and the reproduction right. This part proposes a distinction between the legal phenomenon of derivative works and that of reproductions based, inter alia, on the notions from the non-legal discussion on the significance of the use of prior knowledge for creativity. It also addresses the derivative works right's desired characteristics, specifically the strength of its accompanying remedies. The examination of this aspect will also rely, in part, on the non-legal conclusions as well as on the previous normative legal discussion and includes a new proposed model for the derivative works right, which will be justified and based on the right's normative justifications. Although the notions from the non-legal discussion cannot function as independent justification for the proposed model, the suggested model is also in line with their understanding of creativity.

The reexamination of the scope of the right to make derivative works as part of the bundle of rights offered to the copyright owner is also important on various levels. First, due to the lack of unity in the existing literature and case law with respect to the right's current scope, its desired scope, and its justifications, it is important to offer an extensive model for the right that could lead to better predictability and unity in the field. Second, to the extent that the right could be adjusted to fit both its underlying normative justifications and non-legal understandings of the creative world, the results of an effective reexamination could improve the legal norm. Third, a model for the right to make derivative works based both on knowledge and theories from non-legal fields of creativity and on legal normative theories is important because the legal theories alone lack sufficient tools to afford a granular and stable analysis. Additionally, such a reexamination highlights the benefits that may be gained through review of basic doctrines in copyright law and intellectual property in light of interdisciplinary research and notions from non-legal fields.

VI. An overview of the main arguments

The course of the book is as follows: Chapter 1 presents the discussion on the creative process according to cognitive psychology and extracts notions which may be used in the legal context. Chapter 2 discusses the development of genre theories and shows how modern approaches to genre understand the use of prior knowledge as enabling creativity and facilitating the meaning-making process. It also explains how such notions affect the legal discussion. Chapter 3 reexamines the legal-theoretical justifications of the right to make derivative works while focusing on the Lockean approach, corrective justice, and the personality approach. The conclusion of this examination is later used as a basis for the doctrinal discussion. Chapter 4 reviews the development of the right to make derivative works and the expansion of the reproduction right. It also examines the positive overlap between the two. In this light, it explains why the theoretical conclusions from the previous chapter justify the separation of the derivative works right from the reproduction right and mandate limiting the strength of its accompanying remedies. Chapter 5 portrays the most efficient and fair way to adjust the right to make derivative works to fit its underlying justifications. It suggests redesigning the right's scope and proposes a new remedies model which better fits its normative basis.

1) The cognitive process of creation includes the use of preexisting expressions

Given the versatility and number of different creative styles and methods, a quantitative-empirical study of the subjective process the author undergoes while creating a work seems almost impossible to conduct. Instead, cognitive psychology examines typical creative patterns and the scope of use of prior knowledge, including previous expressions, in the creative process.

As previously noted, cognitive psychology characterizes the creative process. However, despite the lack of uniformity and consensus in the field, at least with respect to a stable and precise definition of what creativity is and what the creative process consists of, an extensive review of the differing views yields several stable notions about the cognitive process of creation. These have serious repercussions on the debate about the significance of using prior expressions in the creative process.

In brief, the process of creation is consistently divided into two main phases, which are themselves sometimes further subdivided. In the first stage, the author uses unfocussed and associative cognition – which could also be described as imagination, epiphany or as the conscious or unconscious – to search for the beginning of a possible "solution." This phase resembles, to a certain extent, the romantic approach to creativity and authorship, which sees the creative process as an almost meta-physical activity. In contrast, in the second stage, authors are required to crystalize their unfocussed lines of thought into concrete products. This phase is almost unanimously described as imposing constraints on the unfocussed thought of the author. These constraints are driven by preexisting professional knowledge and the author's skill in the relevant creative domain. The fact that authors must rely on available preexisting knowledge to crystalize their abstract thoughts also requires an inevitable reliance on significant components from prior works of authorship in the relevant creative domain. Consequently, these function as basic building blocks for their creative process. To the extent that this phenomenon is inseparable from the cognitive process of creation, it is understandable that prior expression use, which leads, to a certain extent, to the making of derivative works, is a necessary and inevitable part of almost every creative process, or to say the least, of many creative undertakings.

2) The creative products – genre theories identify common building blocks in shared creative domains

Examining and characterizing the creative product demonstrates that substantial similarities exist between works that share the same creative domain, in a way that proves that the use of preexisting expressions is also identifiable objectively. This argument follows from genre theories principles which examine the discourse classification rules in a specific creative community. While research development in the field of genre theories originally focussed only on classification of discourse products, it has, as previously noted, progressed. It now addresses a more complex structure of interrelations between the various participants in the discourse and the way in which new classifications develop. Yet this development in no way alters the basic, underlying principles of genre theories. Genre analysis still requires the identification of similarity between different discourse products, a concurrent examination of the common building blocks which were used, and analysis of the way they were used to make a creative product. In fact, to the extent that there is a close link between the characterization of a discourse in one genre, the pedagogy of new participants in it, the actions of existing participants, and the development of new discourse and the creative products; there must be a close link between the way in which creative products are perceived by the "consumers" and the cognitive process of the author. Moreover, classifying the different features of discourse is necessary and has social value in itself. This follows, because the act of classification enables community social interactions around a specific discourse.

3) Reexamination of the justifications for the derivative works right

The conclusion thus far is that there is a mismatch between non-legal understandings of creativity and the legal right to make derivative works. In this light, Chapter 3 reexamines the legal-theoretical justifications to the existence of the right, specifically copyright law's four main justifications: the utilitarian approach, the Lockean approach, corrective justice and the personality approach.

The current literature on derivative works has already reviewed and criticized this right on economic and democratic grounds. Therefore, Chapter 3 presents a shorter discussion of these approaches, including only additions to or comments upon the existing literature. With respect to the economic approach, it reaffirms many of the criticisms of the economic approach and its ability to justify the existing broad derivative works right and relies primarily on non-legal discussion to do so. In addition, it attempts to contest Abramowicz's approach, which justified the right using the principle of rent dissipation in secondary markets. Derivative works do not necessarily create secondary markets for the original works. Their purpose is to develop and make the primary market more efficient. As far as the democratic criticisms are concerned, Chapter 3 considers the limitations cast on the derivative works right by the fair use doctrine. It emphasizes the differences between the two doctrines, specifically with respect to transformative use.[40] It also explains that the fair use doctrine complements the book's proposed derivative works model.

With respect to the Lockean approach, Chapter 3 reviews the right's current broad scope, at least as far as it is based on Locke's justifications for granting right in the fruits of one's labor. It focusses on Locke's two provisos and interprets them based on the non-legal understanding of creativity.[41] The derivative works right may violate Locke's second proviso, also known as the non-waste proviso. It practically guarantees waste by granting first authors a quasi-monopoly with respect to the development of their works and secondary markets but placing no obligation on them to further develop their works. The derivative works right may also violate Locke's first "sufficiency" proviso, which restricts the individual's right to use common property to those that leave enough and qualitatively equivalent resources in common for others. By depriving society of the ability to further develop the primary market of a work or to create secondary markets for it, the derivative works right potentially leaves others with fewer and less valuable resources than existed prior to the first work's creation. This is true even when considering the resources in the public domain which are not considered "reproductions" of the first work. Thus, the Lockean theory cannot justify the current scope of the derivative works right.

With respect to corrective justice, which is based on Kant's doctrine of right, Abraham Drassinower has asserted that there is no justification for a derivative works right at all.[42] However, Chapter 3 suggests a different interpretation of corrective justice, according to which the right could be justified so long as it does not empower first authors to enjoin subsequent authors from producing derivative works. These interpretations are based on Kant's principle of universal right, according to which every person's freedom is subject to the ability of all other persons to enjoy the same degree of freedom. With respect to the derivative works right, then, second authors must be afforded the same freedom to act in the world that first authors enjoy. This must include the ability to use expressions from previous works, including other authors' first works. Chapter 3 proposes and explains a model which allows second authors the right to use expressions from first works, but also imposes on them the obligation to share any revenues from such use with first authors.

In contrast to the external criticisms of the personality approach raised in the literature, Chapter 3 presents an internal criticism which employs a philosophical understanding of the autonomy of expression, together with hermeneutic approaches, to illustrate the personality justification's limitations.[43] It uses Hans Georg Gadamer's hermeneutic model for the act of interpretation, which he divided into three stages – understanding, interpretation and application,[44] to demonstrate that the application of the interpretive result changes the perception of the interpreter and her behavior. To this model, it then adds Roberta Kwall's distinction between the first author's meaning, i.e. the work's subjective meaning to its author, and the work's message, i.e. the way in which the author wishes her work to be perceived by society.[45] These subjective elements should be protected in order to enable first authors to achieve autonomy. When a person is subjected to a message that an author wishes to share with society, this person undergoes an interpretive process which results in changes of the expressions in that message, creating a different meaning than that intended by the first author. Subordinating the second person's interpretation to the first person's message, and to it alone, ignores the second person's right and ability to act and express herself according to her free will.

According to each of the approaches, the independent existence of a derivative works right, in contrast to the reproduction right, is justified but the strength of its remedies should be diminished. This conclusion will be later used to adjust the right to make derivative works to align with its underlying justifications.

4) The existing overlap between the derivative works and reproduction rights

Due to the fact that the right to make derivative works developed side by side with the systematic expansion of the reproduction right, the relationship between the rights has always been unclear. Whether the derivative works right is fully included in the reproduction right remains an open question. Thus, for example, David Nimmer has argued that the right to make derivative works is superfluous because for a work to be "derivative" it must be significantly based on a previous work. According to him, to the extent that the derivative work includes expressions which are substantially similar to the first work, it inevitably infringes the reproduction right and no further claim with respect to the derivative works right is necessary.[46] Other commentators have asserted that this overlap is not complete, since there are cases in positive law in which a derivative work is created without reproduction.[47] However, Chapter 4 argues that in American and English laws, the overlap is almost complete. In English law, it exists due to the explicit statutory language according to which the existence of an adaptation does not preclude the existence of copying.[48] In American law, it exists due to the infringement tests established by the courts with respect to the reproduction and derivative works rights. They create a *de facto* overlap despite the fact that the rights have separate legislative sources.

5) Criticizing the current right to make derivative works

In light of the overlap between the derivative works right and the reproduction right, and due to the mismatch between the derivative works right's strength and its underlying justifications, Chapter 4 criticizes the current right's definition and application. The derivative works right's separate legislative definition and its distinct underlying justifications should lead not only to a separate legal analysis, but also to a complete separation from the reproduction right and a change to its attendant remedies. The crux of the argument is that, following the classification of a certain action as the making of a derivative work, the reproduction right should no longer be invokable and the remedies to which the first author is entitled should thus be limited in comparison to those offered by the reproduction right.

To make this point Chapter 4 first presents existing criticism of the derivative works right and different suggestions for to resolve the difficulties raised. It also points out the deficiencies in such literature. As previously noted, a common criticism is that the derivative works right is overbroad.[49] Some commentators have argued that the derivative works right limits the second author's freedom of speech in an unacceptable manner and therefore should be narrowed. Other commentators have argued that the right to make derivative works is economically inefficient because it hinders creativity more than it promotes it. Although the existing literature has theoretically reviewed the difficulties which the derivative works right raises, it does not offer a sufficient solution to resolve such difficulties. Specifically, it does not deal with both the positive overlap between this derivative works right and the reproduction right, and the independent normative justifications for the derivative works right.

Chapter 4 argues that the right to make derivative works should be completely separated from the reproduction right, and that the strength of its accompanying remedies should be limited. It also asserts that only by reviewing justifications and remedies together can the problems with the current derivative works right be resolved. These aspects are necessarily interrelated for two main reasons. First, much like any other legal right, the strength of the derivative works right is dependent both on its scope of applicability and the scope of its remedies. Second, while the derivative works right's normative justifications do establish it as an independent right, they render its limitations on subsequent authors unjustified at the same time. Therefore, focussing only on one of these two aspects – scope of applicability or the scope of remedies – cannot suffice.

Additionally, although the non-legal conceptions of creativity do not function as an independent normative justification for redesigning the current derivative works right, they do mesh better with a revised model of the right. I argue that this is more than just a happy coincidence. It is an indication that copyright law doctrines better align with deeper, non-legal understandings of the creative process and creativity when they conform to their own underlying normative justifications and fulfill their overarching goal of nurturing the creative world.

6) Redesigning the derivative works right

Having established that two main features of the derivative works right should be adjusted, Chapter 5 explores a way to redesign the right that seeks to match it to its underlying justifications.

First, it proposes a new definition and scope of applicability for the derivative works right that fully separates it from the reproduction right. When second authors combine substantial parts of preexisting works with their own substantial, qualitatively creative additions that are both inseparable from the existing expression and cannot be substituted with existing non-protected expressions – the activity they are engaging in should be considered derivative works making, not reproduction. Thus, the derivative works right's definition should be redesigned to ensure that it applies to such cases, even if they are presently governed by the reproduction right under current case law. To illustrate the suggested definition, several examples of typical actions that ought to be encompassed by the new definition are discussed.

In addition, Chapter 5 establishes a separate and independent discourse on the right to make derivative works that focusses on analyzing its boundaries and underlying justifications, which includes many cases which were previously analyzed and reviewed under the reproduction right. It also explains how the suggested definition, which separates the two rights, allows for a different discussion of remedies, resolving many of the difficulties which have previously arisen when duplicate damages have been awarded for the infringement of both rights simultaneously. It also considers the changes the new definition effects between first and second authors, third parties, and potential infringers.

The normative justifications for the derivative works right require limitation of the strength of remedies it offers today. In fact, they require a transition from the current protection of property rule to a liability rule.[50] To explain the most efficient and fair model to achieve such goal, Chapter 5 also reviews various suggestions for alternative remedies models and explains their deficiencies. The model settled upon proposes establishing a compulsory license for the making of derivative works, which is subject to the payment of fair royalties. Transition to a compulsory license model may raise some difficulties, both theoretical and practical. However, these can be overcome. In addition, practical questions will be addressed – like how royalties should be determined, whether different types of royalties should apply to different types of works, whether first authors should ever have exclusive rights to make subsequent works. The ability to supervise such a model and its potential costs are also examined.

The proposed remedies model enables second authors to use expressions from preexisting works to make derivative works without the first author's consent. However, this right to engage in derivative works creation would be subject to the payment of fair royalties, derived from future revenues of the derivative work. If the parties do not reach an independent agreement as to these royalties, the proposed model provides that the second author may turn to a judicial tribunal to set the rate, subject to a payment of a preliminary fee for the costs of the procedure and the potential goodwill benefits from using expressions from the first work. Lastly, the entire mechanism would be subject to a blocking period during which the first author would maintain the exclusive right to make derivative works herself, or license others to do so.

The advantage of such a model over alternative models lies in its quasi-insurance effect. It is safe to presume that second authors who elect to use compulsory licenses will be able to protect themselves from reproduction claims. First authors will have less incentive to sue than they do now, due to the revenues to which they will automatically be entitled in works characterized as derivative. This is especially true with respect to works that it may be difficult to prove constitute mere reproductions. In addition, first authors will function as gatekeepers to ensure that derivative works are sufficiently creative and original. Open and shut cases of reproduction will still be litigated under the reproduction right, but borderline cases that contain at least some creative and original expression will likely be allowed to exist unchallenged, but subject to royalties. Thus the chances that the model would be exploited for the purpose of making infringing reproductions will actually be lower. The proposed model also resolves many of the derivative works right's theoretical difficulties by removing the restraints it currently places on subsequent authors to use preexisting expression to engage in creativity. In addition, it fits better with the non-legal understanding of creativity in that it does not prefer first authors a priori and equalizes, or at least substantially improves, the position of second authors who explicitly use previous expressions in comparison to second authors whose use of such expressions is more latent.

Chapter 5 concludes with a discussion of the proposed model's relationship with other copyright and intellectual property doctrines, specifically the fair use doctrine, moral right doctrine, and trademark law. Thus, for example, this last section will argue that, to the extent that a specific use is allowed under the fair use doctrine or any other permitted use doctrine, there will be no need for a compulsory license, nor will a user have to wait for the end of the blocking period. In contrast, when a derivative work would infringe the moral right of the first author, the compulsory license is not a cure for such infringement.

Notes

1 17 U.S.C. § 106.
2 Articles 8–15 to the Berne Convention on the Protection of Literary and Artistic Works; WIPO Copyright Treaty art. 6–8, Dec. 20, 1996. For elaboration on the relevant aspects of the TRIPs agreement *see* Daniel Gervais, THE TRIPS AGREEMENT: DRAFTING HISTORY AND ANALYSIS 242–56, 265–72, 292–310 (4th edn 2012).
3 Hereinafter, a wholly original work of authorship will be referred to as a "first work." Likewise, the owner of a first work will be referred to as "the first author." In the same vein, a derivative work based on a first work will be referred to as a "second work," and the derivative work's author will be referred to as a "second author."
4 17 U.S.C. § 101, 106; Copyright, Designs and Patents Act, 1988 s. 21.
5 The question if this would constitute a derivative work is dependent, among other considerations, on the what was exactly taken from the first work. To the extent that the second work uses protected expressions from the first work (such as characters, specific scene and protected plot lines), it would constitute a derivative work, *see, e.g.*, Salinger v. Colting, 607 F.3d 68, 71–72 (2d Cir. 2010). (A sequel to the book "The Catcher in the Rye" was found infringing upon the copyright of J.D. Salinger due to the use of characters from the first work.) However, to the extent that only the general idea underlying the first work was taken, or even if the second work uses only the names of characters from the first work but not their characteristics, the second work would be considered an original work. This point demonstrates the interface between the right to make derivative works, the reproduction right and the fair use doctrine, since the reproduction right protects the owner of the first work from partial reproductions of the works including the reproduction of characters from a full plot, and on the other side, satirical use of the first work or a use that significantly transforms its expression may grant the user or the second author a defense under the fair use doctrine. I will elaborate on these interfaces in parts IV.4 and IV.5.
6 Although the legislative language is unclear under the law in the United States, courts have ruled that a derivative work created without the first author's consent will not be eligible for copyright protection with respect to the second author. *See* Anderson v. Stallone, 1989 U.S. Dist. LEXIS 11109 (C.D. Cal. Apr. 25, 1989); Pickett v. Prince, 52 F. Supp. 2d 893, 906–07 (N.D. Ill. 1999).
7 Paul Goldstein, *Derivative Rights and Derivative Works in Copyright*, 30 J. COPYRIGHT SOC'Y U.S.A. 209, 218 (1983). This notion is so common that Google has chosen it as the slogan for its academic search engine Google Scholar. *See* http://scholar.google.com.
8 Jessica Litman, *The Public Domain*, 39 EMORY L.J. 965, 966 (1990).
9 For a discussion on these types of creativity and the influence legal rules have on them *see* Peter Dicola, *An Economic View of Legal Restrictions on Musical Borrowing and Appropriation*, in MAKING AND UNMAKING INTELLECTUAL PROPERTY 235 (Mario Biagioli, Peter Jaszi and Martha Woodmansee eds, 2011); Peter S. Menell, *Adapting Copyright for the Mashup Generation*, 164 U. PENN. L. REV. 441 (2016).
10 17 U.S.C. § 101.
11 For an elaboration on the historical development of the right to make derivative works *see*: Oren Bracha, *The Ideology of Authorship Revisited: Authors, Markets, and Liberal Values in Early American Copyright*, 118 YALE L.J. 186, 224–33 (2008); Goldstein, *supra* note 7, at 211–15.
12 For elaboration on the parallel development of both rights *see infra* Chapter 4.
13 Copyright, Designs and Patents Act, 1988 s. 21.
14 *See*, respectively, Code de la Propriété Intellectuelle (C. Prop. Intel.), art. L122–4; Urheberrechtsgesetz [Copyright Act] Sept. 9, 1965, BGBL. I at 1273, § 23, as amended, Oct. 1, 2013, BGBL. I at 3728. *See also* 1 André Lucas & Pascal Kamina, *France*, in INTERNATIONAL COPYRIGHT LAW AND PRACTICE § 2[3][a] (Paul Edward Geller ed., 2014); 2 Adolf Dietz, *Germany*, in INTERNATIONAL COPYRIGHT LAW AND PRACTICE § 2[3][a] (Paul Edward Geller ed., 2014).

15 Goldstein, *supra* note 7, at 217, 227.
16 *See infra* part III.
17 Goldstein, *supra* note 7, at 240–1.
18 Patrick W. Ogilvy, *Frozen in Time? New Technologies, Fixation, and the Derivative Work Right*, 8 VAND. J. ENT. & TECH. L. 687, 694–95 (2006). Returning to the Harry Potter example, changing the method of presentation of the first work may happen if the character of Harry Potter will be displayed in the Tate gallery to criticize modern fictional literature, while incorporating the character of Harry Potter in a new book titled "Harry Potter in Space" will bring a change to the original work. This type of distinction may be significant in the context of the interface between the right to make derivative works and the fair use doctrine. *See* R. Anthony Reese, *Transformativeness and the Derivative Work Right*, 31 COLUM. J.L. & ARTS 467 (2007).
19 Goldstein, *supra* note 7, at 241–2; Melville B. Nimmer & David Nimmer, NIMMER ON COPYRIGHT § 3.03 (2016) (hereinafter: NIMMER ON COPYRIGHT).
20 As William Patry has put it, "regrettably the understanding of derivative works is fast approaching incomprehensibility." *See* William F. Patry, PATRY ON COPYRIGHT § 3.46 (2012).
21 The main theories discussed in the literature with respect to the derivative work right are economic analysis, Lockean labor-desert theory, personality theory and the democratic justification to copyright law.
22 For elaboration, *see infra* Chapter 3. This tension is "external" to the derivative work right. For a distinction between "external" and "internal" tensions in the context of copyright law *see* Michael Birnhack, *Copyright Law and Free Speech After Eldred v. Ashcroft*, 76 S. CAL. L. REV. 1275, 1292–1305 (2003).
23 For a discussion on the democratic approach to copyright law *see* Neil Weinstock Netanel, COPYRIGHT'S PARADOX 3 (2008); Netanel, *Copyright and a Democratic Civil Society*, 106 YALE L.J. 283, 347–64 (1996); Yochai Benkler, *Free as the Air to Common Use: First Amendment Constrains on Enclosure of the Public Domain*, 74 NYU L. REV. 354 (1999); Niva Elkin-Koren, *Cyberlaw and Social Change: A Democratic Approach to Copyright Law in Cyberspace*, 14 CARDOZO ARTS & ENT. L.J. 215, 277–83 (1996).
24 William M. Landes & Richard A. Posner, *An Economic Analysis of Copyright Law*, 18 J. LEGAL STUD. 325, 328–29 (1989); William M. Landes & Richard A. Posner, THE ECONOMIC STRUCTURE OF INTELLECTUAL PROPERTY LAW 108–15 (2003); Goldstein, *supra* note 7, at 216. Absent such a right, it is argued, an author of a work will not have any incentive to create it to begin with due to the fact that intellectual creations are public goods and due to other "hitchhiking" problems. This tension is internal to the derivative work right. *See* Birnhack, *supra* note 22.
25 For elaboration, *see infra* Chapter 3.
26 Michael Abramowicz, *A Theory of Copyright's Derivative Work Right*, 90 MINN. L. REV. 317, 357–8 (2005).
27 Pamela Samuelson, *The Quest for a Sound Conception of Copyright's Derivative Work Right*, 101 GEO. L.J. 1505, 1513–15 (2013). The nine examples under the Copyright Act are translation, musical arrangement, dramatization, fictionalization, motion picture version, sound recording, art reproduction, abridgment, condensation. *See* 17 U.S.C. § 101.
28 *See* Daniel Gervais, *The Derivative Right: Or Why Copyright Law Protects Foxes Better Than Hedgehogs*, 15 VAN. J. ENT. & TECH. L. 785 (2013); Chris Newman, *Transformation in Property and Copyright*, 56 VILL. L. REV. 251, 258 (2011); Tim Wu, *Tolerated Uses*, 31 COLUM. J.L. & ARTS 617, 631–2 (2008). Samuelson's support of the derivative work right in its current definition is also based on this approach.
29 Naomi Abe Voegtli, *Rethinking Derivative Rights*, 63 BROOK. L. REV. 1213, 1267 (1997).
30 Paul Edward Geller, *Copyright in Crisis: Principles for Change*, 56 J. COPYRIGHT SOC'Y U.S.A. 165 (2008); Paul Edward Geller, *Hiroshige vs. Van Gogh: Resolving the Dilemma of Copyright Scope in Remedying Infringement*, 46 J. COPYRIGHT SOC'Y U.S.A. 39, 61 (1998);

Orit Fishman-Afori, *Flexible Remedies as a Means to Counteract Failures in Copyright Law*, 29 CARDOZO ARTS & ENT. L.J. 1 (2010); Jed Rubinfeld, *Freedom of Imagination: Copyright's Constitutionality*, 112 YALE L.J. 1, 57–58 (2002); Goldstein, *supra* note 7, at 238 n. 94; Ralph S. Brown, *The Widening Gyre: Are Derivative Works Getting Out of Hand*, 3 CARDOZO ARTS & ENT. L.J. 1, 21 (1984).

31 Christina Bohannan, *Taming the Derivative Work Right: A Modest Proposal for Reducing Overbreadth and Vagueness in Copyright*, 12 VAND. J. ENT. & TECH. L. 669, 696–7 (2010); Voegtli, *supra* note 29, at 1265–6; Netanel, *supra* note 23.

32 Tyler Ochoa, *Copyright, Derivative Works, and Fixation: Is Galoob a Mirage or Does the Form(Gen) of the Alleged Derivative Work Matter?*, 20 SANTA CLARA COMP. & HIGH TECH. L. J. 991, 1020 (2004).

33 Mark A. Lemley, *The Economics of Improvement in Intellectual Property Law*, 75 TEX. L. REV. 989, 1047 (1997).

34 The possibility to use a compulsory license mechanism for derivative works was suggested by a small number of commentators, most of which immediately ruled out such mechanism for unjustified reasons to my concern. *See* Voegtli, *supra* note 29, at 1264–5.

35 Steven S. Boyd, *Deriving Originality in Derivative Works: Considering the Quantum of Originality Needed To Attain Copyright Protection in a Derivative Work*, 40 SANTA CLARA L. REV. 325, 350–77 (2000); NIMMER ON COPYRIGHT, *supra* note 19, at 3.03.

36 Lydia Pallas Loren, *The Changing Nature of Derivative Works in the Face of New Technologies*, 4 J. SMALL & EMERGING BUS. L. 57, 77–8 (2000).

37 The main discussion in the American literature and case law focussed on post-modern art, which aims at, by definition, using preexisting works, and specifically to environmental sculptures and sampling, remix and mash-up techniques in the musical world. *See* Voegtli, *supra* note 29, at 1221–6; Dicola, *supra* note 9; Landes & Posner, *supra* note 24, at 254–69.

38 Most of the literature in this field focuses on post-modern or appropriation art. *See, e.g.*, Philip A. Gunderson, *Danger Mouse's Grey Album, Mash-Ups, and the Age of Composition*, 15(1) POSTMODERN CULTURE 4 (2004); John Shiga, *Copy-and-Persist: The Logic of Mash-Up Culture*, 24 CRITICAL STUD. MEDIA COMM. 93 (2007); Nicholas Diakopoulos, Kurt Luther, Yevgeniy "Eugene" Medynskiy, Irfan Essa, *The Evolution of Authorship in a Remix Society*, PROCEEDINGS OF THE EIGHTEENTH CONFERENCE ON HYPERTEXT AND HYPERMEDIA 133–34 (Simon Harper et al. eds, 2007).

39 For elaboration on the idea of progress in copyright law *see* Michael Birnhack, *The Idea of Progress in Copyright Law*, 1 BUFF. IP L.J. 3 (2001).

40 Transformative use is a term suggested by Judge Pierre N. Leval in his article Pierre N. Leval, *Toward a Fair Use Standard*, 103 HARV. L. REV. 1105 (1990). The term was later adopted by the Supreme Court of the United States in Campbell v. Acuff-Rose Music Inc., 510 U.S. 569, 576 (1994). Transformative use was defined as a use that adds something new of different purpose or character and changes the first expression. For elaboration *see* Neil Weinstock Netanel, *Making Sense of Fair Use*, 15 LEWIS & CLARK L. REV. 715, 724, 746 (2011).

41 For elaboration on the Lockean provisos *see* Robert P. Merges, JUSTIFYING INTELLECTUAL PROPERTY 48–66 (2011).

42 Abraham Drassinower, *Taking User Rights Seriously*, *in* IN THE PUBLIC INTEREST: THE FUTURE OF CANADIAN COPYRIGHT LAW 462, 471 (2005); Abraham Drassinower, WHAT'S WRONG WITH COPYING? 222–4 (2015).

43 For the argument that the individual's autonomy is at the heart of the personality approach to copyright *see* Neil Netanel, *Copyright Alienability Restrictions*, 24 RUTGERS L.J. 374, 374–6 (1993).

44 Hans-Georg Gadamer, TRUTH AND METHOD 306 (2nd edn, Joel Weinsheimer & Donald G. Marshall trans. & revs., 2004).

45 Roberta Rosenthal Kwall, THE SOUL OF CREATIVITY 2–3 (2010).

46 NIMMER ON COPYRIGHT, *supra* note 19, at § 8.09[A][1].

47 *See, e.g.*, Gervais, *supra* note 28, at 844.
48 Copyright, Designs and Patents Act, 1988 s. 21(5).
49 This notion was suggested by Samuelson. *See* Samuelson, *supra* note 27, at 1510 and the literature described in note 24 *id.*
50 Guido Calabresi & A. Douglas Melamed, *Property Rules, Liability Rules and Inalienability: One View of the Cathedral*, 86 HARV. L. REV. 1089 (1972).

1 The cognitive aspects of creativity[1]

I. Introduction

Copyright law reflects the intuitive understating of creativity in the eyes of the law. This is because copyright law's primary goal is to promote creativity.[2] But is the legal understanding of creativity in line with cognitive psychology's understanding of the creative process? This chapter examines whether copyright law is harmonious with cognitive psychology's understanding of creativity. Some scholars posit that theories of creativity fit well with current copyright law.[3] This chapter's goal is to offer a wider assessment of creativity studies and to question whether they indeed fit with copyright law's assumptions about creativity.

This chapter focusses on four main doctrines and concepts in copyright law. The first is the originality requirement in copyright law. The second is the concept of romantic authorship. The third is the idea/expression dichotomy that grants copyright protection to expressions and denies it to ideas. The fourth, which is closely related to the third and is the main topic of this book, is the right to make derivative works. Copyright law treats derivative works separately from original works and creates, to some extent, an identity between derivative works and reproductions. This attitude towards derivative works is not easy to justify, as will be further explained in Chapter 3. This chapter examines whether the cognitive psychology of creativity is consonant with this legal doctrine and how to best apply cognitive psychology's findings to the law.

The copyright doctrines discussed in this chapter are based upon implicit and explicit assumptions about creativity. The originality doctrine, for example, is based upon the express assumption that creative works include an original contribution from the author. By contrast, the idea/expression dichotomy has a more implicit assumption about creativity; it assumes that ideas are more important to the promotion of creativity than expressions. This implicit assumption is evidenced by different normative approaches to copyright law, such as utilitarian analysis and natural rights theories, which suggest that non-protection of ideas is necessary for promoting creativity and that the protection of expressions is too harmful to creativity.[4] The exclusive right to make derivative works is based upon a similar assumption, as will be further discussed in Chapter 3.

This chapter contends that the law's idea/expression dichotomy, which requires the same standard of review for both derivative works and reproductions, is not justified under cognitive psychology's understanding of the creative process, or is at least not a sufficient tool to determine whether a work is creative or not. During the cognitive process of creation, authors utilize their prior knowledge to crystallize abstract thoughts into new ideas. Specifically, authors employ domain-relevant knowledge and memory as building blocks in their creative process. Cognitive psychology posits that both ideas and expressions (in copyright terms) are possible knowledge components that creativity is based on and identifies both types of knowledge as an inherent part of the creative process. This chapter's argument focusses on the descriptive-critical level, and argues that as far as the distinction between derivative works (works based on expressions of previous works) and original works (works that are based on abstract ideas or unprotected expressions) is concerned, there is a mismatch between copyright law and cognitive psychology's understanding of creativity. In fact, it is possible that the basic idea/expression dichotomy in copyright law is also discordant with cognitive psychology. Although a shift to a new copyright regime is premature, a normative reevaluation of the legal justifications underlying the current regime is proper, considering this chapter's conclusions. Additionally, the findings suggested in this chapter could be used as a basis for a normative discussion, under various approaches, in the absence of other empirical data about the affects current copyright law has on creativity, as will be demonstrated in Chapter 3.

Literature on the cognitive psychology of creativity includes theoretical literature as well as empirical and historical studies that seek to outline the various cognitive stages of the creative process and the common pattern of creativity identifiable in authors' cognitive processes. This chapter reviews the existing literature on the cognitive psychology of creativity, discusses its main characteristics, and extracts several substantial notions about the various stages of the creative process and the importance of previous knowledge and memory in the creative process. These notions demonstrate that there is a gap between the way the law understands derivative work and its place in the creative world. This gap warrants a reevaluation of the legal justifications underlying the exclusive right to make derivative works, the scope of this right, and the remedies for infringement.[5]

The notion regarding the centrality of prior relevant knowledge in the creative process and its role as a knowledge component for both ideas and expressions, is one of the grounds on which this chapter argues that the law should conceptually separate mere reproductions from the making of derivative works under copyright. Whereas mere reproductions are properly considered uncreative by cognitive psychology and the law, derivative works are the result of creative activity that is not qualitatively different from making an "original" work. To reflect this distinction between creative and non-creative activities, copyright law should separate the reproduction right from the derivative work right. This conclusion will be further explored in Chapters 4 and 5.

In addition, two other aspects of cognitive psychology could illuminate copyright law. First, the cognitive psychology of creativity could contribute to a better, more precise understanding of copyright law's originality requirement. Copyright should embrace psychology's understanding that not every creative product should be considered entirely original. The second concerns copyright's requirement of an independent contribution by the author. Post-modern copyright law purportedly utilizes a definition of independent contribution that is significantly narrower than the "romantic author" approach, the predecessor to copyright's current understanding of an independent contribution, which was criticized as too broad. The cognitive process of creativity strongly suggests that although a work of authorship has many sources external to the author, the author nevertheless has an independent contribution that cannot be disregarded.

Before delving into the core arguments, it is important to outline several characteristics of cognitive psychology's discourse on creativity. First, this field does not distinguish between creative activities that concern works of authorship in copyright terms and creative activities that concern inventions in patent law terms. Therefore, when necessary, this chapter articulates the differences that may arise in light of this lack of differentiation. Second, the meaning of many terms in cognitive psychology is different from both common parlance and legal terms. Two main terms warrant explanation here: The field of cognitive psychology uses the terms "problem" or "task" to refer to the goal driving the author's creative process.[6] Put differently, these terms mean the task that the creative activity revolves around. The creative environment in which the creative process takes place is referred to as a "domain," and this chapter uses the term "task-domain" often. This term means the creative environment relevant to the task the author seeks to complete. Another important point is the meaning of the term knowledge. In cognitive psychology, this term includes various components of information. Some of these may appear to copyright experts as ideas in their legal sense. However, as this chapter points out, the term *knowledge* in cognitive psychology includes informational components that reflect *expressions* in the copyright sense.[7]

This chapter is organized in the following manner. Part II presents the predominant theories of the process of creation and emphasizes the main characteristics of each group of theories. Part III divides the cognitive process of creation into two main stages: the stage of abstract unfocussed ideation, and the stage of crystallization of a preliminary idea using previous domain-relevant knowledge and memory. Part IV uses theoretical, empirical and historical research to explain the role of prior domain-relevant knowledge and memory in the process of creation. Finally, Part V discusses how the discourse of cognitive psychology and the notions extracted from it may affect copyright law and, specifically, the right to make derivative works.

II. The creative cognition – theories

The birth of the modern understanding of the cognitive process of creation is attributed to the British psychologist Graham Wallas and his book "The Art of Thought", which was published in 1926.[8] In his book, Wallas described various cognitive stages of the creative process that became the basis for current theories of creativity. In the second half of the twentieth century, cognitive psychologists strived to develop a comprehensive model of the creative process. This part presents the predominant theories of the cognitive process of creation. In addition to outlining these approaches, this part shows that, despite their differences, they all dedicate significant discussion to authors' use of prior domain-relevant knowledge, memory, and heuristics in the creative process. For this purpose, this part uses the taxonomy offered in the field of cognitive psychology for the different approaches,[9] while referring to original literature and additional scholarship in order to conceptualize different approaches to the creative process.

1) Stage and componential process theories

The modern stage and componential approaches to creativity are a direct continuation of Wallas' scholarship, and therefore, to understand them, it is important to first describe his stage theory to creativity. Wallas hypothesized that four stages formed the creative process: preparation, incubation, illumination and verification.[10]

The preparation stage consists of a preliminary identification of the problem or task at hand and its definition.[11] Conscious thinking, reliance on the author's prior knowledge, expertise, and his analytical capabilities, and other components that draw from the author's domain-relevant knowledge characterize this stage. The incubation stage is characterized by a lack of conscious thought about the task, and the author often consciously engages in other problems and tasks. At this stage, unconscious processes occur, which consist mainly of associative thinking and the combination of ideas. In the illumination stage, a promising idea breaks into the consciousness of the author, who identifies that an idea is crystallizing in his mind intuitively. Finally, in the verification stage, the author works consciously and examines, refines, and develops the idea that passed into his consciousness during the illumination stage. The author also examines the validity of the idea and crystallizes it into its exact form.

Wallas' stage theory was the basis for empirical studies that sought to verify his theory. In addition, the theory was the basis for more elaborated theoretical models in the same spirit.[12] However, Wallas' division to four stages was too constraining to account for the various characteristics of the creative process, and his focus on the different components included in each stage lacked detail. For example, Wallas did not explain the relationship between the different stages or their significance and position in the creative process. In addition, Wallas did not explain the sub-processes of each stage, which was particularly problematic for the incubation stage. One of the most significant models that was developed on the basis of Wallas' stage theory in order to fill in the gaps was Teresa Amabile's componential model to creativity, which was first introduced in her book "The Social Psychology of Creativity," published in 1983,[13] and was later updated in her 1996 book, "Creativity in Context."[14]

Amabile, as well as Wallas, suggested four main stages in the creative process. Her first stage is the problem or task presentation stage.[15] This stage comes into play when the author is highly motivated to identify a problem or to engage in a task, or when the problem or task are presented by an external entity. The second stage is the preparation stage, which Amabile defined as the stage where the author constructs or activates a task-relevant knowledge database. When the author has sufficient task-relevant knowledge and expertise, this stage may be significantly shortened.[16] The third stage is the response generation stage in which the author generates possible responses to the task or problem by searching, consciously or unconsciously, for possible solution paths.[17] The fourth stage is the response validation stage, which Amabile described as the stage in which task-relevant knowledge and skills have a significant role.[18] In this stage the potential generated responses are analyzed using existing knowledge and formed in a way that will fit the solution on the one hand and be functional on the other hand.[19]

In addition to her four stages, Amabile emphasized three cognitive components that come into play in each of the stages.[20] The first component, and the most important one for the purpose of this chapter, is the domain-relevant skills component. Amabile defined this component as one that contains all possible responses that the author can perceive. A new response is generated from this pool of possible responses and then validated using task-relevant information and knowledge. This component also includes the author's prior factual knowledge about the task-domain that consists of facts, principles, common paradigms, and aesthetic criteria, as well as technical abilities that are necessary for the task-domain.[21] She argued that there is significant importance in the way task-relevant knowledge is stored and coded; information coded by general principles will be more useful to the author than a bundle of facts with narrow applicability.[22] This component was identified by Amabile as mainly within the preparation and response validation stages.

The second component Amabile identified is creativity-relevant skills.[23] She defined this component as the "something extra" that is required for creative activity. It is what determines the amount that the new idea surpasses the old ideas it is built upon. Without creative-relevant skills even authors with excellent task-relevant skills will be unable to create a new product. Amabile offered the following set of characteristics to describe this component: the ability to break through common conceptions; the ability to develop new cognitive systems for problem solving; the ability to understand complex situations; the ability to maintain a wide range of available responses over time; suspension of response validation; the use of the widest categories possible; and precise memory and creative conception of works in the world.[24] This component includes knowledge about the task-relevant heuristics that could operate in both an explicit and conscious mode or in an implicit and unconscious one.[25] Amabile identified this component as related to the response generation stage.[26]

The third component identified by Amabile is task motivation.[27] This component distinguishes between the author's inner task-motivation (i.e., the personal interest the author has in a specific task) and outer task-motivation (i.e., a social or professional constraint that obliges the author to engage with a specific task). While the first, according to Amabile, enhances creativity, the latter inhibits the author's creative abilities. The motivation component affects both the task presentation and the response validation stages.

Cognitive psychologists Mark Runco and Ivonne Chand introduced a five-component model for creativity in 1995.[28] These components are divided into two tiers. The first tier consists of problem finding, idea finding, and evaluation components. The problem finding component includes identifying and defining a problem or task, while the idea finding component reflects creativity and mental flexibility. The evaluation component reflects critical thinking about an idea. The second tier includes knowledge (divided into declarative and procedural knowledge) and motivation (divided into internal and external motivation). Procedural knowledge refers to knowledge of strategies that facilitate accomplishing task-relevant processes (know-how). Declarative knowledge, on the other hand, refers to the author's factual knowledge.[29] Runco and Chand placed these components in the second tier because they contribute to the creative process more than they control it.

Despite the similarities between Runco and Chand's and Amabile's models, some differences should be articulated. While Amabile attributed the task-relevant skills to the preparation and response validation stages, Runco and Chand argued that knowledge (declarative and procedural) affects not only the problem finding stage, but also the idea finding stage. This is significant because Amabile identified a stage in the creative process where prior knowledge has no contribution, while Runco and Chand posit that knowledge affects every stage of the creative process. Amabile's approach and the componential models to creativity were criticized on several grounds. First, because these approaches suggest a wide array of components that are interrelated, they were criticized due to lack of parsimony.[30] Second, these models are difficult to verify empirically because every component must be identified and measured separately to reach a valid conclusion. Third, these approaches do not explain which stage or component is most important to creativity.

Every one of the models in the stage and componential approaches dedicates significant attention to knowledge-based components throughout the creative process. In Wallas' theory, the use of prior knowledge is evident in both the preparation stage, when the author uses his previous education and knowledge, and the validation stage, in which the author validates the creative product in light of his task-relevant knowledge.[31] Under Amabile's approach, prior knowledge plays a significant role in task presentation, preparation, response generation, and validation.[32] In the preparation and validation stages, according to Amabile, the author uses his task-relevant skills, which include factual (semantic) knowledge. Runco and Chand, on their part, emphasized the use of task-relevant declarative knowledge in every part of the creative process.[33]

Under each of these theories, the use of prior knowledge consists of various types of information that could be used as a basis for a work of authorship. Ideas (in their legal sense) are obviously included as well as methods, processes, and other abstract components that are essential to the creative process. However, the description of the task-relevant knowledge under these theories includes the use of knowledge components that reflect concrete and explicit expressions (in the legal sense) formed from works that are stored in the author's memory. Both types of knowledge could be the basis of creative activity under cognitive psychology.

Copyright law only partially matches the cognitive understanding of creativity. With respect to the use of prior knowledge in preliminary phases of the creative process – for example, in the input and processing phases (reflected in the preparation and incubation stages in Wallas' model, or the preparation and response generation stages in Amabile's model) – copyright law allows the use of any type of knowledge that the theories consider. This is because copyright law is not interested in the preliminary phases of creativity; it is concerned only with the concrete final creative product – the output. With regard to the output however, while copyright law allows the use of the knowledge type of ideas (or methods, facts and processes) or unprotected expressions as the basis for creativity, it does not allow the use of protected expressions (with some exceptions, including the fair use doctrine). This is in contrast to the approaches presented above that view expressions as relevant knowledge types for creativity in all of its phases.

In addition, it is important to emphasize that Wallas and Amabile identified stages in the creative process where the author has an individual contribution and prior knowledge does not play a role. This is evident in Wallas' illumination stage and in Amabile's response generation. Even in Runco and Chand's model, which holds that knowledge affects every stage of the creative process, there is specific attention to the author's individual contribution to the creative process in the ideation stage. These findings support copyright law's originality requirement, which affords copyright protection only when the author's expression displays a modicum of creativity original to the author.[34] This is in contrast to post-modern approaches that reject the "romantic author" approach.[35] In this sense, copyright law matches the cognitive understanding of creativity.

2) Creativity as a cognitive process

Kozbelt, Beghetto and Runco, important researchers in the field of cognitive psychology who study the creative process, identified a group of theories that concentrates on cognitive processes that characterize the creative process, which they named "cognitive theories."[36] These approaches aim at identifying cognitive abilities and processes that are necessary for creative activity and focus on the process of creation on the one hand and on the author on the other. The main difference between this group of approaches and the stage and componential theories is that the cognitive theories do not concentrate on the timeline of the creative process or on the chronological stage at which sub-processes take place. Instead, they focus on the type of cognitive processes that are relevant and necessary for creativity.

American psychologist J.P. Guilford, who tried to distinguish between divergent and convergent thinking, developed one of the most important models in this group of theories.[37] Divergent thinking refers to the unfocussed process of associative thought which leads to different directions and may cause an original task-relevant idea to occur.[38] Convergent thinking, in contrast, occurs when cognition seeks to find a correct, applicable, and usable solution that fits task-relevant conventions, mainly using deduction.[39] At this stage, there is significant use of stored memory that affects the creative product.[40]

A similar model was suggested by John R. Suler who referred to two sub-processes in the creative process – primary and secondary – based upon principles of Freud's psychoanalysis.[41] The primary sub-process of thinking usually occurs unconsciously and was described by Suler as more primitive than the secondary sub-process. During this sub-process, memories and past experiences mix together; thought is mainly metaphoric because the borderlines between memories are fuzzy. In contrast, the second sub-process is characterized by conceptual organization of memory. In this sub-process, the author is able to access and control the unfocussed thoughts developed in the primary sub-process and crystallize them into socially meaningful products.

Liane Gabora, a researcher who contributed to this line of theories, observed that the creative process requires phases of unfocussed and focussed thought and the ability to combine the two.[42] Gabora's significant contribution in this context is the use of tools from neuroscience and the cognitive sciences to propose a biological conceptualization of these processes. Gabora explained that the human memory is "stored" in neurons and each neuron is responsible for the storage of several memories. Each memory is split between different neurons. Access to stored memories depends on contextual stimulations; a specific stimulation activates a group of cells containing various neurons that respond to the stimulation. Gabora argued that in a state of unfocussed thought many cell groups and their respective neurons are activated, which are otherwise inactive. These excessive neurons are referred to as "neurds." Thus, Gabora proposed that the purpose of unfocussed thought is to gather neurds to use as a solution for the relevant task or problem. The relevant neurons will pass through to the focussed thought and the author will use them to crystallize a concrete idea. According to this approach, which was named the "honing theory of creativity," unfocussed thought leads to original but impractical ideas that become honed using focussed thought.[43]

Ronald A. Finke, Thomas B. Ward, and Steven M. Smith presented a different theory of creativity called the "Geneplore" model in 1992.[44] The name of the model is derived from its main two processes – generate and explore – that are subject to constraints that depend on the creative product.[45] Fink, Ward and Smith defined the model as more heuristic than explanatory, and its aim is to show that most creative activities could be described in terms of primary production of potential ideas followed by thorough research of these ideas.[46] Different types of idea production processes include restoring memory structures, creating simple associations from these structures, and recombining them or transferring the memory structures to new forms.[47] It is important to clarify that the term "ideas" in the context of the Geneplore model does not have the same meaning as the equivalent legal term; rather, it refers to the production of any part of the creative product.[48] Different types of exploration processes include the search for new characteristics of mental structures, the search for compatible metaphors, the search for new operability of existing memory structures and evaluating the potential to use them in different contexts.[49] This model does not distinguish between generation and exploration processes and posits that the author switches between different modes many times throughout the creative process.[50] Finally, the Geneplore model assumes that the relevant task or the end product can cast constraints on both processes at any point during the creative process.[51] An example of such constraints is restricted resources of limited operability.[52]

These approaches best illustrate the general division of the creative process into two sub-processes: the unfocussed phase, in which abstract ideas are created,[53] and the focussed phase, in which the ideas are crystallized into concrete form. Guilford, Suler and Gabora make an explicit division between these two stages: they show that the focussed phase of creativity is characterized by utilizing prior task-relevant knowledge and memory.[54] Guilford and Gabora stress that stored memory plays a crucial part in creativity. Though they do not explicitly define whether this use of memory includes ideas or expression in copyright terms, they do refer to the use of complete memory units, and it is more than likely that such a use consists of both ideas and expression. Finke, Ward and Smith, on their part, show that knowledge and memory play a significant role in every phase of creativity. In addition, the idea generation part of their model is specifically characterized by the restoration of existing memory structures and recombination in order to produce new creative products. Here too, there is reference to the use of preexisting expression (in copyright terms) as a basis for creativity since these memory structures are capable of bearing concrete expressions as well as ideas. In fact, when a memory structure that holds task-relevant preexisting works is restored, it is more than likely that it will contain expressions rather than mere ideas.[55]

A substantial match between the cognitive approaches to creativity and copyright law is evident here as well. Copyright law allows the use of many types of knowledge and memory components for the crystallization of unfocussed ideas into concrete creative products.[56] Among these are abstract ideas (or methods, facts and processes) as well as unprotected expression (in the public domain or by fair use). However, as far as the use of protected expressions during the output phase of creativity is concerned, there is a mismatch between copyright law's derivative work right and the cognitive theories of creativity.

Aside from that, similar to the discussion of theories about the stages of creativity, the creative cognition theories focus on the independent contribution of the author to the creative product. Notably, Guilford, Suler and Gabora's models include a phase of unfocussed cognition that is not related to the use of prior knowledge.[57] It also appears in the Geneplore model of Finke, Ward and Smith, which articulates the independent cognitive features of the author that are not attributed to prior knowledge.[58] In the context of copyright law, these theories have implications on the romantic author discourse and on the originality requirement.[59] Later sections show that the division to two main sub-processes is also compatible with other theories of creativity.

3) *Creativity as problem solving*

One of the most significant theories on the process of creation posits that it as a problem-solving process.[60] However, in contrast to classical problem solving where the goal is known but the paths to the solution are not, this theory holds that the creative process is characterized by ill-defined goals and problems.[61] Further, although there may be cases in which there is no problem at all, it is usually possible to split ill-defined problems into well-defined sub-problems in a way that fits the classical model of problem-solving theory.[62] Kozbelt, Beghetto and Runco also noted that these approaches focus both on the creative process and the author – the first because these approaches deal with common cognitive psychology approaches that refer to the representation of problem and heuristic searching, and the latter by emphasizing the expertise that is required from the author in the specific task-domain.

Guilford suggested one of the first models of creative problem solving.[63] His model was based on several main recursive stages that are connected with intermediary processes that affect the problem-solving process. The first stage Guilford proposed is the filtering stage, during which the author's attention is directed to a specific input. The next stage is cognition, in which the author recognizes the problem and defines it. At this stage, the author's cognition is open to receiving additional inputs from the environment. The following stage is production in which potential solutions to the problem are produced. Then, another cycle of the cognition and production stages appears in which new knowledge is gathered and additional potential solutions are created. This cycle ends when a potential solution is compatible with the problem. In between each of these stages, there is an intermediate stage of evaluation where the author checks the validity of the input, the potential solutions, and the problem structure. The foundation of the entire process is the author's stored memory, which feeds every one of the different stages. Importantly, when Guilford discussed stored memory, he referred to different types of information, such as visual-figural, symbolic, semantic and behavioral.

Another model for creativity which fits the problem solving and expertise category was proposed by Philip Johnson-Laird, a psychologist professor and researcher focussing, among other things, on the creative process.[64] He theorized that five assumptions underlie the creative process: (1) the outcome of the process must be innovative for the author; (2) the outcome of the process may be innovative for society, but the author's mental process will be the same even if another author has already reached the same outcome; (3) presumably, the creative products are unknown in advance; (4) creativity adheres to preexisting constraints and conventions, whether external or internal to the author, and the author does not function as a closed system but is affected by existing aesthetic values; (5) works of authorship are not composed of "nothing;" rather, they are founded on preexisting grounds that function as raw material even for the most original works.

The problem-solving and expertise approach to creativity is supported by a wealth of empirical and historical studies. Experimental research demystified some of the cognitive processes underlining creative innovation by showing that prior failed solution attempts lead to proper problem representation and heuristic learning that is crucial to creativity.[65] In addition, historical studies based on personal manuscripts of important artists have also shown that expertise plays an integral role in the creative process. American cognitive psychologist John R. Hayes, for example, studied 500 works of 76 great composers and found that only three were composed before the tenth year of the composer's career.[66] As a result, some scholars postulate that there is a "10-year rule," requiring at least ten years of experience to create masterpieces.[67] Other significant experiments have shown how artists and scientists explicitly utilize previous works to improve their creative skills.[68]

The creative problem-solving and expertise approaches best illustrate the importance of task-relevant knowledge to the creative process and the significance of prior knowledge and memory to innovation. These approaches – mainly Guilford's – explain that the use of prior knowledge and memory applied to various types of information also include concrete and material types of knowledge and not only ideas, processes or methods.[69] In this sense, it includes expressions (in copyright terms) as an information type that is at the basis of creativity. Later sections use the historical research that verifies these theories to demonstrate the importance of knowledge and memory in creativity.[70] In addition, these sections show that these approaches fit the general division of the creative process into two sub-processes. However, it is important to note that the creative problem-solving approaches were criticized for two reasons: their inability to explain how authors identify problems at the beginning of the creative process; and their significant focus on expertise and prior knowledge as the only source of creativity.[71] This difficulty is especially relevant to creative activities in which the problem is ill-defined or does not exist because the activation of a heuristic mechanism in the problem-domain cannot account for the first stage of creativity. The problem-finding approach to creativity completes this gap.

4) Creativity as problem-finding

The problem-finding approach came mainly as a reaction to the problem-solving approach to creativity and its shortcoming in explaining how authors identify problems and initiate the required motivation to engage in problem solving. The problem-finding approach is attributed first and foremost to Jacob Getzels and Mihaly Csikszentmihalyi, two leading and ground-breaking creativity researchers, who pointed out the importance of theorizing the problem-finding stage of creativity in 1976.[72] They argued that problem finding is a crucial first step to problem solving and that is it not necessarily separated from the solution itself. To test this hypothesis, they observed 31 art students performing an open task, which required them to draw a set of objects provided by the researchers.[73] This study suggested that the openness of an author to a problem and his investigative behavior while creating and adjusting the structure and content of the preliminary problem indicate that the author is engaged in problem finding while searching for a solution for the first identified problem.

However, Kozbelt, Beghetto and Runco emphasized that the problem-finding approach, as it was much more subjective, was not sufficiently validated through empirical research.[74] In fact, they argued that the research that attempted to explain this approach empirically could be better conceptualized under problem-solving models. Thus, they argued that the distinction between both approaches is explained by scholars' differing emphasis and goals, rather than by the substantive differences in the two scholars' theories. For example, if one is interested in the subjective motivation of authors he would focus on the problem-finding approach; whereas, if one wishes to focus on the cognitive processes that cause the creation of new ideas, he would focus on problem-solving approaches.

In fact, the problem-finding approach is a complementary stage to the problem-solving approach, in the sense that it accounts for the individual contribution of the author within the process of creation while the problem-solving approach does not. If the two approaches are understood as two components of the same creative process, they are compatible with the description of the creative process as a two-phase process of unfocussed and focussed cognitive activity. In the legal context, the problem-finding approach emphasizes the independent contribution of the author to the creative product and conflicts with the post-modern approaches that diminish the author's role in the creative process.

III. Crystallization of the unfocussed thought – the crucial role of knowledge and memory

In spite of the differences between the various theories that seek to explain the cognitive process of creation, they all share general characteristics that have important implications for copyright law in general and, specifically, for the right to make derivative works. This part argues that all the approaches share a division of the creative process into two main sub-processes. Thus, it is possible to characterize the creative process as follows: at the first stage, the author engages in unfocussed thought where she has significant individual contribution to the process; and, at the second stage, the unfocussed thought is crystallized into a concrete creative product in a way that is mainly dictated by prior task-relevant knowledge and memory stored in the author's brain. Each of these processes has implications for copyright law.

1) Unfocused thought – associative thought and abstract ideas

The first characteristic all approaches to creativity have in common is that they refer to a phase of unfocussed attention during which abstract ideas of the creative activity are formed. For example, in Wallas' stage theory, the incubation stage is characterized by unfocussed associative thought.[75] Similarly, the response generation stage in Amabile's model is characterized by abstract cognitive processes, which are driven by highly abstract creative-relevant skills.[76] Runco and Chand also refer to this creative phase in their idea presentation stage, which is described by unfocussed creative thinking.[77]

Further, the unfocussed thought phase is explicitly mentioned in some of the creative cognition approaches. Guilford, for example, referred to it as part of the divergent thinking process, which he described as unfocussed and associative.[78] Similarly, Suler referred to the primary thought process as a metaphorical phase in which memories are not separated from one another.[79] Gabora's model offered a biological description of the unfocussed phase of creativity when she described the formation of "nuerds" during unfocussed stimulation of neuron groups, which import relevant memory and knowledge into the focussed thought stage.[80]

Finke, Ward and Smith's Geneplore model more subtly distinguishes between the two phases. However, significant characteristics of the generation component of the model are compatible with the unfocussed thought description. The generation component includes, for example, associative thought that is followed by new potential ideas.[81] In addition, some characteristics of the exploration component of the model are also compatible with unfocused thought, for instance, the metaphorical thought which the authors attribute to the exploration component.

When considering the problem-solving and problem-finding approaches as a whole, it is evident that they also refer to components that are compatible with the unfocussed thought phase. For example, although Guilford's model appears highly structured and based on analytical phases of knowledge use, it also recognizes the role of illumination and intuition in the creative process.[82] Johnson-Laird's assumption that the products of the creative process cannot be pre-known,[83] along with the notion that ill-defined problems could be split into several well-defined problems,[84] illustrates that the problem-solving approach identifies a stage that is not solely analytic and not necessarily based on knowledge and expertise. Thus, these approaches also fit the unfocussed thought phase of creativity and the problem-finding approaches.

The discussion thus far shows that the predominant approaches to the cognitive process of creativity systematically identify stages and components in which unfocussed thought occurs and produces preliminary abstract ideas at the early stages of the creative process. The more relevant phase of creativity for the purpose of this chapter is, however, the phase in which the abstract ideas are crystallized into a socially valuable concrete product. The next section discusses how each of these theories identifies stages of crystallization of ideas using task-relevant knowledge and memory.

2) The use of task-relevant knowledge

The second characteristic that all approaches to creativity share is reliance on pre-existing task-relevant knowledge and memory in different stages of the creative process. One example is found in Wallas' stage theory. The use of task-relevant knowledge is evident in two main stages – the preparation and validation stages. In the preparation stage, as described by Wallas, the author uses prior expertise and task-relevant knowledge to prepare for the creative process.[85] At the validation stage, the author consciously examines the preliminary ideas in light of his task-relevant expertise. Knowledge plays a crucial role at this point as well. In fact, Wallas himself described the preparation and validation stages as strongly interrelated.

Amabile's more developed stage model explicitly acknowledges the use of task-relevant knowledge. Indeed, this model defines task-relevant skills as one of the three components of the creative process.[86] Like the analysis suggested above with regard to Wallas' theory, Amabile attributes the use of task-relevant knowledge to the preparation and response validation stages.[87] It thus seems that Amabile dedicated a significant and explicit attention to the use of task-relevant knowledge in the creative process. Runco and Chand also explicitly acknowledged the significance of task-relevant knowledge (which they referred to as declarative knowledge) as a main component that affects the problem presentation and ideation stages.[88]

The use of task-relevant knowledge is also emphasized in the creative cognition approaches. Guilford's convergent thinking includes analytical skills and the use of knowledge and memory as he stated explicitly.[89] The secondary thought process described by Suler also fits the use of prior task-relevant knowledge since its purpose is to consciously control and form abstract ideas into concrete products.[90] The same applies for Gabora's honing model of creativity in which the author's memory holds the most significant part.[91] Although Gabora identified the use of memory at the phase of unfocussed thought, she explicitly noted that it is used in the focussed thought phase when memory cells are activated along with the sporadic ideas created by activation of "neurds."[92] The generation process in Finke, Ward and Smith's Geneplore model also consists of task-relevant knowledge use.[93] The researchers defined this process as including the restoration of knowledge and memory structures and adapting them for compatibility with the relevant task.[94]

The problem-solving approach to creativity best illustrates the significance and centrality of task-relevant knowledge and memory to the process of creation. The essence of this approach is the understanding of the creative process as a logical-analytical system to problem solving that is based on task-relevant expertise and previous knowledge.[95] The use of prior knowledge is evident in Guilford's model in which memory storage is utilized during every cognitive activity throughout the creative process. He expressly referred to the importance of knowledge in the creative process and explained that it was characterized by restoring, reproducing and adapting memory structures into a new product.[96] Guilford also articulated the different types of information that are used, including semantic, visual and symbolic knowledge. Johnson-Laird's approach also focusses on task-relevant knowledge and the crucial role of memory in the process of creation. Indeed, two of his five assumptions about creativity concern these components; he pointed out that the creative process must fit predefined creative constraints and be based upon preexisting elements.[97] In addition, Robert Weisberg, an American cognitive psychologist who focussed on creativity studies and the study of geniality, demonstrated the importance of task-relevant knowledge and expertise in a series of experiments.[98]

Thus, the cognitive process of creation is divided into two main sub-processes: (1) unfocussed thought, during which abstract ideas form as a result of the author's associative thought; and (2) the use of task-relevant knowledge and memory during focussed thought for the purpose of crystallizing preliminary abstract ideas into a concrete perceivable form. As noted above, the two sub-processes are relevant to copyright law. The first sub-process is relevant to the discussion on the independent and original contribution of the author to a creative product – copyright law's originality requirement – especially in light of the post-modern discourse on the romantic author approach. The second sub-process is most relevant to the idea/expression dichotomy and the derivative work right because the use of prior knowledge is an inherent part of the creative process and incorporates what copyright law refers to as a derivative work. Further, the second sub-process reveals a mismatch between the law and the cognitive psychology of creativity. The next part will focus on how cognitive psychologists describe the use of prior task-relevant knowledge and the notions that arise from these descriptions, which, as discussed below, have important implications for copyright law and the derivative work right.

IV. The use of task-relevant knowledge and memory in the creative process

The use of task-relevant knowledge and memory is a crucial and inseparable part of creativity under cognitive psychology's predominant approaches to creativity. It is important to discuss the way task-relevant knowledge and memory are formed and used. To this end, this part discusses theoretical notions about the use of prior knowledge that are based on empirical and historical studies of the cognitive process of creativity. This part argues that the use of task-relevant knowledge and memory is not restricted to creative activities such as ideas, processes and methods that are not afforded protection under copyright law and are therefore free to be used for further creative activities. Rather, task-relevant knowledge and memory also include concrete expressions that are stored in the author's memory as part of his visual, semantic and symbolic knowledge. Consequently, the use of expression as a basis for creative activity is not qualitatively different from the use of mere ideas under the cognitive understanding of the creative process. Both elements are an inherent part of the creative process.[99] This observation has significant implications for copyright law, especially the derivative work right.

As emphasized above, the tension between the use of task-relevant knowledge and memory in the creative process and the derivative work right does not necessarily lead to the conclusion that authors should be deprived of an exclusive right to their derivative works. Nevertheless, copyright law's distinction between ideas and expressions is not justified by the theoretical underpinnings of creativity because there is a mismatch between the legal norm and the cognitive understanding of creativity. Accordingly, the legal profession should question whether the law should bridge this gap and fully mirror the cognitive understanding of creativity. It is also important to note that it may be that the creative process is affected by external factors such as culture, economy, religion and the law. This chapter does not argue that the cognitive process of creation is a closed and fixed system; it argues that to the extent the law affects creativity, as may happen due to the existing mismatch presented here, it is important to ask whether this effect is desired and justified. This will be later examined in Chapter 3.

1) Theoretical analysis of the use of knowledge and memory

Runco and Chand dedicated a vast discussion to the role of knowledge and memory in creativity.[100] As to knowledge, they suggested a distinction between procedural and declarative knowledge. Procedural knowledge refers to familiarity with strategies with which certain task-related processes could be accomplished (know-how). When an author chooses a useful strategy, procedural knowledge has a significant contribution to creativity. In a series of studies, Runco, Chand and their collaborators tested the effect of procedural knowledge on creativity. These studies divided participants into two groups and gave each group the same task. One group received general guidelines about how to accomplish the task, while the other group received explicit directions for achieving the task. These studies revealed not only that explicit directions lead to greater innovation, but also that procedural knowledge may overcome thought fixation at the ideation stage of creativity.[101]

Declarative knowledge, on the other hand, refers to factual information stored in the author's memory.[102] Runco and Chand theorized that declarative knowledge contributes to the creative process by supplying the necessary information for the creation of ideas. Support for this theory is found in historical studies that show the need to acquire expertise in a field before achieving substantial creative accomplishments.[103] Runco and Chand argued that declarative knowledge directly affects the ideation stage because an author with greater task-relevant expertise has a wider set of tools to develop preliminary ideas.[104] For example, they argued that when a person is asked to engage in an open task that includes round objects, he will have an advantage if his expertise includes knowledge of round things, such as an astronomer who knows the general features of planets or a biologist who understands molecules or cells. They also emphasized that declarative knowledge is mainly experience-based but could be achieved by relevant environmental cues.

Runco and Chand also explained that both procedural and declarative knowledge are stored in long-term memory, which can be accessed at any moment in order to engage with a task. However, they noted that merely accessing procedural and declarative knowledge would likely lead to an unoriginal and uncreative product. They also posited that the memory in which knowledge is stored could be divided into two types: episodic, defined as a detailed memory of an experience, and semantic, defined as a memory that contains only general characteristics of the relevant experience. Semantic memory is especially relevant to the creative process because it contains "gaps" and therefore does not allow a full reproduction of a relevant experience. Thus, semantic memory allows an author to restore parts of a specific experience and reconstruct other parts to engage in a relevant task. Runco and Chand argued that such reconstruction of memory is a creative activity. It is important to clarify once again that declarative knowledge consists of concrete instances, and, in this sense, includes both ideas and expressions in copyright terms. The result of the reflection on explicit artistic expressions as part of an experience that is stored in the author's memory while restoring it and reconstructing it may be an example of a derivative work in the legal sense.

In fact, Runco and Chand explained that creative thinking is memory-based.[105] They relied on Langley and Jones who argued that knowledge assists creativity by allowing its restoration viaindexes created for each creative-domain. Langley and Jones explained that:

> Humans possess no general creativity factor; so no such component exists to be measured. Instead, humans possess a wealth of knowledge structures indexed by concepts that a person judges as important. The level of creativity that one exhibits will depend on one's knowledge, one's indexing scheme, and the particular situation in which one finds oneself.[106]

Runco and Chand's account of the use of prior knowledge and memory in the creative process is also backed by additional theoretic literature. Roger Schank, an American cognitive psychologist focussing on artificial intelligence and creativity, for example, described in his knowledge structure model that when an author encounters a cognitive input, he processes it in light of his existing knowledge structures, and that input is embedded into memory in a way that allows future access.[107] Dynamic memory, according to Schank, refines this process when inputs are received in the author's memory that relate to existing knowledge structures or past experiences. Thus, an author's prior experiences alter the author's knowledge structure. Accordingly, the author's ability to understand new phenomena and problems in the world is based on a dynamic memory loaded with knowledge of prior experiences. When an author is required to engage with a task, he uses prior knowledge structures and experiences to detect what Schank refers to as an "explanation pattern" he used in the past. He also argued that the creative process is characterized by two sub-processes. The first is the search for a possible explanation pattern and the second is an adaptation process in which the explanation pattern is restored from memory and adapted so that it is compatible with the relevant task. The emphasis on the adaptation and restructuring as a basis for creativity is evident here as well. This theoretical approach could apply to both the adaptation and restructuring of expressions and ideas that are part of an author's knowledge base. Both types of knowledge could be part of the cognitive process of creativity.

The role of knowledge and memory in creativity was also emphasized in Robert Sternberg's three-facet model to creativity.[108] He referred to the components of knowledge acquisition in the process of creation and their effect on creative illumination. Of the three potential causes for illumination presented, two refer to processes similar to those discussed thus far. One cause, according to Sternberg, is "selective combination," in which illumination is created due to a synthesis between separate pieces of stored information. The ability to perform such a process depends on the author's prior knowledge; the wider the knowledge pool, the greater variety of combinations. Additionally, Sternberg referred to "selective comparison," which compares new information to preexisting knowledge and its characteristics to understand and use the new information. He argued that problem solving by analogy is one example of this cause of illumination. Paul Locher, professor of experimental psychology, reached similar conclusions.[109] He reviewed empirical and historical studies on the process of creation, some of which will be elaborated on later, such as brain imaging, X-ray studies of artworks, and archival studies on the creation of historical masterpieces in real time. Based on these studies, Locher argued that the use of procedural and declarative knowledge is essential and central to all stages of the creative process. Sternberg's emphasis on the importance of synthesis between existing knowledge components in the process of creation, along with Locher's focus on the importance of declarative knowledge (which includes both ideas and expression) to the creative process support the argument that no qualitative distinction between ideas and expressions exists.

2) Empirical studies on creativity

The American creativity researchers, Wayne Baughman and Michael Mumford, assumed in their studies that merely restoring an application of prior experiences and knowledge by the author is not likely to lead to creativity.[110] However, they argued that combining and restructuring existing knowledge is a good mechanism for ideation. This argument was based on several studies showing that creative development in many fields requires the combination and restructuring of existing knowledge. They referred to the research of Michele Mobley (and his co-authors), who argued that it is impossible to create something from nothing and that a generation of new ideas has to be based on existing knowledge structures.[111] Mobley hypothesized that if authors are asked to combine diverse categories, their creative products will be more original. To test this theory, 160 participants were asked to work with exemplars of various categories, to combine them in order to create new categories, and to suggest new exemplars for the new categories and write a story that describes them. They found more originality when participants combined more distant categories, but the results also demonstrated that the quality of the products declined when participants worked with distant categories, which was likely due to difficulties that arose when working with unknown categories.

Following Mobley, Baughman and Mumford conducted the following study: 155 participants were given exemplars of undefined categories. They were first asked to identify each category according to the exemplars provided. They were then asked to create a category that united all the categories mapped by them and to find an exemplar for the united category. Finally, the participants were asked to define the new category and to find more exemplars for it. An analysis of their findings led Baughman and Mumford to conclude that under some conditions, tasks involving the combination of categories lead to better and more original creative products. In addition, they noted that the process of combination and reorganization is executed by searching for the characteristics of each category and mapping them, and that only a combination of the two would lead to greater originality.

A line of similar studies focussing on combination and reorganization of categories and the importance of exemplars was conducted by Finke, Ward and Smith.[112] They focussed on the affects that categories and known perceptions have on the creative process. This was based on the perception that new ideas, as creative as they may be, are usually developed as limited expansions of existing perceptions. Their first study, conducted in 1994, consisted of five experiments.[113] In the first experiment, 37 participants were asked to draw an animal they may encounter on a different planet and another animal from the same species, as well as another animal from the same planet but from a different species. The results showed that the vast majority of animals drawn had earthy features (bilateral symmetry, sensory organs, limbs, etc.), which shows that when an author is asked to create an exemplar for a known category, his work will be highly structured. In their second experiment, 180 participants were asked to draw an animal residing on a different planet that is completely different than earth. The participants were divided into four groups, one group did not receive any guidance and the other group was instructed that the animal has either feathers, fur, or lives underwater. This experiment also indicated that there is significant use of prior knowledge about the characteristics of a category in the process of finding a new exemplar for it. Thus, participants in the feathers group tended to draw winged animals and participants in the underwater group tended to draw animals with fins. Participants in the fur and feather groups tended to draw animals with two feet and participants in the feathers group tended to draw animals with a beak. Three additional experiments also produced results showing that participants usually restore known exemplars of earthy animals when asked to draw imaginary animals.

Based on these findings, Finke, Ward and Smith proposed the term "structured imagination" to describe an author's tendency to create new ideas while preserving existing categories and noted, "Imagination is structured or directed by knowledge of the category or categories most related to the individual's goals." Later, Finke, Ward and Smith explained that the use of knowledge in this context refers to both long-tem memory and to knowledge gathered during engagement with the relevant task.[114] To describe the process in which the author uses pre-existing knowledge structures, Finke, Ward and Smith proposed the "path of least resistance" model.[115] They postulated that when an author imagines a new entity, she first determines the task-relevant knowledge-domain and then accesses the existing knowledge in that domain to construct a new entity. Thomas Ward, a cognition and creativity researcher, and Yuliya Kolomyts, a language researcher, both of University of Alabama, expanded this model and noted that when authors develop new ideas in a specific domain, their first inclination is to access specific exemplars from this domain as a starting point, retrieve characteristics from these exemplars, and then import them into developing ideas.[116] This is based on empirical findings of Ward and his followers, which suggested that to develop an exemplar for a new domain, authors develop products that are substantially similar to exemplars of existing domains. It is likely that this tendency is an inherent part of structured imagination.[117] Notably, Ward theorized that the probability of innovative creativity is higher when the author uses larger systems of knowledge instead of mere exemplars.[118] However, Ward and Kolomyts emphasized that while using more abstract ideas would probably lead to more creativity, it would come at the expense of compatibility and usability of the creative products and thus diminish their value.[119] Therefore, it should be expected that the "constraining" effect that reliance on prior knowledge and exemplars has on innovation is necessary to reach meaningful and valuable creative products.[120]

The studies discussed in this chapter thus far focus on creative thought generally and all fields of creative activity, not only those to which copyright law applies.[121] There are very few empirical studies focussing directly on artworks and other works of authorship. Nevertheless, there are numerous studies relevant to this chapter's discussion that examine the process of *making* works of art. Japanese cognitive psychologists Sawako Yokochi and Takeshi Okada attempted to empirically test different theoretical approaches to creativity by studying the process of creating artworks.[122] For this purpose, they observed Chinese Suibokuga, a traditional painter in his sixties with 20 years of experience, for a three-year period.[123]

The painter was asked to draw eight paintings on an empty canvas and eight additional paintings on a canvas containing 15 random lines drawn by two other participants.[124] Yokochi and Okada identified two important characteristics in these studies.[125] First, when the painter worked with the empty canvas, he used the same painting strategy every time.[126] Second, when the painter worked with predetermined random lines, his paintings were less accurate in their composition but much more original in their style.[127] This observation was corroborated by interviews with the painter after the study.[128] The researchers concluded, based on this finding, that the approach of Finke, Ward and Smith was accurate and that combining preexisting knowledge structures containing components from past experiences contributes significantly to innovation.[129]

Another qualitative study conducted by New Zealand cognitive psychologists Mary-Anne Mace and Tony Ward attempted to develop a model for the creative process behind artworks.[130] They conducted semi-structured interviews with authors during the creative process.[131] At the first stage, 16 visual artists were interviewed at three different times during their creative process – first at the beginning of the process, second at the middle of the process, and third at the end of it. The participants were asked to describe their creative process at the relevant stage of the interview and to refrain from reporting general theories about the creative process. After analyzing the findings, the researchers proposed a detailed model for the creation of artworks based on the interviews.[132] According to Mace and Ward, the creation of a work of art does not develop out of a conceptual void; rather, it is a product of thought and ongoing experience.[133] They argued that the author obtains a vast knowledge base of the creative process over time, explicitly and implicitly understanding techniques, skills, genres, theories, aesthetics, *prior works*, and art in its contemporary and historical sense.[134] This knowledge develops along with the process of creation, and the author refers to it at every stage of the process. They later verified the results of this study. It is important to note that Mace and Ward explicitly emphasize that the creative process is also based on explicit knowledge of prior works that the author refers to during the process.[135] They also emphasized that this aspect of the process links the process of creating a current work with previous and future works in the same domain.[136] In this sense, it is clear that the process of creation includes the use of expressions as well as ideas.[137]

In the last three decades, the number of quantitative empirical studies of creativity using methodologies and instruments from neurosciences has grown tremendously. The two main methodologies in this field are the use of fMRI and EEG.[138] One example of such a study is American cognitive psychologist Robert Solso's study, which examines the creative process in real-time using fMRI.[139] Solso measured the brain activity of the British portrait artist Humphrey Ocean while he drew portraits of figures that were presented to him and compared it to the brain activity of another amateur participant performing the same tasks. The two participants were asked to draw the faces of presented figures for 30 seconds each while connected to fMRI.

The results of the study showed excessive activity in the right-rear part of the amateur participant's brain when compared to Ocean's. According to Solso, this shows that Ocean's experience and expertise in face-detection and understanding may have led to less effort in the parts of the brain charged with face-detection. The more interesting result, however, was that Ocean's brain showed excessive activity in the front-central part of the right lobe, which is in charge of associative thinking and manipulation of visual structures.[140] According to Solso, this shows that while the amateur participant reproduced the figures presented to him, Ocean thinks about them and associatively adapts them.[141]

In a different fMRI study conducted by cognition and brain scientist Melissa Ellamil (and her co-authors), 15 visual art students participated.[142] Presented with short book descriptions, participants were asked to draw illustrations for each book's cover on a tablet computer connected to fMRI.[143] Later, they were asked to review their illustrations and evaluate them.[144] The researchers noted that at the production stage of the illustrations, excessive brain action occurred in the medial temporal lobe, which is in charge of the processing of semantic memory and recombination of memory using associations.[145] The researchers explained that this finding fits theoretical approaches that focus on associative processing and recombination of existing knowledge as the basis for creativity.[146]

Studies using the EEG methodology have also validated some of the theoretical approaches to creativity concerning the use of task-relevant knowledge and memory.[147] Austrian cognitive psychologists Andreas Fink and Mathias Benedek reviewed many EEG studies that focussed on creativity.[148] One of their main conclusions was that all studies show changes in alpha power in the author's brain cortex during creative activity.[149] One of the consistent changes that Fink and Benedek showed is an increase in alpha power in the rear part of the parietal lobe of the brain cortex.[150] They concluded that because this part of the brain is in charge of memory, the increase in alpha power should be understood as an attempt to search and restore memory in order to use and recombine knowledge for the creative process.[151]

Despite the differences in the various neuroscientific studies of creativity, many researchers reached similar conclusions about the use of task-relevant knowledge and memory in the creative process. American creativity researcher Keith Sawyer, for example, reviewed the studies published in this field between October 2010 and May 2011.[152] Although he urges psychologists to think critically about the use of neuroscience in creativity studies and to understand its shortcomings, he nevertheless concluded that there are a number of issues where the results are undisputed. For instance, he emphasized that associative thinking – the recombination of preexisting knowledge and task-relevant expertise – is an undisputed part of creativity. In a different literature review, cognitive psychologists Sureyya Yoruk and Mark Runco examined fMRI and EEG studies conducted from 2004 to 2014.[153] They concluded that creativity is characterized by excessive brain activity in the left part of the brain and specifically in the lower parietal lobe, which is in charge of storing semantic memory. In addition, they argued that these areas of the brain are in charge of creating preliminary associations that function as a step toward more distant associations that develop in the right hemisphere of the brain where EEG studies show excessive alpha power. Therefore, they concluded that creativity is characterized by the processing and recombination of semantic memory and task-relevant knowledge contained within such processing.

3) Historical studies

One of the methodologies used in creativity studies is archival research, which studies the creation of works of art by reviewing the personal documents made by artists while they created masterpieces.[154] This section focusses on the studies conducted by Weisberg, a cognitive psychologist focussing on creativity, geniality and expertise, which shed light on the importance of expertise and task-relevant knowledge to the creative process from a historical perspective.

Weisberg's first two case studies are from the field of visual arts, specifically, masterpieces of Pablo Picasso.[155] The first work is *Les Demoiselles d'Avignon* published in 1907. Weisberg analyzed the creative process of this work by comparing X-ray images of the final product to sketches preserved by Picasso. Weisberg described the various stages in Picasso's work as well as the parts in which Picasso used prior works. However, the most important observation for our purposes is the identification of external sources of Picasso's work. Weisberg learned that the nude female figures in Picasso's work were based on and adapted from figures included in other painters' masterpieces. For example, the kneeling female in the bottom-right part of Picasso's painting is substantially similar to the female appearing in Paul Cezanne's work entitled *The Three Bathers*. In addition, the two central female figures in Picasso's work are similar to the two women appearing in Goya's *Nuda Maja* and Manet's *Olympia*. The general composition of Picasso's work is drawn from his colleague, Henri Matisse's work in *Le Bonheur de Vivre*.

Weisberg conducted similar research regarding Picasso's masterpiece *Guernica*. He explained that this work is substantially based on previous works of Picasso. But more importantly, Weisberg also noted that the Guernica, referring to the atrocities of the Spanish civil war, was substantially based on Goya's series of sketches titled "The Disasters of War" from 1816. Weisberg emphasized that several figures and positions presented in Goya's sketches appear, after stylistic adaptations, in Picasso's *Guernica*.

Weisberg found similar findings in musical compositions.[156] He studied many of the early works of Wolfgang Amadeus Mozart and found significant reliance on other composers' works. For instance, Mozart's first four piano concerti (K. 37, 29, 40, 41) did not contain original music at all – they were adapted from the works of five other composers. In addition, Mozart's three consecutive piano concerti (K. 107 nos 1–3) composed in 1772 were in fact the works of Johann Christian Bach (Johan Sebastian Bach's younger son), which were rearranged and orchestrated by Mozart. A similar pattern was identified in Mozart's first symphonies and chamber compositions, which were stylized according to pre-classical styles and based on young Bach's and other German composers' compositions. Likewise, Weisberg found reliance on prior works in Mozart's later compositions.[157] He argued that the finale of Mozart's Jupiter symphony – the last that Mozart composed – is based on five themes that were drawn from other composers' work. Similarly, Mozart's three E-flat horn concerti are substantially based on Antoni Rosetti's horn concerti from the same period.

Weisberg divided his studies into two categories of creativity. The first was described as reproductive creativity.[158] It includes *Guernica*, the structure of which Picasso based on his previous works. He noted that these cases show this type of creativity occurs through the reproduction of prior knowledge without modifying its form and by adapting it to fit new needs through analogical transfer. A second type of creativity is reproductive restructuring. An example of this is Picasso's *Les Demoiselles d'Avignon*, which is speculated to have been substantially restructured after Picasso visited an ethnographic museum and encountered primitive sculpture. Weisberg inferred from these case studies that every work is linked to prior work and that every work has a preceding work, as the past is a crucial basis for innovation.[159] In light of these observations, Weisberg proposed a model that explains the use of task-relevant knowledge in creativity. In contrast to the notion that creativity begins with the reception of input from the environment that is later processed according to stored knowledge (bottom-up model), he contends that task-relevant knowledge forms the perception of input from the environment (top-down model). Thus, when a person identifies a new event in the environment, the mere identification is governed by the preexisting task-relevant knowledge already stored in his memory, which further evidences task-relevant knowledge's critical contribution to creativity.

The studies presented in this part – theoretical, empirical and historical – all point to the same conclusion for this chapter's purposes. They all focus, in one way or another, on the significant role task-relevant knowledge and memory have in the cognitive process of creation and describe in different ways how these components are used by the author. These studies all show that the creative process includes the use of existing knowledge structures inherently and in a concrete way that is identifiable in different stages of the process and its outcomes. The use of knowledge structures is not limited to ideas (in copyright terms); it also includes the explicit use of expressions. Under this reading of the cognitive psychology literature on creativity, there is no qualitative difference between creative activities based upon ideas and those based on explicit expressions. The products of both are considered creative under these approaches. This is the main notion that this chapter tries to extract from the cognitive psychology discourse on creativity. The next part explains how this notion can be applied to copyright law and what implications it may have on different copyright doctrines.

V. The use of prior knowledge and the right to make derivative works

After establishing the notion that the creative process is characterized by two main processes – one of unfocussed thought and generation of abstract ideas and the other of focussed thought and crystallization of abstract ideas – and showing that the use of knowledge and memory (not limited to ideas but also to explicit expressions) is an inherent part of the creative process, this part points out the implications of these notions on the derivative works right and examines to what extent the legal doctrine matches the cognitive understanding of creativity.[160]

The derivative work right grants authors exclusive rights to works that are "based upon one or more preexisting works..."[161] With regard to the application of the current doctrine, Nimmer argues that the right to make derivative works is "superfluous" because the making of a derivative work will (almost) always involve reproduction of the underlying work.[162] On the normative level, most commentators argue that the current, broad definition of the derivative work right is unjustified, as will be further discussed in Chapter 4.

The derivative work right's current definition raises significant questions and difficulties, which focus mainly on the tension between first and second authors, and on the constraints that the right casts on the development of new expressions. The difficulties involve two different aspects of the derivative work right. The first aspect is the scope of the right in light of its statutory definition. This aspect is substantial because it caps the borders of the legal discourse on derivative works and sets its starting and end points and the number of cases to which it applies. The second aspect concerns remedies for copyright infringement. This aspect determines the right's strength to a great extent – that is, the stronger the remedies granted to the copyright holder (or the prohibition on whoever is not), the stronger the right, and vice versa.

In the absence of empirical data that could offer guidance, at least on a utilitarian basis, as to the proper balance between first authors' interests and second authors' interests, it is possible to turn to findings from cognitive psychology's account of creativity.[163] Moreover, as a recent study shows, there is good reason to doubt whether authors are in fact rational agents that respond to market incentives. Stephan Bechtold, Christopher Buccafusco and Christopher Sprigman showed, based on the behavioral experiments they conducted, that authors' decisions to borrow from existing works or create works "from scratch" is not affected by copyright law's incentives, but by their subjective belief about the difficulty of innovation.[164] These findings emphasize the importance of understanding cognitive psychology's account of creativity and applying it to the law in order to create more efficient copyright doctrines. The notion regarding the use of prior knowledge and memory in the creative process and the lack of qualitative differences between ideas and expressions in this context warrant asking whether copyright law's distinction between derivative and original works is justified.

As far as the first aspect is concerned – the scope of the derivative work right – there is a strong link between the legal norm and the cognitive understanding of creativity. If, for example, it turned out that the scope of the derivative work right is very broad, but the reliance on expressions during the process of creation is marginal, it would raise the question of whether such a legal right is needed and justified. In contrast, if the scope of the derivative work right is narrow, vague and applied to a limited set of cases, but the use of preexisting expressions is inherent to the process of creation (as this chapter attempted to show), scholars should ask whether the legal doctrine should better reflect the behavioral aspects of creativity.

But, more important, due to the significance of the use of prior knowledge and memory in the cognitive process of creation (which is not limited to ideas but also includes explicit expressions), a better understanding of the right to make derivative works is warranted. The making of a derivative work is, in its nature, a creative activity under cognitive approaches to creativity and is not qualitatively different than an original work (that is not based on protected expressions). This observation has great importance as far as the scope of the derivative right and its intersection with the reproduction right are concerned. This chapter argues that the reproduction right should apply only to mere reproductions, which are inherently uncreative and therefore qualitatively different from derivative or original works.[165]

To illustrate this point, consider the following example. Assuming that the literary masterpiece "The Catcher in the Rye"[166] is an original work that is creative under copyright law, there are three different alternatives for works based on this work. One alternative is the making of a literary work whose main character is a 16-year-old teenager who runs away from home to the big city and reaches important notions about the life of adults during his journey. This work would probably be considered original under copyright law because it only uses the general underlying idea in the original work, and would also be considered creative under the cognitive approaches presented above. Another alternative is the making of a literary work entitled "60 Years Later: Coming Through the Rye," which presents the relationship between Mr. C. (a reference to Holden Caulfield) and the 90-year-old author who created his character and refers to specific scenes from the original work.[167] This work would fall under the category of derivative works because it uses explicit expression from the original work and contributes additional originality. It would also be considered creative under the cognitive approaches that view the recombination of prior knowledge as part of creativity. A third alternative would be a literal repeat of the original work's text while changing the name of the main character Holden Caulfield to James Sheffield. Under copyright law, this is considered a reproduction despite the marginal changes. In contrast to the two first alternatives, the third option is not considered creative under the cognitive approaches because it is an exact restoration of knowledge without any other creative components.

This example illustrates the gap between the legal categories and the cognitive understanding of creativity. The cognitive psychology approaches do not distinguish between knowledge types such as ideas or expressions as a basis for creativity. They also do not distinguish between the uses of different knowledge types along the timeline of creativity – meaning, in the input, processing, or output stages of creativity. Copyright law, in contrast, is interested almost solely in the output stage and in the final creative product.

At many points, there is a match between the cognitive understanding of creativity and copyright law. Thus, as far as the use of any type of knowledge (ideas or expression) at the time of input and processing is concerned, copyright law allows such use because these stages of creativity are not governed. At the output stage, so long as the use of knowledge led to the creation of ideas or unprotected expressions (whether they are in the public domain or allowed under the fair use doctrine), it is generally not considered an infringement under copyright law as well.

The mismatch between copyright law and the cognitive understanding of creativity is most strongly evident in the use of protected expressions during the output stage of creativity. When this occurs during a creative activity that involves an original contribution of the second author, a derivative work is sometimes made. While the law distinguishes between a derivative work and an original work, under the cognitive understanding of creativity both are creative activities. In contrast, while the law makes almost no distinction between derivative works and mere reproductions, the cognitive approaches to creativity view derivative works as part of creativity but not reproductions. It so happens that while the cognitive approach to creativity views the use of prior expression in the output stage of creativity as an inherent part of the creative process, the legal doctrine sometimes prohibits this behavior and categorizes it as copyright infringement (see Table 1.1).

To illustrate the spectrum of the match between the cognitive process of creation and copyright law, this chapter returns to "The Cacther in the Rye" example.[168] The match between copyright law and the cognitive approaches to creativity is reflected by the fact that the law allows making future works based upon Salinger's book in different ways. Thus, it is possible to make another book that tells the story of a teenager going through complex adolescence in which he critically looks at adult life without it constituting copyright infringement. Such a work would rely substantially on prior knowledge of various types such as ideas, education and aesthetic criteria from the first work. A different type of use that reflects the match between copyright law and the cognitive approaches to creativity is the use of explicit plot lines from the original work during the input and processing phases, so long as the output does not include these expressions. Copyright law also allows the use of explicit scenes and plot lines, and even the character of Holden Caulfield, to express a different mode of expression that substantially changes their original meaning. Under the fair use doctrine, it would probably be allowed to use the character of Holden Caulfield and plot lines from the book to criticize the oppression of minorities in a certain country without it constituting copyright infringement. This would also allow reliance on prior knowledge. The mismatch between copyright law and the cognitive approaches to creativity exists when explicit protected expressions are used to make a new work of authorship – a sequel for example. This was the case in *Salinger v. Colting* where the court ruled that a sequel used explicit expressions from it and therefore infringed Salinger's copyright.[169]

This chapter argues that, in order to relax the tension between the legal doctrine and the cognitive approaches to creativity, it is first necessary to completely separate the reproduction right from the derivative work right. Second, in order to create a full match between the legal doctrine and the cognitive approaches to creativity, a shift in the remedies regime is warranted. These two arguments will be further elaborated in Chapters 4 and 5. This chapter does not argue that these changes to the legal doctrine are justified solely by the cognitive understanding of creativity; they are also justified by intra-legal normative justifications to copyright law, which are further discussed in Chapter 3. I do, however, argue that such changes could better fit the creative behavior of human beings and that, if normatively justified, they should replace the current doctrine which does not fit the behavior it governs.

Table 1.1 The components of the creative process under each of the theories of creativity[i]

Components	*Ideas*	*Methods*	*Facts*	*Expressions*	*Thought*	*Education*	*Technical Skills*	*Aesthetic Criteria*	*Analytical Skills*
Copyright-Law	Unpro-tected	Unpro-tected	Unpro-tected	Protected (if original)	Unpro-tected	Sometimes Protected	Unpro-tected	Sometimes Protected[ii]	Unpro-tected
Preparation		+	+	+		+	+		
Incubation	+				+				
Illumination	+				+				
Validation		+	+	+		+	+	+	+
Preparation		+	+	+		+	+	+	+
Response Generation	+				+				+
Response Validation		+	+	+		+	+	+	
Task-relevant Skills		+	+	+		+	+	+	
Creativity-relevant Skills	+				+				+
Problem Presentation					+				
Ideation	+	+	+	+		+	+	+	+
Evaluation		+	+	+		+	+	+	+
Declarative Knowledge			+	+				+	
Procedural Knowledge	+	+				+	+	+	+

(*Continued*)

(Cont.)

Components	*Ideas*	*Methods*	*Facts*	*Expressions*	*Thought*	*Education*	*Technical Skills*	*Aesthetic Criteria*	*Analytical Skills*
Evaluation		+	+	+		+	+	+	+
Cognition	+				+				+
Generation	+	+	+	+		+	+	+	
Unfocused Thought	+				+				
Focused Thought		+	+	+		+	+	+	+
Generate	+	+	+	+				+	
Explore					+				+

i The + sign in this table indicates that under the relevant stage and the relevant approach, the knowledge type in the specific column is being used. Empty cells indicate that the relevant knowledge type is not being used.

ii Aesthetic criteria would often be considered as methods, facts, or abstract ideas that are not copyrightable. Nevertheless, aesthetic criteria at their early stages in a specific creative field may be considered as explicit copyrightable expression. This is the case when a second author wishes to use explicit expressions from a previous work in the same field because of the aesthetic value he attaches to them. For example, assuming the Picasso was the first to express the female body in a non-proportional way in which the organs are presented as cubes, it is possible to think of such an expression as copyrightable. A second author who applies this aesthetic criterion may be using a protected expression. Whether this would be considered a use of expression or a use of a mere idea depends of the level of abstraction in which the idea/expression dichotomy is referred to.

VI. Conclusion

There is a mismatch between important copyright law doctrines and the cognitive understanding of creativity. Specifically, this chapter focusses on the distinction between derivative works and original works, and the idea/expression dichotomy. To substantiate this claim, it discusses theoretical approaches to creativity as well as empirical and historical studies that focus on the process of creation. Under all approaches to creativity, the creative process could be divided into two main processes. The first is unfocussed thought in which abstract ideas are generated. The second refers to the process of crystallization of the unfocussed thought into concrete perceivable products using task-relevant knowledge and memory. Both explicitly and through a suggested reading of the literature, theoretical approaches to creativity view both ideas and expressions as knowledge components that are inherent to the creative process.

These notions from the cognitive psychology of creativity discourse assist in portraying several potential implications for copyright law. This chapter explains that one implication could apply to the originality requirement in copyright law in that the analysis should shift from the originality of a work as a whole to the originality of its specific components, which courts often do already. It also suggests that post-modern approaches which require an idea of original contribution of an individual author are not consistent with the cognitive process of creation. While the cognitive understanding of creativity shows that many components of the creative process are based on prior knowledge, it also acknowledges a significant independent contribution of the author.

This chapter's main goal is to articulate the argument that the distinction copyright law makes between derivative works (based on protected expressions) and original works (based on ideas and unprotected expressions) is an intra-legal normative distinction and is not based on any justification inherent to creativity. In this sense, this chapter argued that there is no qualitative difference between original works and derivative works under the cognitive approaches to creativity. Likewise, the idea/expression dichotomy also finds no justification in creativity. Therefore, if the distinction between derivative works and original works is merely a normative legal one, the mismatch between creativity and the law could justify a more careful evaluation of the normative intra-legal justifications to copyright law. Such evaluation will be discussed in Chapter 3.

Notes

1 An earlier version of this chapter was published in the Fordham Intellectual Property, Media and Entertainment Law Journal. *See* Omri Rachum-Twaig, *Recreating Copyright: The Cognitive Process of Creation and Copyright Law*, 27 FORDHAM INTELL. PROP. MEDIA & ENT. L.J. 287 (2016).

2 *See* U.S. Const. art. I, § 8, cl. 8 (providing that Congress has the power "[t]o promote the Progress of Science ...."); *see also* Twentieth Century Music Corp. v. Aiken, 422 U.S. 151, 156 (1975) (noting that copyright's "ultimate aim" is "to stimulate artistic creativity for the general public good"); Kelly v. Arriba Soft Corp., 336 F.3d 811, 820 (9th Cir. 2003) ("The Copyright Act was intended to promote creativity,

thereby benefitting the artist and the public alike."); Warner Bros. Inc. v. Am. Broad. Cos., 720 F.2d 231, 240 (2d Cir. 1983) ("It is a fundamental objective of the copyright law to foster creativity."); Julie E. Cohen, *Creativity and Culture in Copyright Theory*, 40 U.C. DAVIS L. REV. 1151 (2007) ("Creativity is universally agreed to be a good that copyright law should seek to promote...."); Ned Snow, *The Regressing Progress Clause: Rethinking Constitutional Indifference to Harmful Content in Copyright*, 47 U.C. DAVIS L. REV. 1, 40 (2013) ("[I]n no uncertain terms the Court has articulated a view of copyright that defines the primary objective of copyright as creativity or originality (which turns on creativity).").

3 *See* Joseph P. Fishman, *Creating Around Copyright*, 128 HARV. L. REV. 1333, 1360–90 (2015). Fishman's argument is based upon the "path of least resistance" approach to creativity and empirical studies based upon it. *Id.* This chapter discusses this approach to creativity as part of its broader theory of creative cognition, along with other approaches to creativity. *See infra* Section IV.2.

4 For elaboration *see infra* Chapter 3.

5 It is important to note that, although this chapter argues that copyright law and the right to make a derivative work right should be analyzed in light of the cognitive understanding of creativity, the creative process – even in its cognitive context– is fluid and not predefined. It is likely that the cognitive process of creation is affected by various factors that are external to the author and only one of these factors may be the law. Nevertheless, the law's effect on creativity should be scrutinized in order to maximize the law's efficacy.

6 *See* Todd I. Lubart, *Models of the Creative Process: Past, Present and Future*, 13 CREATIVITY RES. J. 295, 297 (2001).

7 Two disclaimers are appropriate. First, this chapter is not advocating for a direct link between the use of prior knowledge and memory in the creative process and the creation of derivative works in the legal context. In this sense, it does not argue that every work of authorship is a derivative work because many works are based upon knowledge that the law treats as a mere idea. The claim is limited to the argument that making derivative works – i.e., using prior knowledge that contains explicit protected expression as part of the creative process – is an inherent part of the creative process and is not qualitatively different from making an original work with preexisting "ideas." Second, this chapter does not suggest that the law's distinction between original works and derivative works is impossible to justify normatively. Instead, this chapter posits that this distinction is discordant with cognitive psychology's understating of creativity.

8 *See* Graham Wallas, THE ART OF THOUGHT (1926). Creativity was discussed in ancient times as well. Plato and Aristotle, for example, discussed the sources of creativity and in ancient Greece Zeus and his nine daughters, the muses, were believed to be the source of creative thought. *See* Robert W. Weisberg, CREATIVITY: UNDERSTANDING INNOVATION IN PROBLEM SOLVING, SCIENCE, INVENTION, AND THE ARTS 90–2 (2006). In modern times, the beginning of scholarly thought about creativity is attributed to Freud and Poincaré who saw the source of creativity in unconscious thinking. *See id.* at 92–4.

9 *See* Aaron Kozbelt, Ronald A. Beghetto & Mark A. Runco, *Theories of Creativity, in* THE CAMBRIDGE HANDBOOK OF CREATIVITY 20, 30–5 (James C. Kaufman & Robert J. Sternberg eds, 2010).

10 *See* Wallas, *supra* note 8, at 80.

11 *See id.* at 82–97. The literature on cognitive psychology typically uses the term "problem" to describe the beginning of the creative process. The meaning of this term is not identical to its common meaning; instead, it is more closely related to the term "task." The term refers to a wide range of instances that could lead to creative activity, whether it is a specific professional or logical problem that needs to be solved, and whether it is the beginning of a task (professional, artistic, scientific or otherwise) that is ill-defined. *See* Lubart, *supra* note 6, at 297. This section uses the terms

"problem" and "task" to describe the task an author pursues during the creative process.

12 *See, e.g.*, Sandra E. Moriarty & Bruce G. Vandenbergh, *Advertising Creatives Look at Creativity*, 18 J. CREATIVE BEHAV. 162, 166 (1984) (identifying Wallas' four stages through a qualitative survey of advertisers' work); *see also* Lubart, *supra* note 6, at 297–9 who identified Amabile's approach as a continuation of Wallas' work.

13 *See generally* Teresa M. Amabile, THE SOCIAL PSYCHOLOGY OF CREATIVITY (1983) [hereinafter Amabile, SOCIAL PSYCHOLOGY].

14 *See generally* Teresa M. Amabile, CREATIVITY IN CONTEXT (1996) [hereinafter Amabile, CONTEXT].

15 *See id.* at 95.

16 This chapter uses task-relevant knowledge to refer to knowledge that is relevant to the environment of the creative activity. This means the knowledge and expertise that are related to the specific creative environment and tradition.

17 *See id.* at 55–6.

18 *See id.* at 96.

19 *See id.*

20 *See id.* at 83–6.

21 This component includes knowledge of the general technique that is related to the relevant task and, more importantly, knowledge and familiarity with concrete previous instances that are related to the task and could be used to complete the relevant task. This means that the task-relevant knowledge also includes visual (or audible) memory of previous works known to the author. *See id.*

22 *See id.* at 95–6.

23 *See id.* at 86–90.

24 *See id.* at 88–9.

25 *See id.* at 89. Amabile defined "heuristics" as any principle or instrument that contributes to the reduction of the average solution search time. *See id.* (citing Allen Newell et al., *The Processes of Creative Thinking*, *in* CONTEMPORARY APPROACHES TO CREATIVE THINKING: A SYMPOSIUM HELD AT THE UNIVERSITY OF COLORADO 63, 78 (Gruber, et al. eds, 1962)).

26 *See* Amabile, CONTEXT, *supra* note 14, at 94.

27 *See id.* at 90–3.

28 *See* Mark A. Runco & Ivonne Chand, *Cognition and Creativity*, 7 EDUC. PSYCHOL. REV. 243, 245–6 (1995).

29 *See id.* It is important to emphasize that the term "factual knowledge" does not refer to facts in the copyright sense. The meaning of the term is visual, semantic or symbolic knowledge that includes all task-relevant details in the author's memory. In this sense, factual knowledge could consist of informative factual knowledge as well as concrete expressions of preexisting task-related works. For example, when a painter seeks to paint a sunflower field, several types of knowledge could come into play. Procedural knowledge in this context includes painting methods and techniques, and the painter's professional abilities and expertise. Declarative knowledge in this context consists of several types of information as well. Simple facts include the painter's acquaintance with the sunflower and its visual form in nature. Another type of declarative knowledge is preexisting visual works use of sunflowers in different visual ways and any specific visual images of sunflowers.

30 *See* Todd I. Lubart, *Componential Models*, in 1 ENCYCLOPEDIA OF CREATIVITY 295, 289–99 (Mark A. Runco & Steven R. Pritzker eds, 1999).

31 *See* Wallas, *supra* note 8, at 80, 86.

32 *See* Amabile, CONTEXT, *supra* note 14, at 94.

33 *See* Runco & Chand, *supra* note 28, at 248.

34 *See infra* Section V.1.

35 The "romantic author" approach sees the individual author as the only source for any work of authorship and describes the creative process as an individual endeavor in which the work is created out of nothing. *See infra* Section III.2.

36 *See* Kozbelt, Beghetto & Runco, *supra* note 9, at 31.

37 *See* J.P. Guilford, THE NATURE OF HUMAN INTELLIGENCE 138 (1967); *see also* Weisberg, *supra* note 8, at 95–7.

38 *See* Guilford, *supra* note 37, at 138.

39 *See id.* at 171.

40 *See id.* at 313–15.

41 *See* John R. Suler, *Primary Process Thinking and Creativity*, 88 PSYCHOL. BULL. 144–6 (1980).

42 *See* Liane Gabora, *Revenge of the "Neurds": Characterizing Creative Thought in Terms of the Structure and Dynamics of Memory*, 22 CREATIVITY RES. J. 1–12 (2010).

43 *See* Nicholas Davis & Ellen Yi-Luen Do, *Quantifying the Artistic Experience with Perceptive Sketching Tools: Cognitive Technologies to Support Creativity Researchers Social Process of Creation*, 22 COMUNICACAO E SOCIEDADE 76, 80 (2012).

44 *See* Ronald A. Finke, Thomas B. Ward & Steven M. Smith, CREATIVE COGNITION: THEORY, RESEARCH AND APPLICATIONS 17–43 (1992).

45 *See id.* at 17–28.

46 *See* Ronald A. Finke, Thomas B. Ward, & Steven M. Smith, *Creative Cognition, in* HANDBOOK OF CREATIVITY 189, 191 (Robert J. Sternberg ed., 1999).

47 *See id.* at 191–2; Finke, Ward & Smith, *supra* note 44, at 20; Lubart, *supra* note 6, at 299–300.

48 *See* Finke, Ward, & Smith, *supra* note 46, at 191.

49 *See* Finke, Ward, & Smith, *supra* note 46, at 191–2; Finke, Ward & Smith, s*upra* note 44, at 26; Lubart, *supra* note 6, at 299–300.

50 *See* Finke, Ward & Smith, *supra* note 46, at 191.

51 *See, e.g., id.*

52 *See* Finke, Ward & Smith, *supra* note 44, at 26.

53 *See id.* at 17.

54 *See* Guilford, *supra* note 37, at 108, 116, 139, *see also* Suler, *supra* note 41, at 144–55; Wallas, *supra* note 8, at 81; Gabora, *supra* note 42, at 3, 9–10, 14.

55 *See* Finke, Ward, & Smith, *supra* note 46, at 191–2; Finke, Ward & Smith, *supra* note 44, at 20–1; Lubart, *supra* note 6, at 299–300.

56 *See* 17 U.S.C. § 103 (2012). *But see id.* § 102(b).

57 *See* Gabora, *supra* note 42, at 9; Guilford, *supra* note 37, at 315; Suler, *supra* note 41, at 146.

58 *See generally* Finke, Ward & Smith, *supra* note 44.

59 *See infra* Section V.2.

60 *See* Kozbelt, Beghetto & Runco, *supra* note 9, at 33.

61 *See id.* (defining creativity as an ill-defined problem solving process); Lubart, *supra* note 6, at 297 (stating that the term "problem" in the creative context also refers to a task that the author wishes to engage in); *see also* Jacob W. Getzels & Mihaly Csikszentmihalyi, THE CREATIVE VISION: A LONGITUDINAL STUDY OF PROBLEM FINDING IN ART 84 (1976); David Collins, *A Synthesis Process Model of Creative Thinking in Music Composition*, 33 PSYCHOL. MUSIC 193, 195 (2005); Yingxu Wang, *On Cognitive Foundations of Creativity and the Cognitive Process of Creation*, 3 INT'L J. COGNITIVE INFORMATICS & NAT. INTELLIGENCE 1, 2 (2009) [hereinafter Wang, *Cognitive Foundations*]; Yingxu Wang & Vincent Chiew, *On the Cognitive Process of Human Problem Solving*, 11 COGNITIVE SYS. RES. 81, 85 (2010).

62 *See* Kozbelt, Beghetto & Runco, *supra* note 9, at 33.

63 *See* Guilford, *supra* note 37, at 313–16.

64 *See* Philip N. Johnson-Laird, *How Jazz Musicians Improvise*, 19 MUSIC PERCEPTION 415, 419–20 (2002).

65 *See* Kozbelt, Beghetto & Runco, *supra* note 9, at 33.
66 *See* John R. Hayes, *Cognitive Processes in Creativity, in* HANDBOOK OF CREATIVITY 202 (J.A. Glover, R.R. Roning & C.R. Reynolds eds, 1989); *see also* Robert W. Weisberg, *Creativity and Knowledge: A Challenge to Theories,* in HANDBOOK OF CREATIVITY 226, 230–1 (Robert J. Sternberg ed., 1999).
67 *See* Weisberg, *supra* note 66. The 10-year rule suggested by Hayes was criticized because it does not account for different fields of creativity. *See id.* 231–2. Nevertheless, the idea behind this rule was validated by future studies that examined the length of preparation time artists need before achieving significant accomplishments in their fields. *See id.* 232.
68 For a list of studies, *see* Kozbelt, Beghetto & Runco, *supra* note 9, at 33. The different theories of creativity do not distinguish between authors and inventors, despite the distinction in copyright and patent laws.
69 *See* Guilford, *supra* note 37, at 315.
70 *See infra* Part III.
71 *See* Kozbelt, Beghetto & Runco, *supra* note 9, at 33–4.
72 *See* Getzels & Csikszentmihalyi, *supra* note 61, at 89–106.
73 *See id.* at 85–90.
74 *See* Kozbelt, Beghetto & Runco, *supra* note 9, at 35.
75 *See* Wallas, *supra* note 8, at 86.
76 *See* Amabile, Context, *supra* note 14, at 88–9, 95.
77 *See* Runco & Chand, *supra* note 28, at 245–6.
78 *See* Guilford, *supra* note 37, at 138.
79 *See* Suler, *supra* note 41, at 144.
80 *See* Gabora, *supra* note 42, at 5–6, 10.
81 *See* Finke, Ward & Smith, *supra* note 44, at 20; Finke, Ward, & Smith, *supra* note 45, at 191–2.
82 *See* Guilford, *supra* note 37, at 321–4.
83 *See* Johnson-Laird, *supra* note 64, at 419.
84 *See* Kozbelt, Beghetto & Runco, supra note 9, at 33.
85 *See* Wallas, *supra* note 8, at 88–4; *see also* Collins, supra note 61, at 209 (finding that composers consciously choose between known genres at the preparation stage according to qualitative empirical research).
86 *See* Amabile, CONTEXT, *supra* note 14, at 85–6.
87 *See id.* at 95–6.
88 *See* Runco & Chand, *supra* note 28, at 245–6.
89 *See* Guilford, *supra* note 37, at 313–15, 319.
90 *See* Suler, *supra* note 41, at 145–6.
91 *See* Gabora, *supra* note 42, at 10.
92 *See id.*
93 *See* Finke, Ward & Smith, *supra* note 44, at 19.
94 *See id.*, at 20; Finke, Ward, & Smith, *supra* note 46, at 191–2; *see also* Thomas B. Ward & Yuliya Kolomyts, *Cognition and Creativity, in* THE CAMBRIDGE HANDBOOK OF CREATIVITY, *supra* note 9, at 93, 93.
95 *See* Guilford, *supra* note 37, at 317–19.
96 *See id.* at 319.
97 *See* Johnson-Laird, *supra* note 64, at 419–20.
98 *See* Robert W. Weisberg, CREATIVITY: BEYOND THE MYTH OF GENIUS 113–22 (1993) [hereinafter Weisberg, GENIUS]; Robert W. Weisberg, *Problem Solving and Creativity, in* THE NATURE OF CREATIVITY 148–60 (Robert J. Sternberg ed., 1988).
99 It is important to note that copyright law permits the use of another's expressions in certain circumstances, usually under the fair use doctrine. *See* 17 U.S.C. § 107 (2012).
100 *See* Runco & Chand, *supra* note 28, at 245–9.

101 For the full studies, *see* Ivonne Chand & Mark A. Runco, *Problem Finding Skills as Components in the Creative Process*, 14 PERSONALITY & INDIVIDUAL DIFFERENCES 155 (1993); Mark A. Runco, *Maximal Performance on Divergent Thinking Tests by Gifted, Talented, and Nongifted Children*, 23 PSYCHOL. SCHOOLS 308 (1986); M. A. Runco & S. M. Okuda, *The Instructional Enhancement of the Flexibility and Originality Scores of Divergent Thinking Tests*, 5 APPLIED COGNITIVE PSYCHOL. 435 (1991); Michal Shur-Ofry, *The (Copyright) Law of Genre: A Network Perspective on Copyright Protection of Cultural Genres*, 2 FA. ENT. L. REV. 60 (2008).

102 *See* Runco & Chand, *supra* note 28, at 246–8.

103 *See, e.g.*, Hayes, *supra* note 66. For a discussion of additional similar studies, *see infra* Section V.3.

104 Runco & Chand, *supra* note 28, at 248–9.

105 *See* Runco & Chand, *supra* note 28, at 249.

106 *See id.* (citing Pat Langley & Randolph Jones, *A Computational Model of Scientific Insight, in* THE NATURE OF CREATIVITY), *supra* note 98, at 177, 199.

107 *See* Roger C. Schank, *Creativity as a Mechanical Process*, in THE NATURE OF CREATIVITY, *supra* note 98, at 220, 221.

108 *See* Robert J. Sternberg, *A Three-Facet Model of Creativity*, in THE NATURE OF CREATIVITY, *supra* note 98, at 125, 135–7.

109 *See* Paul J. Locher, *How Does a Visual Artist Create an Artwork*, in THE CAMBRIDGE HANDBOOK OF CREATIVITY, *supra* note 9, at 131, 143.

110 *See* Wayne A. Baughman & Michael D. Mumford, *Process-Analytic Models of Creative Capacities: Operations Influencing the Combination-and-Reorganization Process*, 8 CREATIVITY RES. J. 37, 38–55 (1995).

111 *See id.* at 39 (citing Michele I. Mobley et al., *Process Analytic Models of Creative Capacities: Evidence for the Combination and Reorganization Process*, 5 CREATIVITY RES. J. 125 (1992)).

112 *See* Finke, Ward & Smith, *supra* note 46, at 191–92, 195.

113 *See* Thomas B. Ward, *Structured Imagination: The Role of Category Structure in Exemplar Generation*, 27 COGNITIVE PSYCHOL. 1, 7–31 (1994).

114 *See* Ward, Smith & Finke, *supra* note 46, at 198.

115 *See* Ward, *supra* note 113, at 35; Thomas B. Ward, *What's Old About New Ideas?*, *in* THE CREATIVE COGNITION APPROACH 157, 174 (Steven M. Smith, Thomas B. Ward, & Ronald A. Finke eds, 1995).

116 *See* Ward & Kolomyts, *supra* note 94, at 99–100.

117 *See id.*

118 *See* Ward, *supra* note 113, at 36.

119 *See* Ward & Kolomyts, *supra* note 94, at 100.

120 *See id.* at 101.

121 It is important to note that the theoretical literature on cognitive psychology does not distinguish between works of authorship, inventions and abstract creative thought. This does not diminish the applicability of these theories to creative activities governed by copyright law.

122 *See* Sawako Yokochi & Takeshi Okada, *Creative Cognitive Process of Art Making: A Field Study of a Traditional Chinese Ink Painter*, 17 CREATIVITY RES. J. 241, 241 (2005).

123 *See id.* at 243.

124 *See id.*

125 *See id.* at 244.

126 *See id.* at 245. The researchers noted that in 15 out of the 16 paintings the painter started drawing a tree and only later added other objects. *Id.*

127 *See id.* at 247.

128 *See id.*

129 *See id.* at 250; *see also* Finke, Ward & Smith, *supra* note 46, at 192.

130 *See* Mary-Anne Mace & Tony Ward, *Modeling the Creative Process: A Grounded Theory Analysis of Creativity in the Domain of Art Making*, 14 CREATIVITY RES. J. 179, 180 (2002).
131 *See id.* at 181.
132 *See id.* at 182–8.
133 *See id.* at 182.
134 *See id.* at 188.
135 *See id.* at 189.
136 *See id.* at 182.
137 *See id.*
138 *See* Keith Sawyer, *The Cognitive Neuroscience of Creativity: A Critical Review*, 23 CREATIVITY RES. J. 137, 138–40 (2011). The fMRI uses magnetic traits of oxygenated blood cells in comparison with un-oxygenated cells to examine which parts of the brain are active at a specific time. The fMRI produces an image portraying the difference between the oxygenation levels of different blood cells and shows a model-based image of the active parts of the brain during the sample. The EEG measures electromagnetic pulses created by the activity of neurons in the brain cortex by placing electrodes on the scalp of the participant. *Id.* For an elaboration on the two methodologies and their shortcomings, *see id.* at 140.
139 *See* Robert L. Solso, *Brain Activities in a Skilled Versus a Novice Artist: An fMRI Study*, 34 LEONARDO 31, 33 (2001).
140 *See id.* at 33–4.
141 *See id.* at 34.
142 *See* Melissa Ellamil et al., *Evaluative and Generative Modes of Thought During the Creative Process*, 59 NEUROIMAGE 1783, 1784 (2012).
143 *See id.* at 1784–5.
144 *See id.* at 1785.
145 *See id.* at 1786 Fig. 3, 1791.
146 *See id.* at 1791. For additional studies finding a correlation between creativity and brain activity in the medial temporal lobe, *see* Huimin Zheng, Jiayi Luo & RongjunYu, *From Memory to Prospection: What Are the Overlapping and the Distinct Components Between Remembering and Imagining?*, 5 FRONTIERS PSYCHOL. 1, 10 (2014).
147 *See e.g.*, Andreas Fink & Mathias Benedek, *EEG Alpha Power and Creative Ideation*, 44 NEUROSCIENCE & BIOBEHAVIORAL REV. 111 (2014).
148 *See id.* at 113.
149 *See id.* As explained above, EEG measures electromagnetic pulses created by the activity of neurons in the brain cortex. *See supra* note 316 and accompanying text. These pulses are measured in several frequencies. The frequency between 8 and 12 Hz is referred to as "alpha power." The changes in alpha power are measured before and after a stimulating event occurs. A decrease in alpha power is referred to as event-related desynchronization, while an increase in alpha power is referred to as event-related synchronization. *See* Fink & Benedek, *supra* note 147, at 114–15.
150 *See* Fink & Benedek, *supra* note 147, at 117.
151 *See id.* at 119. For similar findings, *see* Mathias Benedek et al., *Alpha Power Increases in Right Parietal Cortex Reflects Focused Internal Attention*, 56 NEUROPSYCHOLOGIA 393 (2014).
152 *See* Sawyer, *supra* note 138, at 149–50.
153 *See* Sureyya Yoruk & Mark A. Runco, *The Neuroscience of Divergent Thinking*, 56 ACTIVITAS NERVOSA SUPERIOR 1, 11–13 (2014).
154 For a description of this methodology, *see* Locher, *supra* note 109, at 132–4.
155 *See* Weisberg, GENIUS, *supra* note 98, at 193–208.
156 *See* Weisberg, *supra* note 66, at 235–36.
157 *See* Weisberg, GENIUS, *supra* note 98, at 225.

158 *See* Robert W. Weisberg, *Case Studies of Creative Thinking: Reproduction Versus Restructuring in the Real World, in* THE CREATIVE COGNITION APPROACH, *supra* note 115, at 53, 57–69.
159 *See* Weisberg, *supra* note 8, at 112–18. This notion is an explicit expression of the idea of progress in copyright law and is directly related to the difficulties with the current definition of the derivative work right.
160 While this part purports that the derivative works right does not fit the conclusions from creativity studies, other copyright doctrines such as the originality requirement could be justified under creativity studies. For elaboration *see* Rachum-Twaig, *supra* note 1, at 338–43.
161 17 U.S.C. § 101 (2012).
162 *See* 2 Melville B. Nimmer & David Nimmer, NIMMER ON COPYRIGHT § 8.09[A][1] (2015).
163 For a similar approach, *see* Fishman, *supra* note 3, at 1341, and Jeanne C. Fromer, *A Psychology of Intellectual Property*, 104 NW. U. L. REV. 1441, 1458–9 (2010).
164 *See* Stephan Bechtold, Christopher Buccafusco & Christopher Jon Sprigman, *Innovation Heuristics: Experiments on Sequential Creativity in Intellectual Property*, 91 IND. L. REV. 1251, 1297 (2016). For additional discussion on creativity and intellectual property *see* Christopher Jon Sprigman, *Copyright and Creative Incentives: What We Know (and Don't)*, 55 HOUSTON L. REV. 451 (2017); Christopher Buccafusco, Stephan Bechtold & Christopher Jon Sprigman, *The Nature of Sequential Innovation*, 59 WM. & MARY L. REV. 1 (2017); Christopher Buccafusco & Christopher Jon Sprigman, *The Creativity Effect*, 78 U. CHI. L. REV. 31 (2011); Jessica Silbey, THE EUREKA MYTH: CREATORS, INNOVATORS, AND EVERYDAY INTELLECTUAL PROPERTY 79–148 (2015).
165 A reservation is appropriate here. There obviously are reproductive actions, in copyright terms, that use explicit copyrighted expressions without adding original expressions to them which are very creative in the cognitive behavioral sense. One example is the use of an expression while changing its mode of presentation or presenting it in a different context that gives it new meaning. These activities are typically allowed under the fair use doctrine. This chapter does not focus on the interrelations between fair use and reproduction but it seems that the fair use doctrine sufficiently accounts for the cognitive notions regarding the creativity of such activities.
166 *See generally* J.D. Salinger, "The Catcher in the Rye" (1951).
167 These were the facts that led to the decision in Salinger v. Colting, 607 F.3d 68 (2d Cir. 2010).
168 *See generally* J.D. Salinger, "The Catcher in the Rye" (1951).
169 *See* Salinger v. Colting, 607 F.3d 68 (2nd Cir. 2010).

2 Genre theories and copyright[1]

I. Introduction

One of copyright law's primary goals is the promotion of progress and development in arts and the enrichment of the world of expressions. In the field of literary theory, we find theories that deal with genre and seek to explain, among other things, how art develops and how meaningful artistic products are created. This chapter examines if and to what extent the legal norm of copyright law, which governs the world of creativity, fits genre theories. The chapter focuses on three main aspects of the creative world: the author; the audience and creative products; and how creative products act as a mediating element between authors and their audiences. In other words, I will analyze what components serve as the foundation of creativity, allowing authors to create on the one hand and the audience to understand and give value to the creative products on the other, and whether copyright law allows the use of these components. Thus, the discussion is intended to examine whether there is a match between copyright's goal of enriching the creative world and the way genre theories understand the conditions for such enrichment.

Showing a match between genre theories and copyright law would validate current legal rules, as they adequately reflect extra-legal approaches to the enrichment of the creative world. If, however, there is a mismatch between some copyright doctrines and genre theories, then there is reason to reexamine these doctrines. In this sense, there is a shift from the descriptive to the normative aspect of the discussion. Nevertheless, the argument that copyright doctrine should be amended in order to fit the notions of genre theories needs further support; it does not follow simply from the presumption that copyright law must adhere to other fields of knowledge that study creativity. Rather, to the extent that genre theories explain, among other things, the important and significant conditions for the enrichment of the creative world, and to the extent that copyright law aims at such enrichment, I believe any gap between legal rules and extra-legal understanding of the creative world should be bridged. This is because genre theories examine and explain significant components of creativity and could therefore identify rules that encourage enrichment of the creative world, which is the goal of copyright law. Thus, principles of genre theories that explain both the conditions enabling authors to create and enrich the creative world and how an audience gives value to works of authorship and understands them should be reflected in the legal doctrine that governs creativity.

The normative aspect of this chapter could be criticized because it does not explain why genre theories are superior to other theories explaining how the creative world best develops, for example, economic analysis. There are three answers to such criticism. First, the mere fact that there are other normative justifications to copyright law and various normative approaches to identifying conditions that enrich the creative world does not, in itself, diminish the theoretical validity of any other approach. Aside from that, the notions from genre theories are flexible; they can accommodate other normative approaches and allow them to frame secondary rules that will contribute to the development of the creative world, including economic analysis. Second, there is no necessary contradiction between genre theories' understanding of how to best enrich the creative world and that of economic analysis. As I will show, some important doctrines in copyright law (which rely considerably on economic analysis) match the notions of genre theories. The alleged tension mainly concerns the right to make derivative works, which will be discussed below. However, as far as the derivative works right is concerned, its economic justification is controversial even under principles of economic analysis, as will be further discussed in Chapter 3.

Third, and most important, genre theories explain aspects of the creative world where other theories, including economic analysis, fail. In the context of the right to make derivative works, for example, the main reason economic analysis does not provide sound predictions is the lack of empirical data concerning the amount of works that would be created absent this right, the amount of works that would not be created if the author was not awarded this right, and the social welfare resulting from these two groups of works. The ability to collect such empirical data is highly restricted if not impossible. As a result, theories that explain the interrelations between different players on the field of creativity – authors (both first and second) and audience – in a manner that is independent of empirical data could offer a sound solution to various questions in copyright law. Unanswered questions about the justification for the derivative work right and its scope are a key example. In this sense, genre theories are relevant to copyright law because they offer a systematic understanding of the creative world, the interrelations between the different players in it, and the significant conditions that allow its existence and development, which could inform the basic legal rules that should govern creativity.

In this chapter, I will examine the existing literature on genre theories in an instrumental way to demonstrate their implications for creativity. I will present the main characteristics of genre theories and will extract from the literature notions regarding the components that are significant to the enrichment of the creative world. It is important to emphasize that while this chapter concentrates on the literary text as a paradigmatic subject for genre analysis, genre theories apply equally to other non-literary forms of art and creativity such as music, visual arts, films, games and even computer software.[2] As I will show, genre theories recognize that in the heart of the creative world stand common building blocks that are the basis for the existence and development of the creative world in two main aspects. First, the common building blocks are a tool that enables authors to create within certain constraints by using known rules and conventions. This means that the common building blocks are used by the author as available raw materials and enable, through the constraints they cast, the crystallization of ideas into perceivable products, and are simultaneously affected by creativity itself, thus allowing the development of new conventions. In this sense, the common building blocks are both an enabling and constitutive tool for creativity. Second, the common building blocks are also a tool that enables the formation of meaning. For authors, the common building blocks serve as raw materials for creation, while for the audience they function as raw materials for the creation of meaning and as a common language between the audience and authors. The use of common building blocks thus allows not only the making of creative products but also meaningful products that the audience may value. Seen in this light, the common building blocks are a meaning-making tool.

Viewing the creative world through the lens of genre theories could contribute to a better understanding of copyright law, which, as explained above, focuses on the development and enrichment of the creative world. The examination of genre theories and copyright law in this chapter concerns several main copyright doctrines. The first is the idea/expression dichotomy, a central doctrine in copyright law. Under this doctrine, ideas are not protected by copyright while explicit expressions are. Another doctrine, related to the first, is the scènes à faire doctrine, which provides for the free use of any expressions that are necessary to the depiction of particular artistic styles. A third doctrine is the fair use doctrine, which, under certain conditions, allows the use of protected expressions without the owner's consent. The fourth doctrine is the right to make derivative works. This right gives the owner of a copyrighted work the exclusive right to make works that are based upon it.

The argument I wish to establish in this chapter is that although there is a match between some copyright doctrines and genre theories, as far as the right to make derivative works is concerned, there is a significant mismatch. Genre theories do not distinguish between ideas and expression (in copyright terms) and see both as a possible source of common building blocks for creativity. Copyright law matches this notion to a great extent. Thus, the idea/expression dichotomy allows the free use of ideas as common building blocks. Copyright law also allows the use of expression in certain cases. One example is the use of unprotected expressions – i.e., in cases where the copyright term has expired or in cases governed by the scènes à faire doctrine. Another example is the fair use doctrine which allows, under some circumstances, the use of protected expressions as common building blocks.

However, as far as the right to make derivative works is concerned there is a significant mismatch between copyright law and genre theories. The right to make derivative works provides the owner of a work the exclusive right to make works that are based on it. This means that no one is allowed to use protected expressions from existing works to create new works without the copyright owner's consent. According to genre theories, however, using expression to make new works is at the heart of encouraging the creative world, both as a building block that enables creativity from the author's perspective and (maybe more importantly) as a building block that enables meaning-making from the audience's perspective. The argument here is that under genre theories' understanding of the enrichment of creativity, there is a mismatch between genre and copyright law as far as the distinction between derivative works (that use protected expression and thus are forbidden without the owner's consent) and original works (that use ideas or unprotected expression and thus are allowed).

Following this argument, I will claim that as far as genre theories are concerned, there is a qualitative difference between the act of reproduction and the act of making a derivative work, both from the author's inner perspective and from the audience's perspective. Whereas reproduction without additional original contribution does not constitute a new text that contributes to the development of a genre or the creation of a new one, a derivative work (much like an original work) is a text that has a central and important function in the promotion and development of the creative world; its importance to the creative world is not inferior to any other kind of creative text (whether or not it is based on prior ideas of explicit expressions). This notion strengthens the conclusion that a separation between the reproduction right and the derivative work right is warranted due to the different role of both acts in the creative world. In this sense, the argument in this chapter is both critical-descriptive (examining the match between the current doctrine and genre theories), and normative as it justifies the shift to a different copyright regime with regard to derivative works.

This chapter is structured as follows. Part II presents a case study, the development of the detective story genre, which serves as an example of the theoretical debate discussed in this chapter. In Part III, I present the development of theoretical thinking about genre and its theoretical underpinnings to clarify genre's meaning in this chapter. In addition, Part III describes each side of the debate that follows. Part IV characterizes modern approaches to genre by emphasizing each theory's special traits. Next, in Part V, I highlight two aspects of the modern debate on genre, which provides background for a doctrinal debate. Part VI discusses genre's implications for copyright law in general and the derivative work right specifically. Finally, I conclude the debate.

II. The development of the detective story: a case study

The development of the detective story illustrates the theoretical discussion on genre and the common building blocks' significance for creativity.[3] First, the detective story is a relatively recent genre whose development is well-documented since it first appeared in the first half of the nineteenth century. Second, the development of the detective story occurred long enough ago for us to understand its significance in the literary world. Third, although the detective story developed quite some time ago, it is still evolving and relevant today. Additionally, it is a known and popular genre and therefore convenient for discussion. In this section, I focus on the work of Edgar Alan Poe and Arthur Conan Doyle, the two authors who contributed most to the development of the common building blocks of the detective story as a genre. The books and short stories written by these authors show that the common building blocks developed in various levels of abstraction that are all important to creativity, an observation that has implications in the legal context.

Poe and Doyle's preeminent work is an excellent vehicle for presenting the common building blocks of the detective story. Poe is considered the inventor of the detective story; he was the first author to use a detective as a hero and thus "created" the fictional detective-hero character.[4] The detective character debuted as Chevalier C. Auguste Dupin, the main character in three short stories written by Poe: "The Murders in the Rue Morgue," "The Mystery of Marie Roget" and "The Purloined Letter." With regard to Doyle, the influence of detective Sherlock Holmes, the main character in his books, cannot be overstated. As Murch wrote, Sherlock Holmes is among the very few characters in literature who obtained a separate and distinct identity that is known to thousands, many of whom have never read the works in which it appears.[5] In addition to each author's significant influence on the detective story genre, focussing on them is useful due to their chronological proximity –Doyle was the first significant writer in the detective genre after Poe.[6] Poe's first detective story, "The Murders in the Rue Morgue," was published in 1841 and Doyle's first book, "A Study in Scarlet," which introduced Holmes, was published in 1887.

As mentioned above, comparing Poe and Doyle's detective stories reveals various levels of abstraction of the common building blocks of the detective genre. The highest level of abstraction is the common focus on the detective as the central hero of the story. Poe's stories, which revolved around detective Dupin, were the first plots that focussed exclusively on a detective's endeavors. Similarly, Doyle's plots focussed exclusively on the character Sherlock Holmes and his sleuthing. Importantly, when Poe and Doyle published their novels, they were (almost) the only stories with a detective starring as the main character and reappearing in a series of novels.

A lower level of abstraction, but still a rather high one, is the addition of a sidekick – a character who works alongside the detective – that emphasizes the detective's keen investigative skills and helps explain the detective's reasoning to the reader.[7] In Poe's novels, Dupin has a nameless companion who narrates the story. Although Poe's narrator is attentive to Dupin, he possesses only a limited understanding of each clue's significance; thus, he is constantly surprised by Dupin's discoveries. Consequently, Dupin must explain how each clue fits together, which glorifies the detective's character and underscores the detective's thought-process for the reader.[8] The intellectual gap between the narrator and Dupin is best illustrated when Dupin explains that "[t]he necessary knowledge is of what to observe." Doyle's Holmes also has an eternal companion, but he is more well-known and developed than Dupin's companion – Dr. Watson. The more developed character of Watson also emphasizes the uniqueness of Holmes. Watson is famous for always employing "common sense." Further, he is patient and encouraging and serves as a bridge between the detective-hero and the readers because, as Holmes said to him, "you see but you do not observe." Therefore, Watson needs every clue's implications explained to him.[9]

An even lower level of abstraction of common building blocks is in the personality traits of Poe and Doyle's detective-heroes. Poe's Dupin is described by the narrator as a "bi-part soul" whose personality is a combination of the imagination of a poet and the mind of a mathematician.[10] Holmes, on his part, is described by

Watson as having a "dual nature" and a romantic personality possessed by the spirit of science. Dupin is presented as a man living a humble life that does not require him to work regularly and as a loner who has no interest in sexuality. Likewise, Holmes is described as a person living a bohemian lifestyle alone with no interest in intimate relationships. Dupin and Holmes are both heavy pipe smokers and have significant affection for darkness and taking long strolls through the city at night. They both enjoy a preferred treatment from the local police. Dupin has a strong relationship with the French Sûreté, especially with the Prefect of Police, which he helps solve crimes. Holmes is very close to Scotland Yard and has a complicated relationship with Inspector Lestrade. In both cases, the uniqueness of the detectives is highlighted by their success at solving mysteries that baffled official investigation agencies. A last similar personality trait, and maybe the most important one, is the tendency of both Dupin and Holmes to use logical deduction as a tool for mystery-solving. Both detectives express that they observe every detail and then eliminate possible suspects until they solve the mystery.

The lowest level of abstraction of the common building blocks in Poe and Doyle's novels is the explicit and implicit intertextuality of the stories' contents. One example of the use of similar word choice for maintaining one framework of meaning is found in Doyle's use of the terms "observation" and "deduction," which were also chosen by Poe to describe Dupin's thought process. A more lucid example is Poe's explicit reference to Dupin in Doyle's "A Study in Scarlet." After Holmes arrives at an important conclusion, Watson turns to him and says: "You remind me of Edgar Allen Poe's Dupin. I had no idea such individuals existed outside of stories." Holmes replies: "in my opinion, Dupin was a very inferior fellow. That trick of his of breaking in on his friends' thoughts with an apropos remark after a quarter of an hour's silence is really very showy and superficial. He had some analytical genius, no doubt; but he was by no means such a phenomenon as Poe appeared to imagine." The explicit reference to Dupin and his thinking method (that is also characteristic of Holmes himself) is a significant use of common building blocks to convey the meaning to the reader.[11]

But the most significant use of explicit expression as a common building block is found in one scene shared by Poe and Doyle that subsequently served as a basis for similar scenes in modern detective literature. The first scene takes place in Poe's "The Murders at the Rue Morgue." Two women, mother and daughter, are brutally murdered in their fourth-floor apartment. The mother's body was thrown out the window and the daughter's body was shoved into a narrow chimney. Inexplicably, both the apartment door and windows were locked from the inside. Dupin reasoned that the murderer had to climb into the apartment through the window in the outer wall of the building and then close the window from the outside when he fled the scene. Dupin also deduced that the murderer was an orangutan that was brought to the scene by a French sailor who purchased him in Borneo Island, located in Southeast Asia, after he was out from quarantine. In Doyle's "The Sign of Four," the following scene is described. A man was murdered in a third-floor apartment, and the murder scene was found with all the doors and windows locked from the inside. Because the apartment's chimney was too narrow to allow entry, Holmes deduced that the murderer climbed through the roof window by climbing up the building's side and that the murderer closed the window when he fled the scene. The murderer, according to Holmes, was an Aboriginal man described as a "little black man … with a great misshapen head" and "a little blood-thirsty imp" who was escorted to the scene by a former British soldier who escaped from prison in the Andaman Islands in South Asia.[12]

This comparison between the works of Poe and Doyle, emphasizing the common building blocks for both and the detective genre, will serve as a reoccurring example in this chapter through which I will articulate the differences between the various approaches to genre theories and the importance of common building blocks in the creative world as well as their possible implications for the law.

III. The basis for the idea of genre: static approaches of classification and prescription

In this part, I examine the development of genre theories and the different meanings given to the term while describing pre-modern approaches that were the basis for the idea of genre. These approaches are presented together in one part for two reasons. First, these approaches are pre-modern. They begin with the writings of Plato and Aristotle, continue through scholars from the Renaissance and Neoclassical eras, and end with the Romantic and Post-romantic eras. The second characteristic common to these approaches is that in contrast to the dynamic approaches to genre, they recognize genre as a phenomenon that serves one specific purpose. Accordingly, I refer to these approaches as static because they view genre as a finite and predefined system that is not open for change and development. To understand the conceptualization of genre by each of these approaches, it is important to clarify what I do *not* mean when I use the term genre, while showing some significant characteristics of genre that have accompanied it from the beginning of theoretical thinking about genre. The discussion in this section will be thematic despite the fact that there is significant correlation between the different approaches to genre and the time period during which they were prominent.

1) Genre as a logical apriori division of art

Gérard Genette, one of the leading genre scholars of the twentieth century, demonstrated in his book "The Architext: An Introduction" how modern scholars on genre systematically refer to the writings of Aristotle and Plato as the origin of generic thinking and genre theories.[13] Genette referred to the writing of Warren, Todorov, Bakhin and Batteux, which I will elaborate on later in the part that discusses the dynamic approaches to genre. Similarly, Heather Dubrow suggested in her important book "Genre" that the development of theoretical scholarship on genre along the years is vastly based upon Aristotle, to such extent that it seems like a "series of footnotes" refer to him.[14] Therefore, I begin by describing the approaches of these two important philosophers and the generic division of literary texts, which forms the basis for the discussion in the rest of this section.

The first expression of theoretical thinking on genre appears in the third book of Plato's *Politeia*. In a dialog between Socrates and Adeimantus, Socrates tells his student that poetry can be divided into three possible categories.[15] Frow recognized that this statement marked the beginning of the theoretical thinking on genre because Socrates' goal was to map three possible ways to convey poetry or literature: direct narration (storytelling in the words of the poet), narration by imitation (storytelling by characters) or a combination of both. Genette referred to the division proposed by Socrates as the "Socratic triad" and emphasized that it was the basis for what would later be called "genre."[16]

Further elaboration of the Socratic triad is found in the "Poetics of Aristotle."[17] As Dubrow mentioned, three notions about poetics are recognizable in Aristotle's text. First, literary works differ in the medium they use to imitate reality (through rhythm, melody, or a combination of both). Second, he distinguished between works based on the subjects of imitation, meaning whether the characters are in a better or worse condition in comparison to reality (when comedy fits the latter and tragedy fits the first). Third, and most importantly for our purposes, Aristotle divided works according to their manner of imitation. This is a reflection of the Socratic triad because Aristotle made a distinction between direct narration (using personal pronouns or a poetic character) and realistic representation of characters.[18]

Dubrow explained that Aristotle's framework was based on the assumption that each literary subject demands a particular form and style. Therefore, every literary work must fit one perfect model, and the author must create with this model in mind.[19] Genette, on his part, explained why the attempt to use Aristotle's division of literary kinds as a superior a priori one is problematic. Genette argued that what Aristotle and Socrates defined as "form" is actually more similar to what we understand today as "mode" or different modes of enunciation. This analysis led Genette to conclude that the different modes suggested by Aristotle cannot be considered superior or a priori forms of poetry because they could be included in categories of a higher level of abstraction or more specific categories of form.[20] According to Genette, such misunderstanding of the Aristotelian division was the basis for the historical distortion of genre's definition, as will be elaborated below.

2) Genre as prescription

During the Classical era, in the centuries following the work of Plato and Aristotle, the Socratic triad has prevailed; genres are categorized by their mode of narration, and works must conform to a particular genre's model to be regarded as perfect.[21] However, in contrast to Plato and Aristotle's frameworks, which concentrated on theoretical questions about the nature of art, scholars that referred to genre as prescription dealt mainly with codification of different literary works. In this regard, Dubrow mentioned the writing of Horatius in "Ars Poetica" through which many English scholars came to learn about the philosophy of Aristotle. Dubrow explained that Horatius concentrated mainly on defining literary prescriptions that would match the theoretical approaches to the nature of poetry.[22] A similar codification project was held by Quintilian and Diomedes.[23] Thus, it is clear that over a millennium after the writings of Plato and Aristotle, the discussion on genre has become prescriptive and classificatory in its nature. In this sense, the theoretical division to modes of representation has turned into a tool that allows one to decide whether a certain text is poetry.

In the following era, the Renaissance, the concentration on genre became more intense and mainly followed the character of the Classical era.[24] In sum, the Classical and Renaissance eras concentrated on classifying and codifying kinds of works in accordance with the theoretical approaches that form the basis of genre; whereas the Neoclassical era was a clear example of a purely prescriptive approach to genre.[25] Dubrow described the Neoclassical era as concerning repetition and refinement of the generic rules of the Classical era and the examination of works in this light. She argued that the Neoclassicists were seldom interested in the theoretical basis for genre and its origins and took the Classical distinctions for granted as part of their respect for the entire era.[26]

The prescriptive understanding of genre is applicable in two ways. First, it can explain to the author the rules he should adhere to if he seeks to create a work of art within a certain genre. Thus, for example, in the context of the detective story genre, the main character should be a detective; the detective should have a companion that emphasizes his special characteristics and ability to solve mysteries; and the detective should have unique personality traits, such as a bohemian lifestyle, strong analytic abilities, and a creative soul accompanied by the will to live a lonely life away from society. Second, a prescriptive understanding of genre could be applied retrospectively to examine whether a certain text is in fact a work of art in a specific genre. Thus, for example, we could say "A Study in Scarlet" is a detective story because it adheres to the above prescription.

3) Genre as a superior division of modes of nature

In the eighteenth century's Romantic era, the literature on genre revisited the Socratic triad as a unifying literary theory and concentrated on characterizing specific genres and classifying works. Hegel, for example, discussed the three modes – epic, lyric and dramatic – in depth.[27] The reference to the Socratic triad in terms of the relationship between the subjective and objective was at the center of other genre scholarship in the Romantic era.[28]

But Goethe's writing on the three modes is the most important for understanding genre as a superior division of modes of nature. He distinguished between two terms – poetic kinds (*dichtarten*) and forms of nature (*naturformen*). The poetic kinds are genres in the classificatory sense like the romance, the ballad and the satire. In contrast, the three real forms of nature (*drei echte Naturformen*) that Goethe described – the epic (characterized by distant narration), the lyric (characterized by enthusiasm) and the dramatic (characterized by representation of human behavior) – were presented as superior types of genres that divide the world of literature to three sets of expressive potential and include all poetic kinds within them.[29]

Genette explained that Geothe's approach misconstrued the theoretical grounds of Plato and Aristotle's writings. He further argued that the Classical and Neoclassical eras revolved around the Socratic triad only out of respect for the past, and that a significant misconception occurred in the Romantic era when the major scholars considered the three modes as superior categories of genre, or "Archigenres," as he phrased it.[30]

This misconception of the Socratic triad was part of the general zeitgeist of the Romantic era that focussed on the individual and the idiosyncratic.[31] It was the chief cause of approaches that seek to nullify the very concept of genre. These approaches were at the core of the approaches that seek to reject the idea of genre.

4) The rejection of genre

One of the most critical statements of the approach rejecting the idea of genre is found in the writings of the eighteenth-century German philosopher Friedrich Schlegel, according to which "all modern genres are either one or infinite. Every work has its own kind."[32] Bawarshi and Reiff described the genre nullification approach as one that seeks to reject the very existence of genre as the prescriptive force of texts. In fact, according to this approach, a text is better when the author detaches himself from precious generic conventions.[33] One example of this approach provided by Dubrow is Victor Hugo's critique of the Neoclassical reliance on rules in his 1826 preface to "Odes et Ballades":

> On the subject of literary productions, one hears talk every day of the "dignity" of such a genre, the "appropriateness" of another … "tragedy" forbids what the novel "permits" … . The writer of this book has the bad fortune not to understand all that at all.[34]

Hugo suggested an alternative to the prescriptive focus on genre and argued that a poet needs one model alone: nature. Thus, according to Dubrow, Hugo has replaced nature as the origin of the rules of genre (in the Aristotelian a priori sense) with nature as an alternative to genre (in the prescriptive sense), meaning that the only relevant rules for the making of artistic literary works are the rules of nature, and whatever is natural "fits" the genre.[35]

Approaches that reject the concept of genre as a theoretical tool for defining literature were logically refined a century later by the Italian philosopher Benedetto Croce in "Aesthetics." Croce posited that knowledge has two forms. One is intuitive; the imagination realizes it, and it is structured by knowledge of individual phenomena in the world. The other is logical; the intellect realizes it by focussing on universal phenomena.[36] Croce criticized attempts to conceive a theory of artistic and literary phenomena because theoretical thinking breaks the distinction between the aesthetic phase (when work is created) and the logical phase (when work is perceived theoretically).[37]

The last commentator I address in this subsection is the French philosopher Jacques Derrida, who wrote in the second half of the twentieth century. The writing of Derrida is to some extent the borderline between the approach that rejects the idea of genre altogether and the dynamic approaches to genre. In his important article, *The Law of Genre*, Derrida expressed his stance on the Romantic approach to genre, and, to a certain extent, he continues the approach of rejecting the idea of genre and considers it a constraint of the creation of texts.[38] But Derrida did not stop there. He continued with a thought exercise that invites the reader to examine whether it is possible to identify a work of authorship without it carrying a generic character that distinguishes it from other works. His answer was that although there is no genreless text, a text never belongs to a genre.[39] This approach to genre puts Derrida in a crossroads: it holds that genres exist, but only in the sense that texts participate in genre, meaning that texts are examined in light of existing genres but can form new genres. He posited that genre is an important and necessary component in the creative world, and in this sense his writing was the starting shot for modern pluralistic approaches to genre.[40]

The static approaches to genres discussed in this part, which were the basis for the idea of genre, explain what I do *not* mean when I use the term genre in the rest of this chapter. Genre is not just a classificatory tool for prescriptive purposes, as it was considered under the prescriptive approaches to genre. Additionally, I do not refer to genre in the sense of an exclusive a priori division to categories that form the basis of artistic text, as other approaches suggested. Similarly, the term genre does not refer to any other a priori division, such as the Socratic triad. In the next part, I examine dynamic approaches to genre, which provide a better understanding of the term and genre's effect on players in the creative field.

IV. Dynamic approaches to genre

In this part, I examine dynamic approaches to genre proposed in the twentieth century and discuss their different characteristics, which allows me to suggest general notions about the effect genre has on the creative world. I refer to the approaches presented here as "dynamic" because, in contrast to the static approaches discussed above, they do not view genre as a predefined and constant phenomenon. As such, they provide a viable alternative to static approaches, which cannot explain how genres change and develop over time.[41] The purpose of presenting different approaches is not to canvass different ways of analyzing genre. It is also not an exhaustive description of all the modern dynamic approaches to genre or even the most prominent ones, and it is not to suggest that any of the approaches discussed below is more important than the other. Instead, the purpose of this part is highly instrumental. It shows that throughout the twentieth century and specifically in its second half, scholars developed dynamic approaches, which explain how genres evolve and affect the field of creativity and the interrelations between its different players. The discussion of the various approaches in this part is organized by the underlying idea of each of approach, although there is often chronological proximity between the commentaries related to each approach. First, I discuss linguistic approaches to genre that developed from the twentieth century philosophy of language. Then, I discuss the institutional approach to genre, which imported sociological aspects into genre's theoretical framework. Finally, I conclude with metaphorical approaches to genre, which explain the sets of rules that apply to texts by analogies to different systems known from other fields.

1) Linguistic approaches to genre

Because the discussion of genre theories focuses mainly on literary texts, the obvious link between genre and language led to the development of linguistics-based generic approaches.

Canadian literary researcher Northrop Frye was the first to combine theories of linguistics and genre. In his important book, "The Anatomy of Criticism," Frye proposed viewing literary criticism through the lens of science; like all sciences, literature is a closed system that can explain itself using internal logic.[42] One of the main characteristics of literature as a closed self-explanatory system, according to Frye, is the existence of genres and archetypes to which all literary texts could be attributed. The origin of such thought is de Saussure's research and his distinction between *langue* (the system of rules applying to language) and *parole* (a specific utterance of the language), which allowed him to explain language using *langue*. [43] To support the argument that literature is a closed system, Frye detached literature from any exterior aspect and specifically from historical context. As far as genre theories are concerned, Frye's theory—which explains genre as a pre-given historically-independent system of rules that apply to literary texts – is not significantly different from the static approaches of the Classical, Neoclassical, and Romantic eras discussed above.[44] The dynamic aspect of linguistic approaches to genre was only apparent with the introduction of the historical aspect to the systematic understanding of genre.

One of the most prominent commentators that focussed on the historical aspect of genre, aside from its linguistic aspect, is Bulgarian literature researcher Tzvetan Todorov, who was among the most important commentators in the structuralist approach to literary theory and one of the most important writers on genre. Todorov used terms from the field of linguistics (semiotics in particular) to explain his approach to genre, which he suggested in the end of the 1970s. After discussing prior pre-modern and static definitions to genre (while implicitly criticizing Frye), Todorov proposed viewing genre in a more complex way that entails both the systemic non-historical aspects and the historical-empirical aspects of the phenomenon. Todorov defined genre as the "codification of discursive properties." Discursive properties, according to Todorov, are the semantic and syntactic aspects of text that characterize the linguistic aspect of genre.[45] Additionally, Todorov explained that society will eventually decide to code and empirically recognize discursive properties. This decision is historical in the sense that it depends on social institutions.[46]

The approach to genre as a social institution is discussed in further detail below. The linguistic approach to genre added a historical-social aspect to the linguistic-systemic aspect from within the field of linguistics. This development is owed to Marie-Louise Pratt, who emphasized the importance of pragmatics in the study of literary texts, which improved the analysis of semantics and syntax by focussing on the social context of texts. Pratt viewed genre as a speech act,[47] the importance of which is not limited to its evident grammatical properties. Rather, speech's significance lies mainly in its context, namely the "intentions, attitudes, expectations of the participants, the relationship between participants, and generally, the unspoken rules and conventions that are understood to be in play when an utterance is made and received."[48] Other commentators later adopted this approach to genre.[49]

The linguistic approach to genre could be demonstrated using the development of the detective story as follows. When the rule applying to each of Poe and Doyle's stories is examined, one should look at both the formal characters in each text and their social context. For example, Doyle's text includes a detective character that has a specific relationship with his companion, Dr. Watson, who explains to the reader that a detective named Sherlock exists. More importantly, Dr. Watson adds another layer to Doyle's novels, which follows from the books' social context, by alluding to a similar relationship in a different detective story. In this sense, the social context of the text influences how the text functions and the sets of rules that apply to it.

2) Institutional approaches to genre

Another branch of the dynamic approaches to genre is defined as the "social institution" approach to genre. The institutional approach to genre was developed by Rene Weleck and Austin Warren, who explained that genre is an institution in the sense that a church, a university, or a state are institutions.[50] This means that when one tries to understand the "church" as a social institution, one should be interested in more than the characteristics of the church's form and structure and its inner logic; rather, one should also study its influence on the different social players that act in relation to it. Likewise, genre is not just its inner set of rules, rather it is also the way it affects the different players in the field of the genre.

In addition to identifying the link between genre and linguistics, Todorov explained that genre is a social institution. According to Todorov, as mentioned above, genre is the codification of discursive properties. The discursive properties are the inner systems of genre's rules. Codification, according to Todorov, is society's choice to recognize certain discursive properties as important, a choice that is made within social institutions.[51] Todorov demonstrated this in the following way. The understanding of genre could be based on inner rules that apply to texts much like the static approaches to genre in the pre-modern eras and even Frye's formalist approach. Under this understanding, genre can only explain theoretical possibilities of discourse and cannot explain specific empirical instances of discourse. Another alternative is understanding genre as a social-historical phenomenon. Under this understanding, genre refers to groups of texts that are conceived by society (or social institutions) as genres, and the sets of rules that characterize them are examined in relation to these existing groups of texts.[52]

The second alternative suggested by Todorov characterizes genre as a social institution and focusses on both the empirical-historical aspect of genre and its inner sets of rules. In this sense, according to Todorov, genre explains how authors create texts according to an existing genre (and its typical sets of rules) and the audience reads texts in relation to genre.[53] This approach characterizes the writing of Fishelov and Frow on genre, which could be categorized as an institutional approach. Fishelov, who focussed on the literary aspects of genre, theorized that genre combines typical and representative texts, which are accompanied by a set of constitutive rules that apply to different levels of literary text, different authors, and, usually, more than one literary era.[54] In a somewhat similar way, Frow detailed several characteristics of generic texts such as formal properties, thematic structure, rhetoric structure, and physical environment and concluded that genre is a set of conventional and well-organized constraints on the creation and understanding of meaning.[55] Frow also explained that genre is not a character of the text itself or of the reader-interpreter; rather, it is a product of the social relationship between authors, texts and readers.[56] This last definition explains genre as a social institution well. Bawarshi and Reiff, who described similar approaches as "social" approaches to genre, explained that the institutional approach concentrates on the question of how genres organize, classify, normalize, and enable the creation of texts and other non-literary social actions. According to this approach, genre is a social institution, which, along with other institutions, shapes the way we identify, appreciate and experience texts.[57]

This is demonstrated by the development of the detective story: the mere fact that society recognizes Poe and Doyle's texts as part of the detective genre justifies examination of the sets of rules that apply to it (as a social institution), in order to understand how they affect the various players acting within it.

The essence of the institutional approach to genre is, therefore, the understanding that the sets of rules and conventions governing texts affect players in the creative field and that these players influence the rules and conventions. Thus, every generation of authors creates the basis for participation in the field.[58] Seen in this light, the institutional approach to genre and the linguistic approach to genre are two sides of the same coin. The starting point of the linguistic approach to genre is the formal inner sets of rules that apply to texts and their analysis. The entrance of pragmatics into linguistics added the social aspect to this analysis, which takes into account the way society uses these sets of rules.[59] The starting point of the institutional approach to genre is the opposite; it focuses first on the social aspect of genre and on the fact that there is social value in grouping texts together. Additionally, the institutional approach to genre is interested in examining the sets of rules that shape these groups of texts and the way they affect society.

The difference between the static approaches to genre and the dynamic approaches that consider the social aspect of genre is demonstrated by the development of the detective story. Under the static approaches to genre, one should examine each of Poe and Doyle's stories separately with a predefined set of rules and the hierarchy of the different possible methods of presentation. Under the Socratic triad, for example, we could have reached the conclusion that both stories are drama because they aim at the representation of real relationships between characters. Under the same approach, we could also reach the opposite conclusion: Poe's story is a tragedy while Doyle's is a comedy. In any case, the similarities between the stories are not important for genre analysis under these approaches.

Under the dynamic approaches to genre, which consider the importance of the social aspect of texts, the analysis is completely different. According to Todorov's demonstration, for example, because society places Poe and Doyle's stories in the same category, it is proper to examine the set of rules that govern and unite them. Additionally, in contrast to the analysis under the static approaches to genre that examines every text alone, under the dynamic approaches, we would consider parts of Doyle's later text in light of Poe's earlier text because the social-historical context could be important for the understanding of the rules characterizing the genre and the way to use them. Thus, the similarities between the stories – such as the characters of the detective and his companion, some repeating scenes, and the personality traits of the detective – would receive special consideration under dynamic social approaches to genre.

3) Metaphorical approaches to genre

As mentioned above, the dynamic approaches to genre reject the notion that genre is a static ahistorical phenomenon. Due to the difficulty in finding a positive and exclusive definition of genre, some approaches use analogy or metaphor to understand genre. Fishelov reviewed four metaphors for understanding genre, but I will concentrate on only two of them in this section: genres as *biological species* and genre as *family resemblance.* [60]

Under the development of the dynamic approaches to genre, which sought definitions that understand how genres form and develop, the French literary researcher Ferdinand Brunetière proposed examining the development of genre by analogizing genre to Darwin's evolutionary biology of species.[61] The analogy between genres and biological species was severely criticized by genre theoreticians at first, mainly due to three basic problems with the comparison. First, while biological genres usually do not produce hybrids, genres often merge, creating a new mixed genre. Second, in contrast to biological species, it is possible for one individual to change the entire definition of the genre. Third, genres are different from biological species in that they do not necessarily have an evident circle of life.[62]

In light of this criticism, Fishelov offered a renewed approach to genres as biological species that explains the link between the phenomena in a metaphorical way and not through identity or direct analogy. Fishelov explained, for example, that although genres tend to evolve and change in a relatively short period of time compared to biological species, one individual can pass new properties to its offspring in a way that eventually changes the entire species. This observation allows analogy to biological species without leading to a static perception of generic development. Fishelov based this thought on the Darwinian approach to evolution the implications of which will be discussed below. Aside from that, it is important to point out that in contrast to the dynamic approaches to genre discussed above, the metaphor to biological species does not explain the inner structure of genres, the sets of rules that apply to text, or the influence of specific genres on the field of creativity.[63]

I will explore the metaphor of biological species using the development of the detective story. Poe's detective story could be conceived of as an offspring of the crime fiction stories that existed in England and France in the relevant period; it shares common attributes with other texts in that genre, such as the existence of a crime in the heart of the plot. Aside from that, Poe's story includes a new trait that is not shared with the genre it supposedly belongs to: the detective as the main character of the story.[64] Doyle's detective story, which is in a sense a direct offspring of Poe's detective story, also includes a new trait and so do its own direct offspring. All of these offspring develop and strengthen the new trait (the centrality of the detective character), leading to the development of a new genre, the detective story.

The approach that proposes analogy between genre and family resemblance is a follow-up on the family resemblance approach to linguistics that was developed by Ludwig Wittgenstein. Wittgenstein observed that we sometimes categorize items based on their resemblance to each other, even though every member of the category does not actually share a common trait.[65] He proposed that the best way to describe such a system is to compare it to family resemblance.[66] Wittgenstein's idea marked a turning point from the Classical view, according to which groups or classes must be organized by the common traits of all individuals that belong to them, and created a new approach named the *prototype theory*. [67]

Wittgenstein's approach was quickly adopted by genre commentators. Alastir Fowler explained, this approach holds that generic texts are related to each other in a family resemblance way without having one common trait.[68] Fishelov, on his part, argued that Fowler's application of the family resemblance model to genre theories was too simplistic and failed exactly where previous definitions did. According to him, the will to break the boundaries of the perception of genre as a limited predefined set of rules cannot justify a shift to an approach that sees no necessary link between all individual texts that form a genre. Fishelov suggested a different interpretation of Wittgenstein's family resemblance model as it applies to genre theories. Under this interpretation, genres are different categories that share a core of exemplar texts, these texts greatly resemble each other, while other texts share only some traits with the exemplar texts.[69] Another property of genres that Fishelov absorbed from the family resemblance model is the existence of a common ancestry of texts that form a genre. This common trait has nothing to do with texts' similar content; instead, it concerns interrelations with previous texts and assists in assigning texts genres – or families of texts.[70] To demonstrate this using the detective story, we could view Poe and Doyle's stories (and many others following them) as texts that are in the core of the detective story and thus share many common traits. Aside from that, it is possible to attribute to the detective story genre a story that focusses on the detective character and his relationship with his companion without the detective solving a mystery. A story that focusses on solving mysteries without a detective character is also attributable to the detective genre. While both such stories would not share common traits with one another, they would share traits with the texts in the core of the genre and therefore would be considered offspring of common ancestors.

V. Common building blocks as a basis for genre, the tool that links the various players in the field of creativity

The different approaches to genre discussed thus far are representative exemplars for the modern debate on genre, which started in the second half of the twentieth century. This debate is characterized by dynamic approaches to genre that reject static approaches to genre, but differ from one another in the starting reference point to genre and the different aspects of the phenomenon that the different definitions attempt to encapsulate. However, I argue that it is possible to identify basic common grounds that characterize the modern debate on genre – genre as the common building blocks in the basis of texts. The common building blocks approach allows examination of the sets of rules that apply to groups of texts and the analysis of the way these sets of rules affect the creative field and the players acting within it. The rest of the discussion on genre focuses on the common building blocks and the two important roles they have in the creative world: first is the power of these common building blocks as a tool that enables creativity and second is the use of common building blocks as a meaning-making tool. These two aspects relate to different players in the world of creativity; the first relates to the authors who engage in creativity and the second relates to the audience who engages in the valuation and understanding of works of authorship. These two aspects view creativity as sociological/philosophical and help illuminate the legal debate on creativity.

1) Common building blocks as a tool that enables creativity

In this section, I argue that many dynamic approaches to genre view the identification of common building blocks of texts as necessary for the creation of text (or other rhetoric actions) by authors. It is important to emphasize, however, that although the enabling aspect of the common building blocks approach is somewhat "prescriptive," it is not prescriptive in the Neoclassical sense according to which genres are predefined and every text must be created in their light. To the contrary, the enabling aspect of the common building blocks lies in the fact that the building blocks facilitate the creation of new texts within the framework of existing genres while simultaneously allowing the evolution of new genres and building blocks that drive future creativity. In this sense, this approach to genre corrects an ancient misapprehension described by Scottish genre and literature researcher Alastir Fowler: genre is a predefined prescription for the making of texts.[71] The discussion in this section examines how commentators who endorse dynamic approaches to genre understand the common building blocks' contribution to the enrichment of the creative world from the authors' perspective.

Following the critique on the static approach to genre, according to which genres are predefined, proponents of dynamic approaches questioned how genres are created and change over time. Fowler, in the introduction to his important book "Kinds of Literature," argued that every genre has several distinctive properties, which are not necessarily reflected in each and every exemplar of a particular genre (similar to the family resemblance metaphor to genre). According to him, the most representative characteristic of genre is that it changes; such changes are of the most literary importance. Fowler also stated that every text belongs to at least one genre, and one can identify significant generic properties in it (or common building blocks). However, he explained that genre's effect on creativity differs from previous understandings in that it is more than a mere constraint on spontaneous expression. He argued that a proper understanding of genre identifies it as a tool that facilitates creative expression, and that the relationship between texts and their genres is not one of passive participation but rather one of active change. For example, consider the similarity between Poe's detective story and the crime fiction in England and France at that time, much like the discussion on the biological species metaphor above. While Poe's detective story participated in the crime fiction genre, due to the fact that his plot focussed on a crime scene, it also actively changed the genre by making the central character a detective who investigates the crime.

Fowler explained that genre's active changes are a type of communication; therefore, genre should be understood as a speech act.[72] In this sense, the author communicates through a system of common grammatical rules and artistic conventions. This system is similar to the semiotic system that de Saussure defined as *langue*. The text itself is an expression of the system of rules and is similar to *parole*;[73] in this sense, it depends and is based significantly on a preexisting system, but simultaneously changes it and differs from it in a way that creates new rules and conventions that will be used for future textual expressions.[74]

According to Fowler, genres are in a constant state of change, but it is the change of genre itself that gives a text an artistic value. However, Fowler argued that it is not possible to object to the prescriptive aspect altogether. Certain authors need rules and conventions to create, and others need a framework for creativity and a reminder to evaluate their work in light of these rules.[75] Fowler viewed the prescriptive aspect of genre (in its open and dynamic sense) as one that facilitates creativity rather than inhibits it. He stated two main reasons for the lack of harm in prescriptive approaches to genre. First, the author can always (try to) relate its work to mixed, hybrid or ill-defined genres – thus untethering his work from prior conventions. Second, the author can create a new system of rules that will be accepted under the wide generic framework in which he acts, especially when the creative environment is relatively new. In this way, prescriptive genres, in the dynamic sense that allows development and change, encourage authors to break through by expanding the generic boundaries or by variation of the existing generic framework.[76]

Moreover, Fowler argued that genres do not inhibit creativity, they positively support it. Genres give the author a predefined creative space that urges them to use past experience in a novel way. Fowler stated that genre gives the author access to formal examples for possible combinations of common building blocks while also allowing him to rise above existing exemplars. He concluded that it is impossible to forsake the prescriptiveness of genres; the author most interested in originality is the most interested in genre.[77]

The prescriptive aspect of genre (in the dynamic and open sense) as a tool that enables creativity is demonstrated by the detective story. Poe's detective story – the first to put the detective character in the heart of the story – was not written in a vacuum. Poe worked with a certain prescription, the crime fiction genre popular at that time. But his activity within this prescription was not constraining, rather, it was enabling in the sense that Poe could have added a new layer to the existing prescription – thus changing its rules from that point on. Doyle used Poe's new prescription, or at least parts of it, to create his detective story. Doyle's use of the prescription, moreover, was not static and closed, it was open and dynamic in the sense that he too continued to develop the rules of the new prescription.

Todorov also expressed this dynamic approach to genre that emphasizes the significance of common building blocks as a constitutive tool that facilitates creativity and the development of genres. One of his important arguments in this context was his answer to where genres come from. Todorov answered: "Quite simply from other genres. A new genre is always the transformation of an earlier one, or of several: by inversion, by displacement, by combination."[78] But Todorov did not specify exactly how this phenomenon takes place. Fowler, in contrast, did not stop at the theoretical observation regarding the dynamic character of genre; he dedicated a significant discussion to the typical ways genres change.

One way generic change occurs, as noted by Fowler, is when new topics for genre are invented. When a new topic joins the repertoire of a certain genre, a sub-genre may evolve around that topic. The new topics can be transformed from one genre into another or from different mediums.[79] Poe's detective story is a good example of this when it is considered from the point of view of the crime fiction genre. Poe's focus on the detective character added a new subject to the crime fiction genre and developed it in a way that led to the formation of a new genre. Another way genre changes is the combination of generic repertoire that, when successful, may form a new unified repertoire for a new genre. A third way is when an aggregate of works from one or various genres form a distinct genre (for example an aggregate of poems may create a genre of poem cycles). Indeed, the aggregate may sometimes supersede the repertoire of its components. The fourth way Fowler mentioned is based on the scale of the works that form a genre. A new genre can thus be formed by the expansion or contraction of the type of works that constitute an existing genre. The classic example of this is the use of the sets of rules that apply to the short story genre to create a full-length novel. A fifth way genre changes is through changes in the conventional functions of genre, for example by changing the way a character tends to address others or changing the type of characters. Fowler emphasized that such a change may be intentional but could also be unintentional and gradual and thus will form a new generic convention over time. This is illustrated by comparing Dupin and his companion's relationship with Holmes and Watson's relationship; Dupin's relationship is characterized by an official tone and clear hierarchy between the characters, while Holmes's relationship is characterized by sarcasm and humorous remarks. Thus, the detective story genre could have developed both as a dramatic genre and as a comedy. A sixth way Fowler observed is generic mixture: the addition of one genre's properties to another genre, allowing a wider spectrum of works to be created using common building blocks. Hybrids, as Fowler named them, are the most frequent type of generic mixture. They are characterized by a mixture of works from different genres that are so similar in scale and form that one cannot identify the most dominant genre in the mixture.[80] A good example is the combination of rules that apply to the detective story genre and those that apply to the children's story genre, which would result in the genre of detective stories for children. It is interesting to note that the different ways for the change and development of genres that Fowler identified are very similar to the cognitive patterns of creativity identified by commentators in the field of cognitive psychology, as presented in Chapter 1.

Another commentator that focussed on the constitutive aspect of the common building blocks is Fishelov. He also concentrated on the misconception of genre as a predefined static prescription, which is unchangable and leaves no place for the dynamics of genre. Thus, Fishelov suggested that genre is a set of rules that are enabling in their nature more than they are regulatory or restraining, in the sense that they do not refer to a preexisting action but enable a new one.[81] To demonstrate how this approach to genre takes place, Fishelov reviewed different metaphors for genre used in literature. One important metaphor which I discussed earlier is the biological species metaphor. He offered a Darwinian evolutionary approach to genre, according to which organisms are analogous to texts, biological species are metaphors to genres, and the natural environment is a metaphor for the "cultural environment." Fishelov stressed that the evolutionary survival of a genre depends not on the continuity of a "correct" interpretation of it but on its continuous productivity.

Generic productivity, according to Fishelov, is divided into two stages: the primary stage and secondary stage. The primary stage of productivity happens when works that constitute a genre influence and encourage the creation of new works that are perceived as part of the same genre by both authors and readers. The secondary stage of productivity happens when new texts are produced in light of a generic formula. Fishelov gave examples of secondary productivity, including translation, parody, imitation (preserving the form but changing the content), and adaptation (preserving the content but changing the form or the medium).[82] The development of the detective story is an excellent example of generic productivity. Poe's detective story, as noted above, could be conceived of as a development of the crime fiction genre that added the detective character and his personality traits, the companion character, and the murder mystery scene. Doyle's detective story is an example of both the primary phase of generic productivity – it belongs to the same generic compound of Poe's new characteristics – and the secondary phase of productivity – it is compatible with the characteristics presented by Poe and therefore contributes to the survival of the new genre. It is important to note that any one of the characteristics created by Poe, in every level of abstraction, could be the basis for generic productivity and the creation of a new genre. Further, it is interesting that the different forms of secondary productivity proposed by Fishelov are highly compatible with the legal definition of a derivative work.

According to Australian genre commentator Vijay Bhatia, the most significant characteristics of genre are the communicative conventions that constrain the use of common building blocks in a specific discourse, thus allowing formation of stable and predefined rules for participating in the discourse.[83] However, Bhatia also emphasized that the stability of genre is not entirely static. Genre's conventions are based on recurring social-rhetoric utterances, but the recurring utterances are often not identical to the typical utterance – thus requiring the community to respond to these changes using the arsenal of generic conventions in their hands. In this way, experienced participants in the discourse can manipulate their deep understanding of these conventions to break through the borders of genre and satisfy immediate social needs. Bhatia emphasized, however, that such changes are often considered "innovative" or "creative" only by members of the genre; the resulting change is thus never a complete abandonment of convention. In this sense, it is clear that Bhatia also understood the common building blocks as an enabling phenomenon that facilitates creativity and development and not as a restraining and inhibiting phenomenon. At the same time, Bhatia's commentary stressed the common building blocks' importance and genre's inability to detach from them entirely.

Bhatia contended that two main characteristics of genre explain its dynamics and ability to change. He argued that genres across different disciplines have similar properties, which form groups that he defined as "colonies of genres."[84] The colonization of genres occurs when one genre invades another, thus mixing the conventions that characterize both genres. This mixture of conventions, according to Bhatia, leads to the creation of a hybrid that shares the properties of both genres and allows the use of both genres' resources to create a new genre, which is a combination of the underlying genres. Another dynamic characteristic of genre mentioned by Bhatia is the use experienced participants in the genre discourse make of the generic conventions in order to express their "personal intentions" through the common building blocks in a way that "bends" the borders of genre towards the development of a new genre.[85] It is important to note, however, that a new genre that breaks through the borders of an existing one is always dependent on the use of the existing common building blocks.

The discussion above explains that the common building blocks at the heart of genres are a tool that enables creation from the author's perspective and are thus necessary for creativity.[86] This notion is a significant part of the dynamic approaches to genre, which reject that genre is a predefined prescription for the making of texts. It is also notable that the discussion in this section focussed on the enabling aspect of common building blocks from the author's point of view, and the conclusions derived from it are similar to the cognitive psychology of creativity as described in Chapter 1. Aside from that, the common building blocks have a significant impact on another part of the creative field – the audience. The common building blocks at the heart of genre affect the way the audience gives meaning to works of authorship. This aspect will be discussed in the following section.

2) Common building blocks as a meaning-making tool

The dynamic approaches to genre debate the enabling aspect of the common building blocks, which facilitate creativity and the development of genres. This debate focuses mainly on the influence of the common building blocks on the participants of the creative process, the authors. However, some commentators suggest that the common building blocks of texts have significant influence on other participants in the creativity discourse: the audience. Thus, although Todorov dedicated a vast discussion to the prescriptive aspect of genres (in its open and dynamic sense), he also argued that the historical existence of genre has two sides. The first side is the author who creates texts as a function of the existing generic system (even if not in accordance with it). The second side is the reader who understands texts as a function of the same generic system, even if sometimes unconsciously.[87] Similarly, Frow argued that genres do not function only as a classificatory mechanism; instead they mainly function as representative frameworks that play a crucial part in the everyday meaning-making process.[88]

Fowler explained the common building blocks' contribution to the meaning-making of artistic texts through a comparison to communication theory. According to him, non-artistic interpersonal communication preserves messages in a manner that allows their reception and understanding, even though the redundancy of information they contain causes uncertainty. This occurs through the situational context in which the communication occurs. Fowler argued that artistic texts have no real situational context, and they should therefore carry a substitute that will allow the same meaning-making process.[89] He explained that in contrast to everyday communication, artistic texts enjoy a much wider repertoire of possible forms, which are drawn from the basic grammatical forms of the relevant language. This wide repertoire allows the formation of a system of rules (or *langue*) that is wider than everyday language and serves as a substitute for the lack of situational context in two main ways: first, the artistic rules supply an artistic context to the situation, which the text refers to; second, the artistic rules strengthen the semiotic set of communications with additional coding rules that may sometimes replace the codes of the "normal" language or supplement to them. Fowler added that the artistic coding "validates" the work itself and the message it contains, offering credibility and the possibility to enjoy its communicative expression. Thus, a reader's attention is more easily captured by conventional and known properties of texts (generic characters for example) and every convention used by the author influences the meaning of text. This description led Fowler to state that the most important code in the artistic *langue* is genre and that it is used as a meaning-making tool: "It is an instrument not of classification or prescription, but of meaning."

A similar conceptualization of the same idea was suggested by Miller. Miller's starting point was that human actions are based on and directed by meaning. Thus, before one can act, he must interpret the material environment and define the situation in which he acts.[90] She added that we understand situations by comparing them to prior situations or other known situations. According to Miller, we understand the new by identifying relevant similarities, which are referred to as "type." She argued that successful communication can occur only when participants of the discourse share common types. The meaning-making process makes use of the common building blocks in different levels of hierarchy. Miller explained that this process is based on a combination of content (semantics) that is presented in a certain form (syntax) with context (pragmatics). However, at a certain point in the hierarchy of meaning, the content and form merge and become a new type of content in a higher level of the hierarchy, which is also divided into content, form and context. Genre, or the common building blocks, according to Miller, is a merger of content and form in a specific context that plays a crucial role in the meaning-making process. It is important to note that Miller's approach articulates that the common building blocks are not limited to the rules regarding the form in which texts are expressed, they also apply to content or semantics shared by texts that create meaning. This note has implications for copyright law, as will be discussed below.

The difference in Fowler and Miller's conceptualizations of the meaning-making aspect of genres is demonstrated by the detective genre. Regarding Doyle's detective story, its content and form carry a meaning value resulting from Doyle's use of language and the relationships between the different characters in the story. By contrast, a different meaning value results from factors that are not part of Doyle's common use of language when Doyle's work is read in light of a preexisting text in the same genre, Poe's detective story. This could occur, for example, when explicit intertextuality exists in the text, such as Doyle's reference to Poe's detective, Dupin. Thus, when Doyle wrote that Dupin was an inferior fellow, a different meaning value is added that does not result from the understanding that a person named Dupin is inferior. Instead, it results from the fact that Dupin was the hero of a different text. Additional meaning value could also exist without explicit intertextuality. Thus, in light of Poe's story, the reference to the relationship between a detective with certain personality traits and his companion in the context of mystery solving carries a meaning value in additional to the ordinary lexical value. Here too, it is important to emphasize that the additional meaning value may result from various abstraction levels of common building blocks, much like the case of the detective story, such as plot lines, general ideas, explicit personality traits and scenes.

Fowler's argument, according to which the meaning of artistic texts depends on generic types for its existence, was supported by Hirsch's statement that:

> A verbal meaning is always a type since otherwise it could not be sharable. If it lacked a boundary, there would be nothing in particular to share; and if a given instance could not be accepted or rejected as an instance of the meaning … the interpreter would have no way of knowing what the boundary was.[91]

Hirsch's approach could be summarized by one sentence in his book: "All understanding of verbal meaning is necessarily genre-bound."[92] This approach is related to another approach that views the importance of common building blocks from the audience's point of view – the reader response approach in aesthetics and literary theories.[93] This approach holds that genre is a heuristic tool that serves the reader-interpreter or, as Adena Rosmarin put it:

> The genre is the critic's heuristic tool, his chosen or defined way of persuading his audience to see the literary text in all its previously inexplicable and "literary" fullness and then to relate this text to those that are similar or, more precisely, to those that may be similarly explained.[94]

Bawarshi and Reiff explained that genre in this sense functions as a consensus about the guesses and expectations readers assume about a text and according to which their understanding of the text and its meaning is shaped at a certain point in history.[95] This characteristic of genre is substantially based on Hans Robert Jauss, who studied the development of genre in texts of medieval Germany. Jauss concluded that texts create a "horizon of expectations" in the reader that are based on rules the reader learned from previous texts. These common building blocks could be transformed, expanded, amended, or simply reproduced.[96]

The significance of the common building blocks of texts as a meaning-making tool was emphasized in literature that relates to the institutional approach to genre. According to Bawarshi and Reiff, this approach questions how genres organize, classify, normalize, and assist the creation of texts and other non-written social actions. Under this approach, genres are social institutions that shape the way we identify, valuate, and experience texts.[97] One of the central commentators of this approach is Thomas Beebe, who argued that genre is a precondition for the making and reading of texts.[98] Beebe explained that the common building blocks allow the audience not only to understand a text passively but also to use it and actively valuate it.[99] In fact, under this approach, the common building blocks are the tool through which texts are recognizable, receive meaning, and are useful in relation to each other.[100]

In this part, I focussed on the importance of the common building blocks of texts as the main characteristic of genre as part of creativity. I showed that the modern literature on genre explains the important role of common building blocks as a constitutive tool that facilitates creativity both through known patterns and through the development of new ones. In this sense, the discussion on the common building blocks bears a strong resemblance to the discussion of the cognitive process of creation and the basic need to use memory and domain-relevant knowledge. The common building blocks that authors use to create new texts are similar to the task-relevant knowledge that cognitive psychology identifies as a crucial component in the creative process. In addition, and maybe most important for the argument in this chapter, I explained how the modern discussion on genre emphasizes the importance of the common building blocks as a meaning-making tool for the audience, which is independent of the use of common building blocks by the author. This notion is of most importance to creativity because without the ability to give meaning to creative products, they cannot be valuated and thus, to a certain extent, there is no justification for their creation in the first place.

Before I conclude this part, and as a link to the next one, it is important to clarify the benefit of using the common building blocks approach as an organizing idea about genre and creativity with regard to copyright law. The discussion of the common building blocks approach has been mainly theoretical thus far, but it is important to explain what kinds of common building blocks are theoretically possible and exist in the world of creativity. The spectrum of possible kinds of common building blocks is relatively wide. It begins with high levels of abstraction, such as artistic styles, general themes, and what is referred to in the copyright discourse as "ideas." As far as this level of abstraction is concerned, copyright law fits the understanding of the enrichment of the creative world as genre theories view it.

Additionally, common building blocks may be found in much lower and more particular levels of abstraction. Thus, a certain text (or melody, character, painting etc.) may constitute a building block for the development of other text in the same creative environment. As explained above, one way to develop a genre is recombining texts and other existing artistic expression. The rest of this chapter establishes that common building blocks of a lower level of abstraction, "expressions" in copyright terms, are not inferior in their importance to the field of creativity when compared to other building blocks. The development of the detective story is a good example for this argument. These notions have significant implications for copyright law, especially the right to make derivative works, which governs when common building blocks may be used to create new products.

VI. Common building blocks and derivative works

Thus far I have shown that the enrichment of the creative world could be explained by the use of common building blocks in genres. One aspect of common building blocks' importance is their contribution to the creative process and the existence and developments of creative patterns. A second, and maybe the most important, aspect of common building blocks is their contribution to the audience's process of meaning-making. In this sense, genre theories explain the importance of common building blocks and the system of rules that apply to them as a tool. The audience uses this tool to give meaning to creative products, valuate them, and justify their creation and contribution to society. Accordingly, it is important to examine whether these notions are reflected in copyright law.

My argument in this part is that copyright law is aware, even if intuitively, of the common building blocks' importance to the creative world, and copyright law reflects their importance to a great extent. It does so in two main doctrines: the idea/expression dichotomy (and the scènes à faire doctrine that derives from it) and the fair use doctrine.[101] However, I argue that the significant match between genre theories' understanding of the common building blocks' importance to the promotion of creativity and that of copyright law is not complete. The mismatch is most evident with regard to derivative works. The right to make derivative works allows the owner of a work of authorship to forbid the making of works that are substantially based on the underlying work.

Thus, the first author has a de facto right to bar the use of the common building blocks that his work is based on in the making of new works, a constraint that naturally limits the ability of the audience to identify these common building blocks in future (derivative) works. This is demonstrated by the development of the detective story. Doyle's use of common building blocks, such as expressions (the detailed detective character of Dupin and the locked room mystery scene) from Poe's story could be considered a derivative work under current doctrine. Had this doctrine existed and applied when the detective story genre was developing, Poe could have prevented Doyle from using these common building blocks.

According to genre theories, the use of common building blocks as part of the enrichment of the creative world, occurs on different levels of abstraction, including expressions. The right to make derivative works therefore collides with a substantial aspect of the sociological-philosophical understanding of the creative world and thus should be reevaluated.

Copyright law allows the use of certain types of common building blocks of texts and thus reflects the understanding of their importance to the enrichment of the creative world. This is evident in the idea/expression dichotomy that allows authors to use building blocks in the form of abstract ideas. The scènes à faire doctrine allows the use of common building blocks when their use is necessary to creating a work that falls within a particular genre. In addition, transformative use of protected expressions is allowed under the fair use doctrine and thus allows the use of another type of common building blocks. However, copyright law forbids the use of common building blocks in the form of expressions (that are not fair use or stock scenes) in order to enrich the creative world. These cases fall under the definition of the right to make derivative works.

My argument is that the first author's right to bar subsequent authors from using many types of common building blocks to enrich the creative world and promote creativity does not match genre theories' understanding of the common building blocks' importance to the creative world. Thus, the right to make derivative works as a legal norm does not match the sociological-philosophical understanding of creativity and should be scrutinized and reevaluated.

Genre theories can assist in the rethinking of the derivative work right in two main respects. The first is the scope of the derivative work right and its relation to the reproduction right. The second is the strength of remedies available to an owner of a work in relation to the unauthorized making of derivative works based on it. As far as the first is concerned, genre theories can explain why the derivative work right should be separated and distinguished from the reproduction right. The current overlap between the derivative work right and the reproduction right does not reflect a qualitative difference between the two. Genre theories explain why making a derivative work is qualitatively different from the making of a reproduction and thus why the two should be separated.

As I showed, the use of common building blocks – in the establishment of a new genre, its development on the author's part, and the meaning-making of texts on the audience's part – is necessary and significant to the creative world. Common building blocks are important both in using rules and conventions on the one hand (derivation) and on developing the existing rules on the other (originality). Genre theories are indifferent to whether the use of common building blocks is of ideas or unprotected expression or whether it is of protected expressions, as long as the use develops new genres or expands existing ones. In contrast, the use of common building blocks without the development of genres does not contribute to promoting creativity and does not have a significant part in genre theories. Thus, in copyright terms, derivative works are much more similar to original works than they are to reproductions and an overlap between derivative works and reproductions could not be justified. This notion justifies a new derivative work doctrine that would completely separate it from the scope of the reproduction right.

Here too, the detective story is a good example. The common building blocks in Poe and Doyle's stories are of different levels of abstraction, though some amount to expressions in copyright terms. For example, the detective character of Dupin and his detailed personality traits that Doyle used for the creation of detective Holmes, as well as the locked room mysteries in both stories. Despite the fact that Doyle's detective story is different from Poe's and is, without a doubt, an original work on its own, under copyright's derivative work right and reproduction right, Doyle's story would likely infringe modern copyright protections.[102] It seems that under the understanding of the importance of common building blocks to creativity according to genre theories, Doyle's story is better seen as a derivative work rather than as a reproduction.

This point leads me to the second respect in which the importance of common building blocks affects the right to make derivative works: the strength of the remedies available to the owner. Even if we define Doyle's story as a derivative work and not as a reproduction, under the current definition of the derivative work right, it would still amount to copyright infringement. Genre theories could support a different doctrine. The main collision between the current derivative work right and the genre theories' understanding of common building blocks is in the first author's right to prevent subsequent authors from using common building blocks when other doctrines such as fair use or idea/expression dichotomy do not apply. Therefore, genre theories could support a change in the remedies available to the owner of the derivative work right so that the first author could not prevent a second author from such uses of common building blocks.

It is important to clarify that I do not argue that the derivative work right should be completely annulled such that it does not recognize any interest the first author has in potential second works based upon his original expressions. One could definitely think of cases in which such an interest should be recognized. Similarly, I do not argue that there is no value in making a distinction between ideas and expressions or in the scènes à faire doctrine. It also makes sense, in inner-legal logical terms, to set a border beyond which the first author has no more interest in second works. This happens when the second work is based on ideas from the first or when it is based upon stock expressions. However, the findings in this chapter assist in portraying a remedy model for the derivative work right that will match the understanding of the common building blocks' importance to the promotion of creativity under genre theories.

As noted earlier, the implications of genre theories on copyright law and the mismatch between the two concerning the derivative work right includes a normative aspect on top of the descriptive-critical one. This means that the mismatch between the conditions for the enrichment of the creative world under genre theories and the right to make derivative works could be a normative justification for changing the current legal doctrine. This is because genre theories examine and explain the significant necessary components for the enrichment of the creative world, and because copyright law's goal is to promote such enrichment. Therefore, notions from genre theories regarding the conditions that enable authors to create and develop the creative world and enable the audience to value works of authorship and extract meaning from them must be reflected in the legal rules that govern creativity.

VII. Conclusion

Although there is a significant match between copyright law's understating of the way in which the creative world develops and the importance of common building blocks to such development under genre theories, as far as derivative works are concerned there is a mismatch between the two. To support this argument, I discussed different approaches to genre that focus on the development of creative texts and showed these approaches recognize that common building blocks are the foundation of creative development. The common building blocks have two main aspects. First, the common building blocks enable creativity within constraints, rules and familiar conventions from the author's perspective. Second, the common building blocks have an aspect that enables the audience to assign meaning and value to creative products and make them socially valuable. I also showed that the understanding of the enrichment of the creative world by using common building blocks views expressions and ideas as relevant types of common building blocks.

Using these notions from genre theories, I examined the possible implications this debate has on copyright law. As far as the idea/expression dichotomy is concerned – as well as the scènes à faire doctrine, which allows the use of protected expressions that are customary under a recognized genre – I showed that there is a match between genre theories and the legal rules. However, I argued that these doctrines do not supply a sufficient tool and do not allow the use of all types of common building blocks that genre theories recognize. This is because the scènes à faire doctrine does not fully reflect the way in which artistic styles are formed and developed. Further, in many cases, the use of what would be considered a protected expression at a certain period is necessary to creating an artistic style.

As far as the fair use doctrine is concerned, I showed that this doctrine also nicely reflects the importance of common building blocks to the promotion of creativity under genre theories. Transformative use, whether of purpose or content, allows the use of common building blocks in the form of expression to develop the creative world in certain ways. However, I showed that this doctrine does not offer a full response to the spectrum of use of common building blocks that genre theories recognize, due to its limited scope and other factors that are part of the doctrine.

As a result of the examination of these doctrines, I showed that the mismatch between genre theories and their understanding of the importance of common building block to the enrichment of the creative world and copyright law is in the right to make derivative works, which forbids the use of common building blocks in the form of protected expression for the development of the creative world. The main argument was that according to genre theories' understanding of the development of the creative world, the use of common building blocks in the form of protected expression for the promotion of creativity should be allowed. This is because the use of expressions as common building blocks is significant for the development of new genres both from the author's perspective and, most importantly, from the audience's perspective. Thus, my argument was that there is no justification for an overlap between the making of a new work based on protected expression (derivative work), an act which develops the creative world, and the use of protected expressions that does not promote creativity (reproductions). Therefore, the conclusions from genre theories presented in this article support the separation of the derivative work right from the reproduction right and the understanding of the two as qualitatively different. In addition, I argued that there is a collision between the right to make derivative works and genre theories because the derivative work right allows first authors to bar second authors from using common building blocks. Therefore, I argued that genre theories could support and portray a shift in the remedies available under the current doctrine that does not prevent the making of unauthorized derivative works. Such remedies will be discussed in length in Chapter 5.

Notes

1 An earlier version of this chapter was published with the Santa Clara High Technology Law Journal. *See* Omri Rachum-Twaig, *A Genre Theory of Copyright*, 33 SANTA CLARA HIGH TECH. L.J. 34 (2016).
2 Frow stated in the beginning of his book titled "Genre" that his book concerned "kinds or genres of speech, writing, images, and organized sound: forms of talk and writing, of drawing and painting and sculpting, of architecture, of music, and mixed forms like film, television, opera, and drama. It is a book about how genres organize verbal and non-verbal discourse, together with the actions that accompany them, and how they contribute to the social structuring of meaning." JOHN FROW, GENRE 1 (2006). In this article, the term "text" is used in the broader sense proposed by Frow.
3 I am thankful to Dror Mishani for a fascinating discussion about the development of the detective story and for references to the common building blocks in the writing of Edgar Alan Poe and Arthur Conan Doyle. Mishani motivated me to study the detective story.
4 A.E. Murch, THE DEVELOPMENT OF THE DETECTIVE NOVEL 67 (1958).
5 *Id.* at 167. Similarly, Howard Haycraft wrote in 1941 that Sherlock Holmes is the most beloved and renowned detective character in the world. *See* Howard Haycraft, MURDER FOR PLEASURE: THE LIFE AND TIMES OF THE DETECTIVE STORY 60–1 (1941). This notion is still true today, over 70 years later and over 120 years after the publication where Holmes first appeared.
6 Of course, Doyle was not the detective genre's first author after Poe. Police and crime fiction in England and France at the time included detective stories prior to Doyle. *See* Murch, *supra* note 4, at 84–151. However, besides the French author Emile Gaboriau, who influenced Doyle and focussed on the detective character Lecoq, Doyle was the most significant author after Poe to use the detective character. *See id.* at 120–32.
7 Vincent Buranelli, EDGAR ALLAN POE 83 (1961).
8 *Id.* at 83–84.
9 Murch, *supra* note 19, at 179; Buranelli, *supra* note 22, at 83–4.

10 Buranelli, *supra* note 22, at 83–4; George Grella, *Murder and Manners: The Formal Detective Novel, in* 4 NOVEL: A FORUM ON FICTION 30, 35 (1970); Murch, *supra* note 19, at 178. Dupin, for example, is an amateur poet and Holmes is an amateur violinist. *See* respectively Buranelli, *supra* note 22, at 83 and Grella, *supra* note 25, at 35.

11 In this case the intertextuality is two-fold. In addition to the express reference to Dupin and Poe's novels, Doyle actually refers to one of Poe's strategies for conveying meaning in "The Murders at the Rue Morgue." There, Dupin turns to the narrator to explain the necessary traits of a good detective and says: "Vidocq, for example, was a good guesser, and a persevering man. But, without educated thought, he erred continually by the very intensity of his investigations. He impaired his vision by holding the object too close. He might *see*, perhaps, one or two points with unusual clearness, but in so doing he, necessarily, lost sight of the matter as a whole." This is a reference to the story of Eugene Francois Vidocq who was a French criminal in the first half of the nineteenth century and later became a criminologist and private detective and even cooperated with the crime detection unit of the French Sûreté. Dupin's characters were based to a certain extent on the actions of Vidocq.

12 For a discussion on the comparison, *see* Stephen Bertman, *Kindred Crimes: Poe's "The Murders in the Rue Morgue" and Doyle's "The Sign of Four,"* 15 EDGAR ALLAN POE REV. 205, 206–7 (2014). It is important to note that this example of the use of common building blocks is one of many in Poe and Doyle's writing. Moreover, these similarities were not only recognized retrospectively. The first to note the many common building blocks in the various stories of the two was Simon Sidney Teiser, who already in 1901 referred in his article *Is Doyle a Plagiarist?* to the many similarities and emphasized that they exist in actual scenes and not only in general plot lines. For elaboration, *see* Simon Sidney Teiser, *Is Doyle a Plagiarist?*, 44 U. VA. MAGAZINE 468 (1901).

13 Gérard Genette, THE ARCHITEXT: AN INTRODUCTION 3–6 (Jane E. Lewin trans., 1992).

14 Heather Dubrow, GENRE 47 (1982). For a similar observation that recognizes the importance of Aristotle's writing on the theoretical thinking of genre, *see* Rick Altman, FILM/GENRE 20 (1999).

15 Plato, THE REPUBLIC: BOOKS I-V 231 (Paul Shorey trans., 1999).

16 Genette, *supra* note 12, at 8–9. Genette also stated that the Socratic division refers only to narrated poetry and therefore does not apply lyric poetry at all. *Id.*

17 Aristotle, POETICS 15–16, 17–18 (Gerald F. Else trans., 1990).

18 Dubrow, *supra* note 35, at 47. *See also* Frow, *supra* note 5, at 56.

19 Dubrow, *supra* note 35, at 48. According to her, this was the starting point of Aristotle's followers and critiques along the years.

20 Genette, *supra* note 12 at 10–21.

21 Genette, *supra* note 12, at 23–7.

22 Dubrow, *supra* note 35, at 50.

23 Genette, *supra* note 12, at 24–7. *See also* Frow, *supra* note 5, at 58.

24 Dubrow, *supra* note 35, at 52–62.

25 Alastir Fowler, KINDS OF LITERATURE 26 (1982) ("No one can dispute that much neoclassical genre criticism was crudely prescriptive"). *See also* Frow, *supra* note 5, at 58.

26 Dubrow, *supra* note 35, at 69–71.

27 2 Georg Wilhelm Friedrich Hegel, AESTHETICS: LECTURES ON FINE ARTS 1038–45 (T. M. Knox trans., 1975). *See also* Dubrow, *supra* note 14, at 72; Frow, *supra* note 1, at 60.

28 Friedrich Schlegel, for example, considered the epic as subjective-objective, the dramatic as objective, and the lyric as subjective. He later considered the epic as objective, the lyric as subjective, and the dramatic as objective-subjective. *See* Friedrich Schlegel, LITERARY NOTEBOOKS 1797–1801, at 175, 204 (Hans Eichner ed., 1957). For further discussion, *see* Genette, *supra* note 13, at 38–9.

29 Frow, *supra* note 1, at 60; Genette, *supra* note 13, at 62–4.

30 Genette, *supra* note 13, at 62–4. Genette explained the term "archigeneres" as follows: "Archi– because each of them is supposed to overarch and include, ranked by degree of importance, a certain number of empirical genres … –genres, because … their defining criteria always involves a thematic element that eludes purely formal or linguistic description." *Id.* at 64–5.

31 *See* Dubrow, *supra* note 35, at 72.

32 Schlegel, *supra* note 28, at 116. This is my own translation. Originally: "Der Modernen Dichtarten sind nur Eine oder unendlich viele. Jedes Gedicht eine Gattung für sich." *See also* Frow, *supra* note 2, at 27. Bawarshi and Reiff attributed the approach that rejected the concept of genre to Schlegel. He further argued that the greatness of the Romantic poetry is that it is more than genre; it is in effect the art of poetry itself. *See* Anis S. Bawarshi & Mary Jo Reiff, GENRE: AN INTRODUCTION TO HISTORY, THEORY, RESEARCH, AND PEDAGOGY 20 (2010).

33 Bawarshi & Reiff, *supra* note 32, at 20.

34 Victor Hugo, ODES ET BALLADES 22 (1947). The English translation appears in Dubrow, *supra* note 14, at 74. It is interesting to note that Hugo founded the Association Littéraire et Artistique Internationale (ALAI) in 1878, which led to the signing of the Berne Convention on the Protection of Literary and Artistic Works on September 9 1886. *See* Graham Duttfield & Uma Suthersanen, GLOBAL INTELLECTUAL PROPERTY LAW 26 (2008); Orrin G. Hatch, *Better Late than Never: Implementation of the 1886 Berne Convention*, 22 CORNELL INT'L L.J. 171, 173 (1989); ALAI, *General Information – History* (Jul. 6, 2016) http://bit.do/ALAIHistory.

35 Dubrow, *supra* note 14, at 74.

36 Benedetto Croce, AESTHETIC AS SCIENCE OF EXPRESSION AND GENERAL LINGUISTIC 1 (Douglas Ainslie trans., 1953). Croce defined these two forms of knowledge as aesthetic (intuitive) and intellectual (logic). Moreover, he argued that the latter form is always subordinated to the former because it has to do with "things" in the world that are per se intuitive. *Id.* at 22.

37 *Id.* at 35–6. *See* also Dubrow, *supra* note 14, at 83–4. Croce's writing influenced scholars in the twentieth century, and especially that of Maurice Blanchot who stated that "a book no longer belongs to a genre, every book arises only from literature." Maurice Blanchot, LA LIVRE A VENIRE 293 (1959). The English translation appears in Frow, *supra* note 2, at 27. *See also* Bawarshi & Reiff, *supra* note 32, at 21. A similar approach was suggested by Philippe Lacoue-Labarthe & Jean-Luc Nancy that reviewed the literary theory of the German Romantic era and showed that the approach to literature in that time was of "equivocity" in the sense that every work belongs to all kinds or genres at the same time in a way that brings the perception of genre to collapse. This phenomenon was described by them as the "literary absolute." *See* Philippe Lacoue-Labarthe & Jean-Luc Nancy, THE LITERARY ABSOLUTE: THE THEORY OF LITERATURE IN GERMAN ROMANTICISM 121–7 (Philip Barnard & Cheryl Lester trans., 1988).

38 Jacques Derrida, *The Law of Genre*, 7 CRIT. INQ. 55, 56 (1980). Frow suggested Derrida accepted the premise that genre is a prescriptive and classificatory tool that cannot go hand in hand with the uniqueness of individual texts. *See* Frow, *supra* note 2, at 26.

39 Derrida, *supra* note 38, at 64–5.

40 Bawarshi and Reiff argued that although Derrida saw genre as a constraint on texts, he should be read with reference to Croce and Blanchot, and more precisely in contrast to them; they rejected genre altogether, while Derrida explicitly argued that texts cannot exist without genre. *See* Bawarshi & Reiff, *supra* note 32, at 21.

41 Fowler, *supra* note 25, at 24.

42 Northrop Frye, ANATOMY OF CRITICISM 15–17 (1957).

43 For elaboration on the influence of de Saussure's research on formalistic approaches to literary theory, such as Russian formalism, new criticism, and structuralism, *see* Terry Eagleton, LITERARY THEORY: AN INTRODUCTION 84–5 (2nd edn 1996).

44 This is why Bawarshi and Reiff defined Frye's theory as a Neoclassical analysis of genre. *See* Bawarshi & Reiff, *supra* note 32, at 16. In the context of literary theory, however, Frye's approach was a significant innovation because it completely detached the author's role from the meaning of the text; it left the text itself as the subject of examination, thus diverting from the Romantic literary theory. *See* Eagleton, *supra* note 43, at 80–1.

45 Tzvetan Todorov, GENRES IN DISCOURSE 16–18 (Catherine Porter trans., 1990) (1978). Bawarshi and Reiff explained that Todorov's approach is structuralist. They defined the structuralist approach to genre as a literary-historical one, in the sense that it understands genres as a historical context dependent cultural phenomenon and not as an a priori theoretical phenomenon, as it was viewed in the Classical era. *See* Bawarshi & Reiff, *supra* note 32, at 14–19.

46 Todorov, *supra* note 45, at 19.

47 A "speech act" is the linguistic term for an utterance that generates an action that changes reality, rather than merely describing reality. The source of this linguistic term is the British philosopher of the language John Austin, who was the first to define a speech act as an utterance that does reflect a statement of truth (positive or false) and constitutes at least part of an action in reality. *See* J. L. Austin, HOW TO DO THINGS WITH WORDS 1–7 (F.O. Urmson & Marina Sbisa eds, 2nd edn 1962).

48 Marie Louise Pratt, TOWARD A SPEECH ACT THEORY OF LITERARY DISCOURSE 86 (1977).

49 For elaboration on the influence of the linguistic concept of speech act and its adoption by commentators on genre, *see* David Fishelov, METAPHORS OF GENRE 119–26 (1993). *See also* Rick Altman, *A Semantic/Syntactic Approach to Film Genre*, 23 CINEMA J. 6, 12–13 (1984); Carolyn R. Miller, *Genre as a Social Action*, 70 Q. J. SPEECH 151, 155 (1984). Miller explained that genre does not classify the semantics or syntax of texts, it classifies their pragmatics (i.e. the rhetorical action the discourse performs). *Id.* at 152.

50 Rene Welleck & Austin Warren, THEORY OF LITERATURE 226 (3rd edn 1963).

51 Todorov, *supra* note 45, at 19.

52 This is the "modern" characteristic of genre, according to Welleck and Warren, as opposed to the pre-modern approaches of genre. According to them, "Modern genre theory is, clearly, descriptive. It doesn't limit the number of possible kinds and doesn't prescribe rules to authors. It supposes that traditional kinds may be 'mixed' and produce a new kind (like tragicomedy). It sees that genres can be built up on the basis of inclusiveness or 'richness' as well as that of 'purity' (genre by accretion as well as by reduction). Instead of emphasizing the distinction between kind and kind, it is interested – after the Romantic emphasis on the uniqueness of each 'original genius' and each work of art – in finding the common denominator of a kind, its shared literary devices and literary purpose." Welleck & Warren, *supra* note 50, at 245.

53 Todorov, *supra* note 45, at 18–19.

54 Fishelov, *supra* note 49, at 8.

55 Frow, *supra* note 2, at 6–10.

56 *Id.* at 102.

57 Bawarshi & Reiff, *supra* note 32, at 23–8.

58 In this context, Frederic Jameson's definition fits well. He explained, "Genres are essentially literary institutions, or social contracts between a writer and a specific public, whose function is to specify the proper use of a particular cultural artifact."- Frederic Jameson, THE POLITICAL UNCONSCIOUS: NARRATIVE AS A SOCIALLY SYMBOLIC ACT 103, 106 (1981).

59 As part of his discussion on the institutional approach to genre, Fishelov explained that the meaning of such approach is that the phenomena analyzed through this framework should be understood not as mere facts but rather as institutional facts that depend on the cultural meaning derived from a set of institutional rules that are shared by the members of a community that revolves around an institution. *See*

Fishelov, *supra* note 49, at 87. Fishelov showed that this approach was demonstrated by Culler, who argued that "actions are meaningful only with respect to a set of institutional conventions." Jonathan Culler, STRUCTURALIST POETICS 5 (1975).

60 Fishelov, *supra* note 49, at 51.

61 *See* Ferdinand Brunetière, L'EVOLUTION DES GENRES DANS L'HISTOIRE DE LA LITTÉRATURE: LEÇONS PROFESSÉES À L'ECOLE NORMALE SUPÉRIEURE 9–31 (1914). Brunetière referred to five significant issues in the development of genres: the existence of genres; the differences between genres; the fixation (or life term) of genres, changes in genres; and the transformation of genres. *Id.* at 11–13.

62 *See* Fishelov, *supra* note 49, at 19–22 (providing examples).

63 Fishelov himself was aware of these limits. *Id.* at 19.

64 This trait is at a very high level of abstraction. It could also be demonstrated by traits of lower level of abstraction, like the personality traits of the detective or the way in which mysteries are solved in the story.

65 Wittgenstein gave the example of games. Thus, according to him, the terms of board-games, card-games, ball-games, Olympic Games, and others do not share one trait that is common to all. Rather, these games' resemblance to each other links them. *See* Ludwig Wittgenstein, PHILOSOPHICAL INVESTIGATIONS 31 (G.E.M. Anscombe trans., 3rd edn 1986).

66 *Id.* at 32. Wittgenstein suggested another metaphor to illustrate the idea of family resemblance as a unifying term for the definition of individuals in a group – the *fibre* metaphor. He noted that "[i]n spinning a thread we twist fibre on fibre. And the strength of the fibre does not reside in the fact that one fibre runs through its whole length, but in the overlapping of many fibers." *Id.* For an application of this metaphor on classification in the sense of genre, *see* Chana Kronfeld, ON THE MARGINS OF MODERNISM: DECENTERING LITERARY DYNAMICS 62–4 (1996).

67 George Lakoff, WOMEN, FIRE AND DANGEROUS THINGS: WHAT CATEGORIES REVEAL ABOUT THE MIND 5–6, 16–17 (1987).

68 Fowler, *supra* note 25, at 41.

69 Fishelov, *supra* note 49, at 59–63.

70 *Id.* at 65–8.

71 This is also the name of the first chapter in Fowler's seminal book on genre. *See* Fowler, *supra* note 25, at 26–32.

72 *Id.* at 18–20.

73 For the difference between *langue* and *parole*, *see* Ferdinand de Saussure, COURSE IN GENERAL LINGUISTICS 7–15 (Charles Bally & Albert Sechehaye eds, Wade Baskin trans., 1959).

74 Fowler, *supra* note 25, at 20.

75 *Id.* at 26–8.

76 *Id.* at 29. It is important to note that there is no contradiction between Fowler's prescriptive approach and the dynamic approaches to genre discussed above. Fowler's approach views genre as an open and dynamic prescription that does not limit the creation of texts to predefined static rules and is open to understand changes resulting from diversion of texts from the existing rules.

77 *Id.* at 29–32.

78 Todorov, *supra* note 45, at 15.

79 Fowler, *supra* note 25, at 170–4.

80 *Id.* at 181–8.

81 Fishelov, *supra* note 49, at 14, 18.

82 *Id.* at 35–9. It is important to note that the derivative work right in copyright law is often referred to as the "adaptation" right. Despite the resemblance between adaptation in Fishelov's terms and the right to make derivative works, there is not full overlap between the two. Maintaining the content of a text while changing its medium or form is just one type of action that could result in a derivative work. Aside

from that, a derivative work could be made by what Fishelov defined as "imitation," which means maintaining the form while changing the content.

83 Vijay Bhatia, WORLDS OF WRITTEN DISCOURSE: A GENRE-BASED VIEW 23–5 (2004).

84 *Id.* at 57–8. In this sense, Bhatia's approach is similar to those of Fowler as far as the change of genres is concerned. *See* Fowler, *supra* note 25, at 170–88.

85 Bhatia, *supra* note 83, at 87.

86 It is important to note that while the enabling aspect of the common building blocks in the creative world is important and significant for authors, this does not make it necessary. It is possible to think of creative activities that are possible regardless of the existence of common building blocks. However, such creative activities would most likely be meaningless or lack value for the audience, due to the meaning-making aspect of the common building blocks that will be discussed later. In this sense, the importance of the enabling aspect of common building blocks to authors is of high importance.

87 Todorov, *supra* note 45, at 18–19.

88 Frow, *supra* note 2, at 19. For another modern approach to genre that views it more as a "source of meaning" than a "set of rules," *see* Sungsoon Wang, *Text Types and Dynamism of Genres, in* DISCOURSE, OF COURSE: AN OVERVIEW OF RESEARCH IN DISCOURSE STUDIES 81, 83 (Jan Renkema ed., 2009); John Swales, *On Models of Applied Discourse Analysis, in* RESEARCH AND PRACTICE IN PROFESSIONAL DISCOURSE 61 (C.N. Candlin ed., 2002).

89 Fowler, *supra* note 25, at 21–2.

90 Miller, *supra* note 49, at 156–60.

91 E.D. Hirsch, Jr., VALIDITY IN INTERPRETATION 50 (1967). *See also* Fowler, *supra* note 25, at 24.

92 Hirsch, *supra* note 91, at 76.

93 For elaboration on the reader response approach to genre, *see* Bawarshi & Reiff, *supra* note 32, at 22–3.

94 Adena Rosmarin, THE POWER OF GENRE 25 (1986).

95 Bawarshi & Reiff, *supra* note 32, at 23.

96 Hans Robert Jauss, TOWARDS AN AESTHETIC OF RECEPTION 88 (Timothy Bahti trans., 1982).

97 For elaboration on the "cultural" approach to genre, *see* Bawarshi & Reiff, *supra* note 32, at 23–8.

98 Thomas O. Beebe, THE IDEOLOGY OF GENRE: A COMPARATIVE STUDY OF GENERIC INSTABILITY 250 (1994). Bawarshi and Reiff explained that these characteristics give genre a functional value and turn it into a tool for the promotion of culture and hence also an ideological phenomenon. *See* Bawarshi & Reiff, *supra* note 32, at 27.

99 Beebe, *supra* note 98, at 14.

100 Bawarshi & Reiff, *supra* note 32, at 27.

101 For elaboration on how the use of common building blocks is partly accommodated by the fair use and scènes à faire doctrines *see* Rachum-Twaig, *supra* note 1, at 77–84. For other literature utilizing the concept of genre for intellectual property analysis *see* Michal Shur-Ofry, *The (Copyright) Law of Genre: A Network Perspective on Copyright Protection of Cultural Genres*, 2 FA. ENT. L. REV. 60 (2008); Dan L. Burk & Jessica Reyman, *Patents as Genre: A Prospectus*, 26 LAW & LIT. 163 (2014); Annemarie Bridy, *Fearless Girl Meets Charging Bull: Copyright and the Regulation of Intertextuality*, UC IRVINE L. REV. (forthcoming, 2018).

102 *See*, for example, *Salinger v. Colting*, 607 F.3d 68, 71–2 (2d Cir. 2010), in which the court decided that a sequel to "The Catcher in the Rye" infringed J.D. Salinger's copyright. It is important to note that in spite of the criticism of this decision, according to which fair use should have been found, sequels in general amount to copyright infringement. For a criticism of the decision, *see* Rebecca Tushnet, *Content, Purpose, or Both*, 90 WASH. L. REV. 869, 877 n. 96 (2015).

3 Re-examining the justifications for the derivative works right

I. Introduction

In the previous chapters, we saw that there is tension between non-legal understandings of creativity and the derivative works right. Could this tension be relieved by turning to the normative legal justifications for the right? This chapter seeks to examine this question and answers in the affirmative. In Chapter 1, we saw that according to cognitive psychology and creativity studies, prior domain-relevant knowledge and memory are a significant and integral part of the creative process, and that such knowledge includes the use of both ideas and expressions, in copyright terms. Chapter 2 explained that the understanding of the development and enrichment of the creative world under genre theories also justifies the use of common building blocks that include preexisting expressions. The current derivative works right, according to which the first author could prohibit others from using expressions from the first work to make new additional works based on it, conflicts with these understandings.

A mere tension between a behavioral norm and the law does not necessarily lead to the conclusion that the legal norm is wrong. It may well be that despite the fact that people behave in a certain way, the law has good normative justifications to change such behavior and attempt establishing a different one. However, in the lack of convincing normative justifications, the power of the law to intervene with behavior is weaker. In addition, a better understanding of the behavioral norms and the field of knowledge underlying a specific legal norm, based on non-legal fields, could lead to a better application of the normative basis for the legal norm. Accordingly, this chapter will reexamine the normative justifications for the derivative works right.

The first question to be reviewed in light of the legal normative justifications to copyright law is whether a law under which second authors are free to make derivative works without the first author's consent is justifiable. The second question is whether the first author should be entitled to some interest with respect to derivative works based on her work, and if an independent derivative works right is justified.

The theoretical examination in this chapter is intended to review whether the current derivative works right is in line with its underlying normative justifications due to the discussion on the non-legal approaches in previous chapters. Therefore, the discussion on each of the main approaches to copyright law will be internal, meaning it will examine the effects of each approach on the derivative works right based on its own premises and internal logic.

The first approach to be reviewed is the economic analysis of copyright law. The derivative works right was extensively discussed under this approach and the main opinion is that the current right is difficult to justify, in contrast to the reproduction right. However, one economic approach brought by Michael Abramowicz does justify a strong derivative works right based on a rent dissipation model. To the best of my knowledge, this argument has not yet been refuted in the literature and I ask to criticize it and show why even under Abramowicz's model there is a weak justification to a strong derivative works right.

Since economic analysis does not lead to clear-cut conclusions with respect to the appropriate scope of the derivative works right, the remainder of this chapter will focus on alternative non-utilitarian approaches to property: normative approaches based on the theories of John Locke, Immanuel Kant and Georg Hegel, each of which proposed a different understanding for the basic natural justification to private property. These approaches are more challenging to my argument with respect to derivative works, and specifically with respect to the remedies model I will suggest in Chapter 5, since as being deontological in their nature (perhaps with the exclusion of Locke), their perception of a right is categorical and binary in the sense that the two possible alternatives are those of the existence of a right and its non-existence. Thus, the first challenge would be to show that under each approach the first author could not prohibit the use of expressions to make derivative works. The second challenge would be to show that under each approach, instead of a "no right" alternative, the first author could still enjoy some interest (even if only monetary) with respect to derivative works, regardless of her inability to prohibit their making. The discussion will also draw on the conclusions from previous chapters with respect to the creative process, conclusions that could offer a better application of such approaches to copyright law and the derivative works right.

Locke's labor-desert approach was extensively discussed by copyright scholars. With respect to the derivative works right, the limited debate on Locke's approach is insufficient and at times wrong, and I ask to fill this gap here. I will focus on Locke's two provisos for private property, dealing with leaving enough and as good in the public domain and preventing waste. With respect to the first proviso, I will develop the thoughts already raised in the general context of intellectual property, mainly by Wendy Gordon, and extend them to derivative works. With respect to the second proviso, I suggest a new understanding in the context of derivative works, in light of the non-legal understandings of creativity.

The corrective justice approach, based largely on Kant's doctrine of right, was seldom discussed with respect to copyright law until recently, and was usually included in general discussions on personality approaches to copyright. The discussion here will not focus on Kant's approach to personhood, rather on his perception of universal rights and their application to private law in the corrective justice approach developed by Ernst Weinrib. The discussion will be based on a current application of the corrective justice approach to copyright law by Abraham Drassinower. With respect to the derivative works, I argue that the freedom to use preexisting expressions to make new original works, subject to a revenue share model, fits better with corrective justice than the categorical prohibition on making derivative work, and is just as good as a complete freedom to use such expressions without any derivative works right.

The modern formulation of Hegel's doctrine of right, which is mainly based on Margaret Radin's property and personhood reading, is commonly referred to as the personality approach to intellectual property. The discussion on the personality approach with respect to copyright law mainly focussed on justifications for moral rights and to a limited extent to economic aspects of copyright. This discussion was very limited with respect to the derivative works right and found that it is justified to the extent that a strong connection between the author and her work exists. I suggest a general criticism on the understanding of Hegel's doctrine of right as based on personal connection between a person and an object, as well as an internal criticism that will explain why the derivative works right is unjustified under this approach. This last criticism will be based on a refreshed reading of Hegel's doctrine of right in light of conclusions from the field of hermeneutics.

The main conclusion I wish to establish in this chapter is that under each of the main normative approaches to copyright, there is no sound normative justification for the current derivative works right. To the extent that this conclusion is persuasive, there is a good justification to outline a new doctrine for the derivative works right, which takes into account non-legal understandings of creativity, if they fit the normative analysis. Outlining such new doctrine will be at the center of the following two Chapters.

Part II will discuss economic analysis as a normative approach to copyright and will mainly focus on Abramowicz's justification to the derivative works right and my response to it. Part III will focus on Locke's approach and will explain how his provisos cannot support the current derivative works right. Part IV will review the corrective justice approach, explain its applicability to the derivative works right and will suggest a better way to understand derivative works under it. Part V will discuss Hegel's doctrine of right and its development by Radin, and will suggest a general criticism on the conflation of the two as well as an inner criticism on its application to the derivative works right.

II. The economic approach

Economic analysis has two main aspects, one normative and the other descriptive-functional. The normative aspect of economic analysis is reflected in its perception of good which is expressed by the maximization of social welfare, or more concretely maximizing the aggregate individual preferences of humans.[1] The descriptive-functional aspect is depicted in the use of economic tools for cost-benefit analysis intended to explain how certain goals could be achieved in the most efficient way and predict how different legal rules would lead to different social outcomes. Economic analysis is a central approach to copyright law, especially in United States jurisprudence, and its descriptive-functional aspect is used in various other jurisdictions. This part will briefly discuss the main stream of current economic analysis of copyright law, which largely rejects a strong derivative works right, and will then turn to discuss Abramowicz's analysis and my criticism on it.

1) The incentive-access approach

Economic analysis assumes that copyright's main goal is the enrichment of the world of expressions and the respective social welfare.[2] The basic economic analysis of copyright was referred to as the incentive-access tradeoff and can be formulated as follows: for an author to choose to create a work of authorship, two types of costs must be considered – the preliminary investment in making the work, which is a fixed cost, and the cost of making copies of the work and disseminating it to the public.[3] For the work to be created, economically speaking, it is often required that the expected income from the work exceed its overall cost. Since intellectual products are public goods in the sense that they are non-rivalrous and non-exclusive, and since the marginal cost of making copies is usually negligible, it is expected that once a work is created and published, competitors will enter the market and sell unauthorized copies of the work for a price that is close to the marginal cost of making copies. In these circumstances, the author will not be able to make enough profit to recoup her investment and will not create the work in the first place.[4] Thus, the author must be granted property rights in the work to allow enough incentives to create and potentially recoup investment.

In addition to the incentive side of the equation, the social value created by the works of authorship together with the social cost of granting a quasi-monopoly in them must be considered. This is the access side of the equation. If the property right granted to the author is too strong, it will increase the costs of making new works which are often based on preexisting works. In addition, the cost of consuming the work is expected to be high under a monopoly, and absent perfect price discrimination, will lead to the creation of insufficient supply of copies for the demand in the market. This may lead to a deadweight loss that effectively means that people who are willing to pay for the work will not be able to enjoy it.[5]

The incentive-access approach led to the conclusion that the most favorable copyright regime is that which leads to the maximum access to works without affecting the sufficient incentive to create them in the first place. Thus, this approach seeks to review the scope of the various components of the right to adjust it to the above formulation. With respect to the derivative works right, Landes and Posner argued that "the case for giving the owner of a copyrighted work a monopoly of its derivative works as well is a subtle one,"[6] since the assumption that the first author would not create the first work absent control over second works is speculative. Naomi Voegtli further explained that aside from the lack of justification for such incentive, the derivative works right leads to excessive social costs on the access side since it increases the costs of making second works and further disseminating them.[7]

Landes and Posner's additional arguments for a strong derivative works right, such as the benefits in controlling the timing of publication to prevent authors from withholding the publishing of the first work, and the reduction of transaction costs due to a centralized control over the secondary work,[8] were largely and rightfully refuted. Voegtli observed that the first argument is only applicable to a very small portion of works.[9] Stewart Sterk added that the social cost from ineffective behavior with respect to publication timing could occur both under a strong derivative works right and without it, since first authors may withhold publications of second works until they fully extract the value from the first work.[10] Sterk also rightfully argued, with respect to the second argument, that it is only because of the derivative works right that secondary markets should even be contracted around,[11] and Voegtli added that it is the derivative works right itself that creates transaction costs.[12]

It is evident, therefore, that commentators largely agreed that the incentive-access approach could not sufficiently justify the current strong derivative works right. However, other economic approaches to copyright let to the argument that the current derivative works right is indeed justified.

2) *Product differentiation and rent dissipation*

The incentive-access approach to economic analysis of copyright is based on the premise that copyright grants a quasi-monopoly and leads to monopolistic behavior of authors. However, copyright does not grant an actual monopoly to authors due to the fact that ideas are not protected and therefore other authors are allowed to create in the same environment of ideas and produce works that are, to a certain extent, substitutes for the first work. For example, the fact that the Harry Potter book series is copyright protected does not prevent other authors from writing books based on the idea of the existence of a young wizards' school that will compete in this market. This understanding is in the center of Christopher Yoo's product differentiation approach to copyright.[13] Under this approach, despite the fact that authors enjoy a quasi-monopoly in the short term, in the long term new players are expected to enter the first work's market and offer works that are partial substitutes, thus leading to monopolistic competition. Such competition will lead, in the long run, to a decrease in prices of copies and will decrease the deadweight loss created by the quasi-monopolistic copyright.[14] One of the consequences of this approach, according to Yoo, is that aside from thinking about limiting copyright's scope one could think about using copyright law to remove entry barriers and allow new entries to the market to reduce the deadweight loss.

Another complementary approach is the rent dissipation approach to copyright proposed by Abramowicz. He explained that an economic rent reflects the benefit exceeding the opportunity cost with respect to a specific resource. An activity in which participants ask to appropriate a portion of an existing market is referred to as rent seeking, and cases in which the entry costs to such market reduce the potential rents is referred to as rent dissipation. Abramowicz articulated that not all types of rent seeking are economically inefficient, because sometimes the entry to a market creates social benefits that exceed the entry costs. In the copyright context, Abramowicz explained that every author is considered a rent seeker but in most cases the entry to the market creates a higher social benefit than the entry costs, meaning that the social value of the work created exceeds its cost of creation. However, according to Abramowicz, the economic literature established the premise that rent seeking may be inefficient. To emphasize this point Abramowicz proposed the example of gold mines. Assuming that a gold mine is valued at 100,000, absent a property right in the mine and assuming that the entry costs are 1,000, it is expected that 100 participants will enter the market. In this case, the social value of the mine (100,000) will be entirely off-set by the total entry costs (100,000), and no social value will exist. This is an example of rent dissipation.

In the copyright context, Abramowicz argued that taking the idea of rent dissipation seriously must lead to the conclusion that a strong copyright, which protects ideas as well as expression is necessary. However, he argued that rent seeking is even more inefficient when works tend to be highly substitutive to other works as in the case of derivative works.[15] He explained that the main concern is that derivative works will be substitutes for one another and not for the first work. In this case, if everyone was allowed to make derivative works from a first work, such as translation, complete rent dissipation would occur in the market for derivative works. The solution, according to him, is centralizing the right to make derivative works – granting a property right – with the first author who has the best incentive to maximize the benefits from the secondary market.[16]

Abramowicz did point at some difficulties with the derivative works right but argued that they are all economically negligible. First, the first author may refuse to grant licenses with respect to derivative works she does not approve of. He argued that this could be resolved using the fair use doctrine. Second, the first author could charge monopolistic prices for derivative works creating additional deadweight loss, but he argued that the legislator already struck the right balance between the costs and benefits of derivative works. Third, this may lead to underdevelopment of derivative works, but he argued that as long as there is demand in the market, such works will eventually be produced. Fourth, first authors may postpone the making of derivative works, but this concern is unlikely since their costs of creation are not expected to decrease over time.[17]

I will now explain why the Abramowicz model is based on unstable premises, the rejection of which undermines his entire model.

3) A criticism on Abramowicz and differentiation in derivative works

The first problem with Abramowicz's model is his first premise that there is no substitutionality between first and second works. Taking the example of "Harry Potter and the Chamber of Secrets" it could easily be seen that a movie version of the book would compete, to a great extent, with the market of the book itself. As many consumers may choose to watch the movie version following the reading of the book, others may watch the movie and refrain from reading the book at all. Another example could be the making of an abridgement of the first work.

Potential consumers of a literary work may prefer to read a 100-page version over the original 1,000-page version. On the other hand, derivative works could encourage consumers to pay for the first work in cases where they would not have done so if not for the derivative work. If this assumption is correct, then on top of adding a factor to Abramowicz's model – the positive effects of the derivative work on the first market – it affects other factors in the model. First, with respect to the benefits of control over the timing of publication, to the extent that derivative works may compete with the first work, the first author may wish to postpone publication until the full value has been extracted from the first work before any competition from the derivative market exists. Additionally, ignoring the contribution of derivative works to product differentiation is ignoring the positive effects of derivative works on the access side of the incentive-access paradigm. Thus, making derivative works that are partial substitutes for the first work will reduce the monopolistic power of the first author and the respective deadweight loss that will result from more competitive pricing.[18] In this sense, eliminating the prohibition on the making of derivative works adds social value in two ways – reducing the costs of creation for second authors and adding competition to the market of the first work.

A second problem with Abramowicz's model is that he assumes that the first author could most efficiently manage the market for derivative works. This is a difficult assumption to make, especially if we understand that the derivative works market may compete with the market for the first work. First, this argument assumes that the first author has perfect information on the derivative works market. However, in contrast to other resources, the market for creative works and creativity is highly dependent on the players participating in it. The size of the resource in the context of the derivative works market is dependent, to a great extent, on the number of participants and their creative abilities, among other external factors. Therefore, as opposed to more objective resources like goldmines, it is hard to assume that the first author has all relevant information to make efficient decisions with respect to the derivative works market. Second, if we accept the assumption that derivative works may compete with first works, the first author is in a conflict of interests and therefore may not make the most efficient decisions with respect to the utilization of the derivative works market if such decisions could lead to greater revenue from the first work.

The third and main problem with Abramowicz's model is in his assumptions with respect to differentiation between derivative works. For rent dissipation to occur in the rent seeking for derivative works, we must assume that the marginal benefits from every additional derivative work is decreasing. For this to be a valid assumption we must accept one of the following alternatives:

Under one alternative, decreasing marginal benefits from derivative works will occur when they are full substitutes of each other. This is difficult to accept under the product differentiation approach, since it is difficult to believe that product differentiation exists in the market for the first work but not in the derivative works market. For example, as much as there is potential differentiation between all children's books on young wizards' schools, including the Harry Potter, series there is potential differentiation between all movie versions of "Harry Potter and the Chamber of Secrets" or between every literary sequel thereof. This alternative appears, therefore, unreasonable and thus the rent dissipation model that applies to goldmines, in which each ounce of gold equals another, does not apply to creative markets.

Under the second alternative, we can think of decreasing marginal benefits from derivative works if we assume that in the sub-market of a specific derivative work (e.g., the sub-market for movie versions of a first book or the sub-market of English translations of foreign works), there is very limited substitution between each derivative work. Under this assumption the potential value of derivative works in a sub-market is finite and therefore the marginal benefit decreases with every work. This is an unreasonable assumption as well, first because it is not at all clear that there is a finite number of sub-markets for each derivative works market of every first work. Second, because also within a specific sub-market it is difficult to assume that all movie versions of a book will be substitutes for every other movie version. If this assumption is not accepted, then we cannot assume that the marginal benefit from every derivative works is decreasing and therefore rent dissipation does not occur. This is in fact a very similar model to that of product differentiation in the first market, which Abramowicz himself accepts.

These problems add to the general difficulties raised by Abramowicz himself which were not sufficiently resolved with respect to derivative works. Thus, there is no reason to believe that all entrants to a derivative works market will be similarly situated in the rent seeking race. It is hard to imagine that on the exact moment of publication of a first work, all possible derivative works will start being created. In any other circumstance where time or position gaps exist in the various sub-markets, adequate signaling to potential rent seekers will prevent them from investing entry costs for a lost cause thus preventing rent dissipation. To that, we must add the fact that under a legal doctrine that does not limit the making of derivative works, each second author will be granted copyright in her additional originality and thus be granted a property right that will prevent others from using the new contribution or substantially similar contributions. This will signal to other authors and either prevent entry or force differentiation, which in any event will prevent rent dissipation.

To sum this part, it appears that the economic analysis of copyright, under its own premises, cannot sufficiently justify a strong derivative works right and in fact supports its limitation. The only substantiated concern is with a too-rapid development of the derivative works market. In Chapter 5, I will propose a new remedies model for the derivative works right that better fits its underlying economic analysis and resolves the above concern. The main problem with economic analysis of derivative works is that absent convincing empirical data on the amount of works created due to the incentive of a strong derivative works right, the amount of works that would not be created without it, and the relation between the value of the above groups, we cannot reach a conclusion with respect to the proper scope of the right.[19]

Absent such empirical data and a clear conclusion from the existing economic analysis of the right, there are several alternatives. First, assuming that the normative goal of the discussion is enriching the world of expressions and promoting creativity, we can search for alternative data on the conditions that promote such a goal. This was presented in Chapter 1 in which we saw what the substantial components of the creative process under creativity studies are and how they can affect the derivative works right. Second is turning to other normative approaches and reviewing the question using their tools. In Chapter 2 I suggested reviewing the derivative works right using tools from genre theories that focus on the creative field, the relationship between different players in the field and the way in which it develops. The remainder of this chapter will review the derivative works right under additional significant normative justifications to private property, which are mainly right-based.

III. Locke and the labor-desert approach

Locke's labor-desert approach is one of the central right-based approaches to private property in western culture and in Anglo-American jurisprudence specifically. It thus has been extensively applied to intellectual property and copyright. In this part I will focus on the question whether and to what extent the current derivative works right is justified under this approach. This question was addressed, to a limited extent, in the literature, as I will further explain. I argue that the current broad derivative works right is unjustified under this approach and that a more limited right, that allows the making of derivative works subject to payment, fits better with Locke's approach.

Since the Lockean approach was extensively debated, I do not mean to discuss it in length or offer a new reading of his approach to private property. I will first briefly describe the basic principles of his approach and choose interpretations that result from attempts to understand his approach in the most favorable way that maintains its inner logic.

1) Locke's justification to private property

Locke's basic starting point is that before the political state in which people consented to a specific regime and designed laws, they were in the state of nature where a basic law existed – the natural law – that granted any person natural rights. The natural law, according to Locke, is based on four premises: (1) the natural resources in the world were created for the use of human beings; (2) human beings are superior to all animals but equal to each other; (3) the human kind is obligated to preserve itself (each person for herself and then for all other human beings); and (4) human beings must work to provide for themselves and prosper.[20] This means that in the state of nature, all resources were granted to mankind in common.[21] The common way to understand this communality is a state of "negative" commons. The joint ownership is negative in the sense that although all resources belong to mankind in common and each person is free to use the joint resources, none has the exclusive right to use them. This is in contrast to a positive joint ownership under which each person has a positive right to a non-specific portion of all natural resources.[22] Under a negative ownership, no person has a specific right to the natural resources and therefore the possibility for each person to obtain private property rights in a specific resource exists.

Locke offered two main arguments for the moral power that justifies the acquisition of private property in a natural resource, based on a unilateral action of a person. The first justification is based on a divine order for people to provide for themselves from natural resources, which is mainly a theological justification. The second justification on which I will focus is based on the connection between a person's right in his personhood and the specific resource a person chose to appropriate. A person has a natural property right in her own person and therefore in her labor, the argument goes. Therefore, when a person mixes her labor with a natural resource, the mixed product becomes the property of that person and is removed from the common state. Therefore, such mix of labor and resource morally justified private property – this is the mixing argument. In addition to the mixing argument, Locke explained that the labor of a person with respect to a specific resource creates added value and since the labor is the main cause for such added value, it justifies private property in the resource – this is the added value argument.[23]

For example, when a person picks an apple from a natural tree, according to the mixing argument she deserves property rights since her labor was mixed in the picking or transporting of the apple. According to the added value argument, property is justified because the person's act contributed the principal value to the apple, since an apple on a natural tree is lacking any value until picked.

The mixing argument was subject to extensive criticism in the literature, specifically by Jeremy Waldron and Robert Nozick, who asked important questions on the ability to mix labor and objects and the extent to which the labor is actually related to the appropriated resource.[24] John Simmons suggested a formulation of the mixing argument that I believe survives such criticism. According to him, labor is a purposive action that is not limited to the intent to act for a specific purpose but also to the beginning of the physical process that leads to the action. In other words, Simmons suggested to perceive labor not as matter that could be mixed with a resource, rather as a purposive action meant to provide for the needs and joys of life of people. Therefore, mixing can occur without any physical change of the resource but merely due to the fact that it is now subject to the actions and plans of a specific person.[25] With respect to the apple example, a picked apple becomes the property of the person who picked it not because labor was physically mixed with the apple, rather due to that person's choice to act in relation to the apple and subject it to her needs. This perception of the mixing argument is also well in line with the added value argument that complements it. While the mixing argument explains the interest of a specific person in a specific resource, the added value argument justifies excluding the mixed resource from the common state. This is because the added value from the labor is significantly higher than the value of the resource in a natural state, and therefore the damage to the freedom of all other persons with respect to such resource is much lower than the potential damage to the appropriating individual if the resource will be expropriated from her.

In addition to the basic justification for private property in natural resources, Locke imposed two provisos limiting valid private property acquisition. The first proviso is that after the exclusion of a resource from the common state there will be left enough and as good resources in common for other persons to mix their labor with and provide for their needs. This is referred to as the *sufficiency proviso*. The second proviso determines that private property is invalid when a person appropriates more resources than those she can consume in a manner that brings such resources to waste in her possession. This is referred to as the *waste proviso*. If the two provisos are met, private property in natural resources is valid according to Locke.[26]

2) Locke and derivative works

Locke's approach was extensively applied to copyright law doctrines.[27] It was used to justify the originality requirement,[28] the independent work doctrine,[29] the idea-expression dichotomy,[30] and copyright duration.[31] However, the derivative works right was almost never reviewed under the Lockean approach. The exception is Naomi Voegtli's application of the approach to the derivative works right. According to her, Locke's approach cannot justify the current broad derivative works right for two main reasons. First, it cannot explain the scope of the copyright granted to the first author based on her labor. Second, the approach is insufficient to explain why the first author is entitled to a benefit on the account of future second authors. According to her, it is not clear why a property rule granting first authors ownership in the labor of second authors is justified.[32]

This is an unpersuasive criticism as it does not follow the inner logic of Locke's approach. This criticism is mainly based on the fact that the derivative works right grants the first author rights on the account of the second author's future labor. However, the moral power of a person's labor under Locke's theory only justifies the first appropriation of a specific resource from the commons. Therefore, referring to the second author's labor as a justification for property rights in another person's private property is impossible under Locke's theory. Allow me to explain.

According to Locke, when a person is granted private property in a natural common resource due to mixing her labor in it, another person's unauthorized actions with respect to such resource become wrongful. It appears that Voegtli agrees that under Locke's theory, the first author's labor entitles her to private property in the expressions of the first work. The making of a derivative work necessarily uses such expressions. Therefore, if the first author has property in them, the second author cannot use them without authorization. The labor that the second author invests in the making of an unauthorized derivative work does not change the fact that she labors on an already private resource rather than on a common resource. The only possibility to suggest an alternative array of property rights with respect to derivative works which is coherent with Locke's approach is to examine whether the two provisos are met in such circumstances. I will now turn to discuss the two provisos with respect to the derivative works right.

a) *The sufficiency proviso*

The most interesting and important interpretation of the sufficiency proviso in the context of intellectual property law was suggested by Wendy Gordon, who asked to challenge the premise that private property in intellectual products will always leave enough and as good in the public domain and meet this proviso.[33] According to her, the assumption that no-one loses from the appropriation of things that would have never been created but for such appropriation is wrong. She argued that even if something is new to the world, the exclusion of parts of society from it at a later stage may be harmful. This could happen when a person creates something that society becomes dependent on over time. Her example was the invention of an enzyme, the addition of which to drinking water has substantial health benefits that the public becomes dependent on for the purpose of absorbing water. If such inventor would have decided to enforce her patent right and prevent mankind from using the enzyme, and as a byproduct the consumption of drinking water, this may leave the public without enough and as good.[34]

Robert Merges argued that Gordon's analysis is theoretically important, but objected the use of such argument for the purpose of contracting the scope of intellectual property rights. He argued that the proponents of expanding Gordon's idea are ignoring the fact that in most cases new intellectual creations do not significantly affect the public and granting property in them does not lead to the harm described by Gordon. Hence, the sufficiency proviso is met.[35]

Lior Zemer proposed to expand Gordon's approach and understand Locke's approach as taking into account the public interest when granting property, especially in the copyright context. This is mainly due to Locke's own treatment of copyright in his essay *Liberty of the Press.* [36] With respect to the sufficiency proviso, Zemer suggested that leaving ideas always in the public domain does not necessarily meet the sufficiency proviso due to the ambiguity with respect to the border line between ideas and expressions. He argued that due to Locke's goal to benefit the public at large, the public cannot be prevented from using existing works, for example for making derivative works, and that the sufficiency proviso should be interpreted literally – meaning leaving exactly enough and as good for the public to use.[37]

Even if Zemer's broad reading may be acceptable in other contexts of copyright, such as the fair use doctrine or the idea-expression dichotomy, I do not believe it fits the derivative works right. Gordon's argument with respect to circumstances in which excluding the public from private resources could not meet the sufficiency proviso, could certainly fit certain cases in which the making of derivative works should be free, for example when a specific work has become a main cultural asset. In such circumstances, it could be argued that the public should be allowed to freely express itself with respect to such works even if this involves the use of protected expressions that amounts to a derivative work. However, this justification cannot explain why the making of derivative works should always be allowed.

I suggest another way to understand why the sufficiency proviso could change the way we think about derivative works in general, based on Waldron and Simmons' reading of the proviso, that albeit the differences between them well explains the proper application to derivative works. Waldron explained the sufficiency proviso as a condition that has to be met alongside the appropriation and not as a limitation on the ability to appropriate. In other words, the sufficiency proviso may entitle a person to a specific use right with respect to another person's property but not prevent the latter from having property at all. An example could be the right to accommodation. Under this interpretation, for the sufficiency proviso to be met it is not necessary that every person will have property in adequate real estate, rather that every person will have the ability to rent or lease apartments. Thus, according to Waldron, the meaning of the sufficiency proviso is that every person should have the opportunity to obtain private property to the extent that this allows all other people to adequately provide for themselves.[38]

In contrast, Simmons did assume that the sufficiency proviso limits the ability to appropriate. However, Simmons proposed that we understand such limitation more moderately. He argued that the sufficiency proviso cannot be understood as prohibiting appropriation in every case where such appropriation leaves society with less resources to exploit, rather that it limits appropriation to the fair share to which every person is entitled. Simmons explained the fair share idea as the fulfillment of the right of every person to an equal opportunity to obtain private property which is tied with every person's right to purposively execute her wills and aspirations.[39]

Despite the differences between the two approaches, they could merge with respect to the derivative works right, especially in light of the non-legal understanding of creativity as suggested in the previous chapters. As we saw, the cognitive process of creation includes the reliance on prior domain-relevant knowledge. Similarly, the development and establishment of genres are dependent on the use of common building blocks and intertextuality. These understandings about creativity are in line with Waldron and Simmons' approaches. Under Waldron's approach, to the extent that the derivative works right does not allow adequate opportunity to participate in the creative world, due to the fact that it prohibits second authors from using prior knowledge and existing common building blocks, it should be limited so that the sufficiency proviso is met and enough creative space and freedom is left to second authors. According to Simmons' approach, it could be explained why, in order to allow each person the basic opportunity to obtain property rights in meaningful expressions, access should be granted to common building blocks, even if part of which are appropriated by first authors. Granting a broad derivative works right to the first author will grant her control which is beyond her fair share of the commons, and at the same time exclude others from the opportunity to engage in creativity and become owners in a specific creative domain, thus violating the sufficiency proviso. This analysis could lead to two plausible perceptions of the derivative works right that could meet the proviso.

One alternative is eliminating the derivative works right altogether. This is in line with approaches that argue that when the sufficiency proviso is violated, private property cannot be obtained. Accordingly, if the derivative works right does not allow equal opportunity to acquire property in the world of creativity, according to Simmons's approach, no person should be entitled to acquire a derivative works right with respect to expressions she created. For example, if we believe that the derivative works right in Edgar Allan Poe's detective story and the character of Dupin (as discussed in Chapter 2), does not allow equal opportunity to create and develop the detective story genre, Poe will not be entitled to such right. The implication of this alternative is that although the first author did acquire property rights in the expressions she created by using common natural resources by mixing her labor, such property does not include the right to exclude others from such expressions for the purpose of making new expressions.

A second alternative, which I believe fits better with Locke's approach, could be conceptualized in two ways. The first is that the sufficiency proviso limits the broad derivative works right acquired by the first author, for example due to distributive considerations, and the right is contracted due to the balance between the first author's right to property and external limitations on it due to other authors' rights. The second is that the sufficiency proviso only allows the first author to acquire a more limited derivative works right to begin with, as it considers the inherent balance in the definition of the right. The results of both conceptualizations are similar. When the first author mixes her labor with a natural common resource (ideas), she acquires private property in the product of such mixing (expression). The property acquired with respect to the expression does not allow other authors to use such expressions or to mix them with their labor without the first author's consent, as these are already private property and not common resources. Therefore, mixing the work of the second author with such expressions cannot justify their acquisition of property in the derivative works created. However, according to the above analysis, regarding the ability to make derivative works based on the first author's expressions, a broad derivative works right does not meet the sufficiency proviso. The proper solution in this case is limiting the scope of the derivative works right to the extent necessary to meet the sufficiency proviso. This is best reflected in protecting the first author's right with respect to the making of derivative works under a liability rule instead of property rules, for example by using a compulsory license model that allows second authors to use the expressions of the first author for the purpose of making derivative works without her consent, subject to payment of adequate royalties.

This is well in line with Waldron's interpretation of the sufficiency proviso. As explained, Waldron considers that the sufficiency proviso does not limit the mere acquisition of property, rather mandates granting equal opportunities for others to provide for themselves using the appropriated resources. Therefore, acknowledging the derivative works right of the first author while allowing others to use protected expressions for the purpose of making derivative works subject to payment meets the sufficiency proviso.[40] This could also be in line with Simmons's understanding of the sufficiency proviso but the conceptualization must be different. According to Simmons, the sufficiency proviso requires that the derivative works right of the first author does not include the right to exclude others from using protected expressions to make derivative works. In addition, the fair share concept of Simmons is not in contrast to the possibility that second authors must pay a fair payment to the first author that, on the one hand, does not exclude them from using the resource, but on the other hand does not excessively damage the first author. Thus, protecting the derivative works right using liability rules best supports the sufficiency proviso also under Simmons's approach.[41]

b) The waste proviso

In contrast to the sufficiency proviso, the waste proviso was not explicitly applied to the derivative works right in current literature. This may be a result of Nozick's approach that the waste proviso is redundant with the sufficiency proviso, since if enough and as good is left for others, there can be no waste,[42] and even due to Locke's own conception that waste seldom occurs under a money-based economy.[43] Another argument for easily skipping the waste obstacle is that waste cannot occur as long as the acquired goods are used, or potentially used, by their owners.[44] I believe that the waste proviso is a separate and independent condition that limits the acquisition of property and that it has even stronger implications to the derivative works right which help articulate its independent importance.

Justin Hughes suggested we understand the waste proviso in the context of intellectual property in general in two ways. The first is understanding waste in relation to the potential use of the resource, by whomever is not the owner, in the present. The second is understanding waste in relation to the future use of the resource by its owner. Hughes referred to the first conception as social waste and to the second as individual waste.[45] Each of these conceptions of the waste proviso has a different effect on the derivative works right and requires separate examination considering other copyright doctrines as well, and specifically the reproduction right.

SOCIAL WASTE

Lior Zemer argued that in the context of copyright, the waste proviso is reflected in copyright duration, since upon expiry the work and underlying expressions return to the public domain. This argument is based on the premise, which is unique to copyright, that ideas (or expressions) do not spoil. Indeed, ideas do not spoil, but as Peter Drahos explained we may well think of cases in which the opportunity to exploit ideas or expressions will disappear over time, as well as the ideas and expressions themselves.[46] In other words, the social importance of an idea depends on its timing. I argue that the question of social waste of copyright is not necessarily limited to copyright duration, rather to the various types of uses of protected expressions.

Gordon Hull suggested social waste of copyright could be understood under three conditions: first, there must be some (present or future) demand for using a work and insufficient supply; second, the work must already exist; and third, the property right itself is the reason for lack of supply.[47] This is a quasi-market understanding of waste. When a de facto monopoly does not supply existing market demand (by under-production or excessive pricing), waste occurs and therefore it must be expropriated from the monopoly-causing property.[48]

Another alternative understanding of social waste is using the conclusions on the role of common building blocks from genre theories explained in the previous Chapter. Simmons explained that the waste proviso is based on Locke's wish to guarantee that any use of appropriated goods is a productive use. According to him, a person that does not productively use her owned goods does not respect other people and prevents them from the opportunity to fulfill their personhood using such goods.[49] It is arguable that since any work is also a building block for the development and expansion of its genre, and for the production of other works that will contribute to the meaning of both first and second works, and since any work contains expressions that are relevant knowledge for a second author to engage in creativity, granting the first author the right to exclude others from making derivative works necessarily leads to a waste of potential creative development (and its meaning) and a constant insufficient supply even if the first author is not economically monopolistic. This understanding of how the creative world develops must lead to the conclusion that the derivative works right violates the waste proviso by definition, at least to the extent that it allows first authors to prohibit the making of derivative works.

INDIVIDUAL WASTE

The conclusions from the previous chapters contribute to the understanding of individual waste as well. The individual conception of the waste proviso allows, at least under a simple reading of Locke's text, the aggregation of resources for personal welfare and improvement in quality of life, as well as for commerce and capital gains.[50] But this should be understood in a more limited way as well, both generally and with respect to the derivative works specifically. Waldron explained that part of a person's right to the fruit of her labor is the right to decide how such goods will be used. The mirror image of this is that the destruction of goods is prohibited under the waste proviso. According to him, complete non-use will never meet the waste proviso even if it generates gain for the owner, since such gain must result from using the goods.[51] This is also true under Simmons's productive use approach.

One example in the copyright context would be cases where the owner of a digital work sold in copies (and the cost of such copies is near zero), limits the amount of copies sold only to increase the value of each copy. Another example would be a case where a person creates software only to prevent potential competitors from entering the market in which she operates for the purpose of increasing the prices of other products sold by her. The created software itself is not used by that person nor is it distributed by her, and its mere purpose is to allow her to gain more revenues from other works.

With respect to derivative works, my argument is that since the making of derivative works is not only a different type of use than the making or distributing of copies, rather a completely different type of right, its use must be reviewed under the waste proviso independently from the use of any other rights in the copyright bundle. Using the protected expressions in their entirety for copying, distributing, viewing or any other utilization is one type of use that could be made by the author. However, using the underlying expressions for the purpose of making new expressions is a different type of action that is not just one specific use with respect to first work. Therefore, using the derivative works right only to prevent such use from others does not qualify as use of the derivative works right.

There is a qualitative difference between the exploitation of protected expressions in their entirety for gain, which meets the waste proviso, and the non-exploitation of the derivative works right for any purpose whatsoever (whether to increase the revenues from the first work or for other personal reasons). Therefore, the non-use of the derivative works right cannot be considered a productive use under Simmons's definition and violates the waste proviso.

Consider, for example, the making of a movie version of a fiction book or the making of a sequel to such book. The publishing of the book and the sale of copies are obviously productive uses that do not violate the waste proviso with respect to the book itself and the reproduction right. However, the decision not to make any movie version of the book is a waste of this type of action and of the derivative works right. Similarly, deciding not to make sequels for the book also wastes this type of action. It must be noted that there may be circumstances in which some exploitation of the derivative works right will be sufficient to meet the waste proviso with respect to other potential ways to use it. For example, if the author of a book decided to make a sequel, her decision not to make an alternative sequel is not necessarily a waste. However, the decision not to make a sequel to the sequel may still be considered a waste. Similarly, postponing the making of sequels to the first book only to increase the prices of copies of the first book is a waste with respect to the derivative works right.

The first author may wish to productively use her expressions for the making of derivative works, and in this sense will not violate the waste proviso. But it is a safe assumption that the first author will not make all possible productive uses of her expressions for the purpose of developing the creative discourse and therefore will almost always waste the potential development of the creative world and violate the sufficiency proviso. Therefore, the first author's property must be limited with respect to the making of derivative works, at least to require her to use the work for this purpose within a specific timeframe. The suggestion here, in fact, is to limit the exclusive derivative works right in time, meaning that if the first author does not make derivative works during such time others will be entitled to do so. This suggestion assumes a certain grace period during which the first author will be exclusively allowed to make derivative works. This could also be mixed with the suggestion to protect the derivative works right with liability rules, for example by using compulsory licenses, as suggested with respect to the sufficiency proviso, so that when the grace period expires, the first author could still make derivative works but others will be allowed to do so too subject to fair payment.

To conclude the discussion in this part, Locke's sufficiency and waste provisos are the most suitable tools to review the current derivative works right, and in its current definition, the right is unjustified under each of the provisos. Although the sufficiency proviso could lead to the conclusion that the derivative works right must be eliminated altogether, a more nuanced understanding of the provisos leads to the justification of a more limited derivative works right. My suggestion in this context is shifting to a liability rule protection that will preserve some of the first author's right with respect to derivative works but will allow others to make them without her consent, and thus meet the sufficiency proviso. In addition, according to the waste proviso, it is justified to limit the duration of the derivative works right and to grant the first author a short grace period to make derivative works exclusively. Thereafter, anyone could make derivative works based on the first work, either freely or subject to a liability rule. This could support a variety of remedies models for the derivative works right, and specifically compulsory licenses as will be suggested in Chapter 5.

IV. The corrective justice approach

This part will explain how the corrective justice approach, based on the writings of Ernst Weinrib, justifies the limitation of a broad derivative works right and prefers a model that allows the making of unauthorized derivative works subject to certain revenue share. The discussion in this part will focus on the corrective justice approach which is a main normative approach to private law, and its application to copyright law suggested by Abraham Drassinower. Since corrective justice is highly based on Kant's doctrine of right, I will dedicate a short discussion to its basic premises and characteristics. However, the discussion here is not Kantian and I do not suggest that it necessarily fits with Kant's doctrine of right.

1) Corrective justice and private rights

Weinrib's interpretation of private law has been one of the most influential right-based analyses of law to date. Relying on Aristotelian corrective justice and Kant's doctrine of right, it explains that private law should be understood as a corrective mechanism for injustice.[52] This corrective mechanism, however, presupposes correlativity and focusses on the interrelations between the plaintiff and the defendant and the rights and duties they have with respect to one another. In other words, this means that "liability reflects the conclusion that the defendant and the plaintiff have respectively done and suffered the same injustice." Hand-in-hand with the Kantian concept of personality – which treats human beings as purposive entities who are free to act as long as they do not interfere with the rights of others[53] – correlativity serves as the inner, normative justification for legal rights and duties.[54]

The concept of personhood plays a significant role in the corrective justice approach as it is the normative basis for the rights and duties of individuals. It is based on Kant's conception in his doctrine of right, based on which he defined the "right" as follows: "Right is therefore the sum of the conditions under which the choice of one can be united with the choice of another in accordance with a universal law of freedom."[55] Kant's universal right approach is based on the premise that a right could only exist where it reflects a state in which the free will of every person could exist alongside the free will of any other person.[56]

Kant's universal right focusses on relationships between individuals. To the extent that a person's act that is in line with all others' freedoms – meaning, part of her right – is restricted by the right of another person, the latter wrongs the former. From this Kant derived the principles with respect to the rights of individuals in external things, such as property. According to Kant, a person can claim that something is hers if she can claim that others' acts with respect to such thing will limit her freedom that is in line with the freedom of others. Therefore, Kant explained that property is not a right in an external thing, rather the right of a person towards other persons with respect to such thing.[57]

A right to external things could only exist in a civil condition according to Kant, as it requires a common will of all people, since a unilateral will cannot limit other people from acting. The common will guarantees that all people will be entitled to manifest their wills and their ability to have rights with respect to external things, thus fulfilling the universal right principle. In sum, Kant's doctrine of right (including property rights) is correlative since it focusses on the existence of a right in a relationship between two (or more) individuals, and universal since it requires that the right of each person conform with the rights of all other persons and the existence of a formal equality with respect to the possibility to acquire rights.

2) Corrective justice and derivative works

Arthur Ripstein suggested that Kant's doctrine of right cannot justify copyright since he himself excluded intellectual works from the concept of property.[58] Merges, on the other hand, argued that Kant never formally excluded intellectual works from the concept of property and that the doctrine of right could justify rights in abstract things.[59] While this divide is important for a Kantian discussion of copyright, the discussion here is focussed on corrective justice. The doctrine of right and corrective justice focus on the right of individuals with respect to each other and whether they have rights with respect to the acts of others and therefore could be definitely applied to copyright.

Based on the premise that corrective justice applies to copyright, Drassinower explained various important copyright doctrines, such as the idea-expression dichotomy and fair use, using corrective justice principles.[60] In his book, "What's Wrong with Copying?" Drassinower suggested a unified explanation of copyright law under corrective justice. According to Drassinower, originality in copyright law is a manifestation of a person's right to speak in her own words. He argued that copyright law reflects a system of communicative actions in which each person has a right to speech in one's own words to the extent that such right is guaranteed for all other persons.[61] The mirror image of this is that copyright infringement occurs when there is compelled speech, meaning, speaking in the name of another without her permission.[62]

Drassinower's corrective justice explanation of copyright fits well with the conclusions from previous chapters regarding the non-legal aspects of creativity. As we saw in Chapter 1, the creative process is based on an individual contribution of the author in terms of associative development of abstract ideas as well as on the use of preexisting domain-relevant knowledge and expressions that crystalize such ideas. Kant's doctrine of right, as formulated by Drassinower, fits well with this understanding of creativity in the sense that to the extent that a creative activity is concerned, such activity will be allowed even if using preexisting expressions since it is part of each author's right to act in the creative world. An uncreative activity, however, is not part of such right and therefore literal copying would be prohibited. This is also true to the understanding of genre theories as discussed in Chapter 2. We saw that using preexisting expressions is essential to enrich and develop the creative world and should be part of each author's right to act in such environment. However, using existing expression in a manner that does not develop creativity should not be part of such right.

Drassinower's approach suggests a binary conclusion. One option is that a person infringes copyright by copying a protected expression (compelling speech) and therefore the first author could prohibit such use.[63] Another option is that the first author's right does not extend to certain acts of the second author, such as using ideas or even fair uses of expressions, and therefore the second author's acts could not be limited and she has an absolute freedom to so act (speak in her own words). How should derivative works be understood under this framework?

Drassinower discussed the application of this theory to derivative works. He argued that the derivative works right does not fit the basic principle according to which a person has a natural right to speak in her own words as well as with the dialogical nature of copyright. Therefore, according to him, the derivative works right should be eliminated and the use of existing expressions for the making of new works should be free.[64] This is, of course, a valid option and it is well in line with the Kantian analysis of the derivative works right.[65] However, I wish to suggest an alternative conception of the derivative works right under corrective justice.

3) A new model for derivative works under corrective justice

Much like the discussion on Locke's sufficiency proviso, I argue that while the conclusion that the derivative works right is unjustified under corrective justice is viable, a more limited version of the right could be justified under this approach. By that I mean a derivative works right that allows second authors to make derivative works without authorization from the first author while maintaining an independent existence for the right (in contrast to the reproduction right) and a certain interest of the first author to revenue share from the second works. I will attempt to explain this argument based on Drassinower's corrective justice analysis of copyright.

As explained, Drassinower's analysis leads to a binary yes or no right, meaning either an action compels speech and is therefore infringing or it is merely the right of a person to speak in her own words and therefore allowed. I argue that there is a third alternative in which the second author has the right to use expressions from the first work to make derivative works (and speak in her own words) while the first author still has some right in the derivative works right. This is a quasi-joint-ownership between the first and second authors while no rights are infringed.

How could this be aligned with corrective justice? The basic rule in corrective justice is that a person is free to act to the extent she does not violate others' freedom. Thus, at a first glance, if we conclude that the second author has the right to use prior expression to speak in her own words, she could not be infringing the first author's right and therefore has no duties towards her. I believe that an alternative model for such interrelation could be justified in the case of derivative works.[66]

The first step in my analysis is identical to Drassinower's and accepts his normative assumptions: the second author is free to make derivative works based on the first work without wronging the first author. This fits the understanding of copyright as a communicative activity, as explained by Drassinower, and with the non-legal understanding of creativity as explained in the previous chapters. However, the use of the derivative work by the second author may cause her to have a duty towards the first author, but not because she made the derivative work without authorization, rather because of a joint ownership created with respect to the derivative work.

I must clarify what I do not mean by this. This joint ownership cannot be formed due to the second author mixing her labor in the first work. As I previously explained with respect to Locke's approach, a unilateral action with respect to something that is already appropriated cannot justify acquisition with respect to such thing, which is already the private property of another.[67] How could such joint ownership be formed then?

This articulates the question of whether copyright is an external thing or merely an action of a person. It is difficult to discuss joint ownership when the ownership refers to the separate actions of individuals. In contrast, joint ownership in external things is easier to understand. I suggest to distinguish between two aspects of an author's right to her work. In the most abstract description of a work as an intellectual product, it could be conceived as a right of the author to act. But this right to act also includes the right to make concrete copies (physical, digital or otherwise) of the work and control the use of such copies. These are obviously external things that the author has rights in. Thus, we can think of the author's right to speak in her own words as including the right to make concrete embodiments of the work and control them.

This distinction leads to the second step of the model. The second author is free to make derivative works based on expressions from the first work as part of her right to speak in her own words and act as an author in the creative world. The second author's new original expressions are her work of authorship and by using them she does not compel speech on the first author since her speech does not conflict with the speech of the first author. However, communicating the speech of the second author to the public requires the inclusion of expressions from the first work together with the new expressions of the second author. While the second author's right allows her to include the first expressions and disseminate them in concrete copies, each such copy is jointly owned by both the first and second authors. Due to the fact that the second author's right does not include the right to appropriate the expressions of the first author, and since both expressions cannot be separated, the first author must have the right to jointly own the concrete embodiments of the second work to reflect her right in her own speech. This requires the second author to share any future revenue made from the derivative work with the first author, otherwise the former will wrong the latter by becoming unjustly enriched.[68]

For example, take the case of writing a sequel to the Harry Potter book series. Assume that an author decides to write a sequel to the series that begins at the ending point of the seventh book in the original series. Such author writes new original plotlines and these are her original contributions that do not conflict with the original expressions from J.K. Rowling's books. However, to express such new plotlines in a concrete form, the author must include characters from the original series and perhaps some prior plotlines that are protected expressions of Rowling. If we prevent such author from using these protected expressions for the purpose of expressing her new work, she will be prevented from communicating it in a concrete form. Thus, she must be allowed to use Rowling's prior expressions, while Rowling will be entitled to joint-ownership in the concrete forms of the second work.

Two issues arise here. First, how will the revenue share be fulfilled when the second author decides to distribute the derivative work for free while enjoying reputation and cultural gains? Second, what is the role of moral rights in such a model?

With respect to the first point, to the extent that the reputation and cultural gains of the second author result from using the reputation of the first author, this is a wrong that should be compensated for under corrective justice. This could be done using various mechanisms, including under a compulsory license model. For example, a fixed fee could be determined to reflect the reputation gains of the second author from using the jointly owned work on top of ongoing royalties. With respect to the second point, moral rights (if applicable) must exist in conjunction with this model. This is because if we want to take the author's right to speak in her own words seriously and not be subject to compelled speech, we must allow her to choose whether or not the work will be attributed to her. I will elaborate on both these points while discussing the proposed remedies model in Chapter 5.

It may be argued that this analysis should also apply to the fair use doctrine which may also result in such joint ownership. The answer to such argument lies in the idea of transformativity which is at the heart of fair use. United States Courts have clarified that when assessing the first factor of the fair use doctrine, the most significant question is whether the use is "transformative" or not.[69] Transformative use "adds something new, with the further purpose or different character, altering the first [expression] with new expression, meaning, or message."[70] Further, a use can be transformative in two significant ways, transformative of purpose and transformative of content.[71]

When a second author uses a preexisting expression to engage with the public in a transformative way – meaning, changing the purpose, context, meaning or message of the first expression – although the first author's expression is *identifiable* in the concrete form of the object representing the second author's speech, that expression is not a *representation* of the first author's engagement with the public. Thus, the concrete form of the new intellectual object represents only the second author's transformative expression and is wholly owned by her. She is thus under no duty to share her gains with the first author.

However, while some derivative works constitute transformative use, and therefore should be governed by the fair use doctrine, not all derivative works will merit its application – so the two categories do not fully overlap.[72] As Judge Pierre Nelson Leval of the Second Circuit recently stated, while the changes in certain derivative works in comparison to the first work "can be described as transformations, they do not involve the kind of transformative purpose that favors a fair use finding."[73]

Three different variations on a Harry Potter novel demonstrate the distinction between three categories – infringement (compelled speech), transformative derivative works (fair use) and non-transformative derivative works. A reproduction of the book without the author's consent, even one with minor alterations, clearly infringes, and falls into the category of compelled speech. In contrast, placing an image of the Harry Potter character in a modern art exhibition as a criticism of today's youth's diminishing interest in novels likely falls under the category of transformative use. It constitutes fair use because this act is clearly outside the scope of the author's original speech. Adapting the novel "Harry Potter and the Chamber of Secrets" into a motion picture, however, fits into neither category. While this act clearly involves additional authorship and creativity, and thus results in something obviously more than a mere reproduction, it also falls short of transformative-ness, as it clearly does not change the basic purpose, meaning or message of the first author's speech.

This understanding of derivative works under corrective justice distinguishes between derivative works and fair use as follows. In the case of non-transformative derivative works, the concrete copies representing the second author's speech also represent the first author's speech because they both participate in the same discussion, and the purpose and context of the new expression are not different. In contrast, in the case of transformative use, the concrete form of the new object represents only the speech of the second author. In other words, a derivative work of a protected expression elaborates and develops an existing discussion with the pubic, while a transformative use initiates a new one.

To conclude this part, we saw that two formulations of the derivative works under corrective justice are possible. The first, as suggested by Drassinower, is that the derivative works right is unjustified and should be eliminated. The second is that corrective justice could justify a more limited independent derivative works right that allows second authors to use expressions from first works without authorization, while granting first authors joint ownership in the concrete embodiments of the second work that entitles them to shares of the second author's revenues.

V. Hegel and the personality approach

Another right-based approach to private property is the personality approach. It is based on Hegel's doctrine of right that focusses on the connection between an individual's person and external things she may have right in. I will first briefly explain Hegel's doctrine of right and its application to copyright law while emphasizing that the application of Hegel's approach to copyright is more extensive than how current literature treats it. I will then review the derivative works right under this approach.

1) Hegel's doctrine of right

Hegel, much like Locke and Kant, focussed on one's person as the basis for rights. According to Hegel, free will is manifested in the personality of a person. Hegel's concept of personhood is, however, different than Locke's in one main aspect.

While Locke believed that an individual has a right to her body and self-control, Hegel argued that a person has rights only in his abstract personhood. Hegel understood rights as possessions, meaning property or ownership, first in one's person and then in the physical and external manifestations of such person. Actions that contradict the manifestation of a person's possession in herself or her willful actions that correspond with the actions of others, constitute wrongs.[74]

Hegel believed that the abstract existence of personhood alone does not fulfill its purpose, and therefore argued that a person must externally manifest her free will to fulfill her self-purpose. To do so, she must embed her personality and will in external things. According to Hegel, unappropriated things are "empty" and do not hold any personality or rights. A person, being a purposive entity, has the right to embed her will in all empty things and make them her own.[75] Thus, Hegel needed to explain how could a person embed her personhood in external things. The first appropriated external thing is one's body. For all other external things, Hegel explained that acquisition of property could occur when a person manifests her will with respect to an external thing. Three phenomena could lead to such manifestation – possession, use and transfer. For our discussion, the question of possession is of most importance. Hegel explained that while physically possessing a thing could establish acquisition of property, a more profound way to embed personality in a thing is a change of its physical status. By this, Hegel, much like Locke, focussed not merely on the physical labor on an external thing, but rather on subjecting an external thing to the will of a specific person. In other words, as explained by Waldron, Hegel understood embedding personality in external things as a change in external things that could not be accounted for without identifying the will of the person that brought such change.[76]

Thus, according to Hegel, the only way to manifest the abstract personality is to embed it in external things. In addition, each person has a right to the extent it is necessary to develop and manifest her abstract personhood. These two principles lead to the existence of a person's natural right to private property in external things. As Waldron explained, this is necessary because only private property could completely fulfill the development of personality and its external manifestation, since only private property could create a commitment between a person's will and external things that could allow such person to set her goals and limit her own freedom with respect to such goals in the future.[77]

Before discussing the application of Hegel's theory to copyright and derivative works, I must dedicate a few words to one popular formulation of his approach in modern literature. Margaret Jane Radin's *Property and Personhood* suggested a personality-based property theory relying on Hegel's doctrine of right. In short, Radin used Hegel's premise that external things are required for self-fulfillment to suggest that the scope of property rights should be directly related to the type of relationship the owner has with a specific thing. According to her, the loss or expropriation of some things would cause their owners severe grievance and damage, while other things are not so highly linked to the personhood of the owner. She suggested to distinguish between the first category of personal property and the second category of fungible property. Under this intuitive approach, according to her, the basic justification to private property is the personality-based connection between person and object.[78] Radin linked her approach with Hegel's and explained that personhood as an abstract idea could be understood as the way an individual acts as a social creature. Thus, personhood could be understood according to psychological or societal intuitions like those she suggested. The final stage of her model was to suggest that personal property will receive strong property protection while fungible property will receive weak protection or no protection at all.

2) *Hegel and derivative works*

Hegel himself discussed the application of his approach to intellectual products, asking two main questions – are intellectual products empty external things and how could they be transferred as property? With respect to the first question, Hegel believed that intellectual products could be considered external things only if they have been manifested externally or embedded in external things. With respect to the second question, it is implied in Hegel's texts that he believed that intellectual products have two forms of external manifestations – the concrete physical embodiment and the abstract ability to reproduce and disseminate them – and that the author could choose whether to transfer one or both aspects to others.[79]

Neil Netanel mainly focussed on the question of alienability of copyrights under the personality approach and the relationship between economic and moral rights in continental law. His references to Hegel were used to emphasize Hegel's dualist approach that justifies two sets of rights in a work – economic and moral – while the economic rights are alienable and subject to commercialization.[80] Justin Hughes, in contrast, focussed on a more robust application of Hegel's personality approach and its formulation by Radin to intellectual property. His main argument was that not all forms of intellectual property could be justified by the personality approach and that only intellectual products that significantly reflect the personality of the author justify protection.[81]

Hughes' application of personality theory to intellectual property, and his argument regarding its inability to justify many forms of intellectual property rights, is echoed in copyright literature. It is thus customary to understand Hegel's personality approach as justifying full and complete control over protected works, but only with respect to works that show strong relationship to the author's personality. It is also customary to argue that personality theory struggles to justify economic rights in contrast to moral rights.

This is also echoed in the only analysis of the derivative works right under the personality theory, presented by Naomi Voegtli. Voegtli argued that in the context of derivative works it is unclear why copyright in the derivative work should be granted to the first author. She gave the example of a second author changing a first work so extensively so that the first expressions are hardly recognizable. In these circumstances, according to her, the second author, that has a stronger personal relation to the second work, must be granted copyright.[82] I believe that this argument is flawed and is based on an incorrect understanding of Hegel's theory.

First, the perception that justifying copyrights based on the personality approach is limited to works that show close personal relationship to the first author, and to the granting of moral rights alone, does not fit with Hegel's doctrine of right. The source of this argument may be the identity that was wrongly attributed to Hegel's and Radin's conceptions of personality. Hegel, in contrast to Radin, never discussed personality as the psychological-societal attributes of a person, rather as the universal and abstract manifestation of a person that is the basis for rights and duties with respect to external things. In this sense, Hegel never limited a person's interest in external things to the degree in which such things express her personality traits. For Hegel, the interest a person has in an external thing depends on her will (or the application of her personhood) to fulfill herself as a purposive creature by using such thing. This principle is not at all related to psychological or sociological questions, and therefore the above suggested limitations do not fit Hegel's doctrine.[83] In other words, under Hegel's approach, any external thing – whether a wedding ring or a fungible commodity – is part of one's personhood to the extent she chooses to fulfill her goals using it. If a person sells her wedding ring she chooses to subject it to the personhood of another in the same sense as when she sells her laundry machine. Accordingly, when both ring and laundry machine are in her possession, they receive the same degree of property protection.

Second, even if Voegtli's argument could be understood in a more abstract form, under which the derivative work is an external manifestation of the second author's personhood and is required for the manifestation of her free will and her ability to develop her personhood, it does not explain why the first author, who already embedded his personhood in the first work, cannot exclude the second author from doing so. As we saw, Hegel's doctrine of right does not include distributive limitations on the acquisition of property and allows people to embed their personhood in empty external things that are not subject to the personhood of others. In the case of derivative works, such as a sequel to the Harry Potter series, it appears that actions with respect to existing plotlines and characters are actions with respect to an external thing that was already appropriated and are thus prohibited without the owner's approval. I will now turn to suggest an argument that begins at a similar starting point but is more suitable for the inner logic of Hegel's doctrine of right, that could support a more limited derivative works right.

3) Message, meaning and interpretation – the personality of the second author

As part of Hegel's hesitations with respect to the alienability of intellectual products, he asked under which conditions could a second author use the expressions of a first author to express herself and appropriate such expressions without performing plagiarism. The answer, according to Hegel, should be left to discussions of honor and morality.[84] In this section, I will attempt to outline the first ideas to a more concrete approach explaining the relationship between the first and second authors under the inner logic of Hegel's approach.

For this purpose, I will use perceptions from the fields of communication studies and hermeneutics to demonstrate how the derivative work should be understood under Hegel's abstract personality idea, and subsequently to demonstrate the boundaries of the justification for copyright under such approach. The hermeneutic model I will use is the "cycle" of interpretation suggested by Hans-Georg Gadamer in "Truth and Method,"[85] as well as terms related to the interpersonal communicative process.

The act of authorship and its expressions, as Drassinower described it, is essentially a communicative act. Thus, for the purpose of this discussion, I wish to conceptualize the series of communicative actions with respect to a work of authorship under terms from the field of communication that focus on the relationship between message and meaning. In her book *The Soul of Creativity*, Roberta Kwall focussed on message and meaning in the legal context of the creative world. She suggested to distinguish between these terms from the viewpoint of the author, where the meaning for the author symbolizes her subjective relation to the work while the message symbolized the load of knowledge and the meaning the author wishes to communicate to the public.[86] Kwall used these terms for intra-legal purposes with respect to copyright law, but message and meaning play a role in the literature on the interpersonal communicative process. Zohar Efroni suggested a communicative model according to which communication begins with a message transmitted by a sender through a communication channel, that is eventually received by the recipient that extracts meaning from it.[87] Here too, message and meaning are distinguished and the message (the objective product of the sender's internal expressions) eventually becomes the meaning for the recipient.

The meaning-making stage – the stage in which the message formed by the subjective interpretation of the sender attracts meaning by the recipient – is the interpretation stage. Gadamer's approach for interpretation, which was extensively used in the literature in the second half of the twentieth century, is a good tool to demonstrate the interpretation stage. According to Gadamer, interpretation (or understanding) begins when a certain text is addressed to us. In communicative terms, this is the point in time when the message is received by the recipient. Gadamer divided the interpretative process into three main stages – understanding, interpretation and application. He explained that understanding always requires some expectation with respect to the text to allow for an intelligible reading. However, such expectation is updated during the understanding stage and is not constant. This is what Gadamer referred to as the interpretative cycle. This dialectic process was conceptualized by Gadamer as "application".[88]

Gadamer's dialectic is most evident in the concept of application. Application, according to Gadamer, is an inseparable part of meaning-making alongside understanding and interpretation. Gadamer's main conclusion regarding the application stage is that in the process of meaning-making, the interpreter does not apply predetermined universal principles to a text in order to understand it, rather understands the universal principle itself through the text and the previous traditional load carried by the interpreter. Application creates a change in the interpreter's cognition at least in the sense that when she will begin a new interpretation, she will bear a different mindset than the one she had prior to the previous interpretation.[89]

Now, we must turn to apply these notions to Hegel's doctrine of right. I do not suggest that the terms used in Gadamer's hermeneutics or in communication studies are identical to those of Hegel. Rather, I suggest using the notions from the Gadamerian discussion as a metaphor that could explain derivative works and the relationship of first and second authors in Hegelian terms. We saw that according to Gadamer and communication studies, when the recipient (second author) is exposed to a message (and meaning) that the sender (first author) asked to share as part of the communicative process underlying the creative world, the recipient undergoes an interpretive process to extract meaning from the received message, a meaning that could be different than the subjective meaning of the sender. To the extent that the second author decides to act according to such new subjective meaning, which is different from the message of the first author, by making a derivative work, we can no longer speak of acting with respect to something external that the personality of another is embedded in, in Hegelian terms. The difference between the meaning of the second author and the message of the first author explains why the external thing that the second author is subjecting to her will is an "empty" thing that she is free to acquire and embed her personality in. A legal rule that determines that the first author could prohibit any derivative uses of her first expression is in contrast to the basic principle in Hegel's doctrine of right, according to which the way to fulfill a person's basic abstract right in her personality is by externally manifesting it. This is because the second author only acts with respect to an external thing that the personality of the first author is not embedded in, and therefore is not yet appropriated. This line of thought should lead to the conclusion that the derivative works right is unjustified under Hegel's doctrine of right.

This understanding of the derivative works right under Hegel's approach is well in line with the non-legal understanding of creativity. Thus, for example, when the interpretive process of the second author leads her to a different meaning, this should be considered a creative activity based on domain-relevant knowledge under creativity studies. As this is understood as an act that is a substantial part of the creative process and of a person's ability to express her personality as an author, determining that such act should be allowed fits well with creativity studies. In contrast, if the second author interprets the first author's message using the same meaning of the first author, there is no creative activity at all and therefore prohibiting such activity is not in tension with creativity studies. This is also true to the conclusions from genre theories. The new meaning of the second author is in fact a use of the first author's message as a common building block to develop the creative world, and allowing it would fit well with genre theories.

However, in contrast to the Lockean and corrective justice approaches, it is difficult to formulate a valid argument that explains why the second author should be free to act but the first author should still have some interest in the derivative works created. This is mainly due to the lack of distributive components in Hegel's doctrine of right. Indeed, Gadamer's discussion may raise the possibility that the idea of joint ownership between the first and second author could fit here too. In fact, Gadamer himself suggested a similar notion:

> the meaning of a text is not to be compared with an immovable and obstinately fixed point of view… In this sense understanding is certainly not concerned with "understanding historically"… Rather, one intends to ***understand the text itself.*** But this means that the interpreter's own thoughts too have gone into re-awakening the text's meaning. In this the interpreter's own horizon is decisive, yet not as a personal standpoint that he maintains or enforces, but more as an opinion and a possibility that one brings into play and puts at risk, and that helps one truly to make one's own what the text says. I have described this above as a "fusion of horizons." We can now see that this is what takes place in conversation, in which something is expressed that is not only mine or my author's, but common.[90] [emphasis in original]

However, according to Hegel's doctrine of right, such joint ownership does not seem to be possible, since if we acknowledge that the personality of one author (first or second) is embedded in the derivative work, the other author cannot embed his personality in it without the consent of the other. This is where the idea of ethical life comes into play. In contrast to Locke who perceived private property as the basic condition for a civil state and as something that society should preserve, Hegel understood private property as inferior to other moral justifications that arise in the civil state. Therefore, to the extent that societal needs require us to form such joint ownership between first and second author (e.g., based on Gadamer's hermeneutics, the non-legal understandings of creativity and even economic analysis of copyright), this could be politically justified under Hegel's more extensive discussion that exceeds the scope of this part.

VI. Conclusion

This chapter offered a reexamination of the normative justifications to copyright with respect to the derivative works right. Its purpose was to review whether the derivative works right in its current form fits with these justifications and whether a different formulation of the right, that fits non-legal understanding of creativity, could be justified under such normative approaches. The review focussed on right-based theories to copyright since most utilitarian literature concluded that the derivative works right is difficult to justify.

We saw that under each of the main normative approaches to copyright law – economic analysis and right-based justifications based on the theories of Locke, Kant and Hegel – a legal regime that allows second authors to freely make derivative works is justified. This is in line with the non-legal understanding of creativity as discussed in the previous chapters. Therefore, since both intra-legal justifications to copyright and non-legal understandings of creativity support the freedom of second authors to make derivative works, my argument is that there is a strong justification to adjust the current legal framework of the derivative works right to these justifications. It must be noted that the justification is strong not because one specific theory supports it. The conclusion that several main copyright theories, each based on different normative premises, reach similar outcomes with respect to the derivative works right, together with the fact that such outcomes fit well with the non-legal understanding of creativity, adds up to a strong justification to change the current legal framework. In addition, we saw that most intra-legal approaches justify a legal rule according to which the first author maintains some interest in derivative works based on the first work. In other words, there is a strong justification for an independent derivative works right that is separate from the reproduction right. Therefore, my argument is that the derivative works right should not be eliminated, rather remodeled to fit both the normative justifications to copyright and the non-legal understanding of creativity. The remodeling of the derivative works right doctrine, which will focus both on scope of applicability and strength of remedies, will be outlined in Chapters 4 and 5.

Notes

1 This is based on the Benthamian maxim that "it is the greatest happiness of the greatest number that is the measure of right and wrong." *See* Jeremy Bentham, A FRAGMENT ON GOVERNMENT vi (1776).

2 This is reflected in the United States constitution that authorized congress "To promote the Progress of Science ..." *See* U.S. Const. art. I, § 8, cl. 8.

3 *See, e.g.*, William M. Landes & Richard A. Posner, *An Economic Analysis of Copyright Law*, 18 J. LEGAL STUD. 325, 327–9 (1989); William M. Landes & Richard A. Posner, THE ECONOMIC STRUCTURE OF INTELLECTUAL PROPERTY LAW 37 (2003).

4 This formulation does not account for other financing models for creativity such as governmental funds, crowd-funding or reputation gains. *See* Stephen Breyer, *The Uneasy Case for Copyright: A Study of Copyright in Books, Photocopies, and Computer Programs*, 84 HARV. L. REV. 281, 302–6, 309 (1970); Robert M. Hurt & Robert M. Schuchman, *The Economic Rationale of Copyright*, 56 AM. ECON. REV. 421, 424, 427 (1966); Landes & Posner, *supra* note 3, at 48. It also does not account for cases in which copies are not substitutes for the originals or are uniquely expensive. *See* Breyer, *id.*, at, 302–6; Hurt & Schuman, *id.*, at 427; Landes & Posner, *id.*, at 40–3.

5 For elaboration on the incentive-access approach *see* Christopher S. Yoo, *Copyright and Product Differentiation*, 79 N.Y.U. L. REV. 212, 226–31 (2004). *See also* Stan J. Liebowitz & Stephen Margolis, *Seventeen Famous Economists Weigh in on Copyright: The Role of Theory, Empirics, and Network Effects*, 18 HARV. J.L. & TECH. 435, 440–2 (2005); Stan J. Liebowitz, *Copyright Law, Photocopying, and Price Discrimination*, in 8 RESEARCH IN LAW AND ECONOMICS: THE ECONOMICS OF PATENTS AND COPYRIGHTS 181, 183–88 (John Palmer & Richard O. Zerbe, Jr. eds, 1986).

6 Landes & Posner, *supra* note 3, at 354.

7 Naomi Abe Voegtli, *Rethinking Derivative Rights*, 63 BROOK. L. REV. 1213, 1241–5 (1997). This is echoed by other commentators such as Stewart Sterk, *Rhetoric and Reality in Copyright Law*, 94 MICH. L. REV. 1197, 1215–17 (1996); Glynn S. Lunney, *Reexamining Copyright's Incentives-Access Paradigm*, 49 VAND. L. REV. 483, 650–3 (1996).

8 Landes & Posner, *supra* note 3, at 354–5.

9 Voegtli, *supra* note 7, at 1245.

10 Sterk, *supra* note 7, at 1217.

11 *Id.*

12 Voegtli, *supra* note 7, at 1246.

13 Yoo, *supra* note 4.

14 For elaboration on the model *see, id.*, at 236–46.

15 Michael Abramowicz, *A Theory of Copyright's Derivative Work Right*, 90 MINN. L. REV. 317, 348 (2005).

16 *Id.*, 358–60.
17 *Id.*, at 361–2.
18 For the effect of lower entry barriers on deadweight loss *see* Christopher S. Yoo, *Copyright and Product Differentiation*, 79 N.Y.U. L. REV. 212 (2004).
19 For a similar argument (that led to different conclusions) *see* Joseph P. Fishman, *Creating Around Copyright*, 128 HARV. L. REV. 1333, 1341 (2015).
20 Jeremy Waldron, THE RIGHT TO PRIVATE PROPERTY 143–7 (1988)
21 John Locke, TWO TREATISES OF GOVERNMENT § 25 (1689) (Cambridge University Press, 1960).
22 For elaboration *see* Waldron, *supra* note 20, at 155–7; A. John Simmons, THE LOCKEAN THEORY OF RIGHTS 239–43 (1992).
23 Locke, *supra* note 21, at §§ 27, 40–3; Waldron, *supra* note 20, at 177–8; Simmons, *supra* note 22, at 243–52.
24 For elaboration on such criticisms *see* Waldron, *supra* 20, at 184–91; Robert Nozick, ANARCHY, STATE AND UTOPIA 174–75 (1974) (asking whether a person who spills a can of tomato juice to the ocean appropriates the entire ocean or just loses her tomato juice).
25 Simmons, *supra* note 22, at 271–7.
26 For Nozick's criticism on the two provisos *see* Nozick, *supra* note 24, at 175–6.
27 *See* Justin Hughes, *The Philosophy of Intellectual Property*, 77 GEO. L.J. 287 (1988); Robert P. Merges, JUSTIFYING INTELLECTUAL PROPERTY (2011); Seana Shiffrin, *Lockean Arguments for Intellectual Property*, in NEW ESSAYS IN THE LEGAL AND POLITICAL THEORY OF PROPERTY 139 (Stephen R. Munzer ed., 2001); William Fisher, *Theories of Intellectual Property*, in NEW ESSAYS IN THE LEGAL AND POLITICAL THEORY OF PROPERTY 168 (Stephen R. Munzer ed., 2001); Alfred C. Yen, *Restoring the Natural Law: Copyright as Labor and Possession*, 51 OH. ST. L.J. 517 (1990); Lawrence C. Becker, *Deserving to Own Intellectual Property*, 68 CHI.-KENT L. REV. 609 (1993); Wendy J. Gordon, *A Property Right in Self-Expression: Equality and Individualism in the Natural Law of Intellectual Property*, 102 YALE L.J. 1533 (1993); Benjamin G. Damstedt, Note, *Limiting Locke: A Natural Law Justification for the Fair Use Doctrine*, 112 YALE L.J. 1179 (2003); Lior Zemer, *The Making of New Copyright Lockean*, 29 HARV. J.L. & PUB. POL'Y 891 (2006).
28 Becker, *supra* note 27, at 614–15.
29 Edwin C. Hettinger, *Justifying Intellectual Property*, 18 PHIL. & PUB. AFFAIRS 31, 44 (1989).
30 Gordon, *supra* note 27, at 1581–83.
31 Hughes, *supra* note 27, at 323–5.
32 Voegtli, *supra* note 7, at 1248–9. This line of argument corresponds with the general criticism of Locke's mixing argument. It is also based on the premise that Locke's approach is based on the concept of reward for labor. This is a misconception of Locke's approach that is mainly a right-based approach and not a utilitarian one (i.e., property is justified due to a natural right of humankind in their own person and not as a utilitarian award for their labor). Therefore, Locke's approach does not necessarily offer a reward for second authors only for their labor.
33 Gordon, *supra* note 27, at 1566. *See* also Zemer, *supra* note 27, at 926–7.
34 *Id.*, at 1567. In similar vein, Michal Shur-Ofry suggested, based on network analysis of creativity, that copyright protection should be adjusted according to the popularity of works. *See* Michal Shur-Ofry, *Popularity as a Factor in Copyright Law*, 59 U. TORONTO L.J. 525 (2009).
35 Merges, *supra* note 27, at 54–5.
36 Zemer, *supra* note 27, at 898–905; John Locke, *Liberty of the Press* (1695), reprinted in LOCKE: POLITICAL ESSAYS 329 (Mark Goldie ed., 1997).
37 Zemer, *supra* note 27, at 933–4.
38 Waldron, *supra* note 20, at 214–18.
39 Simmons, *supra* note 22, at 288–94.
40 Gordon also explained the liability rules could be used to meet Locke's provisos. *See* Gordon, *supra* note 27, at 1572–6. Shiffrin argued that compulsory licenses fit well

with Locke's understanding of property in the context of copyright law. *See* Shiffrin, *supra* note 27, at 157 n. 45.

41 In this context, *see* Molly Van Houweling's argument that adopting a liability rule protection for derivative works supports distributive argument as it only subjects successful second authors to the property rights of first authors. *See* Molly Shaffer Van Houweling, *Distributive Values in Copyright*, 83 TEX. L. REV. 1535, 1569 (2005).

42 Nozick, *supra* note 24, at 175–6.

43 Locke, *supra* note 21, at § 47.

44 Merges, *supra* note 27, at 56–7.

45 Hughes, *supra* note 27, at 327.

46 Peter Drahos, A PHILOSOPHY OF INTELLECTUAL PROPERTY 51 (1996).

47 Gordon Hull, *Clearing the Rubbish: Locke, the Waste Proviso, and the Moral Justification of Intellectual Property*, 23 PUB. AFFAIRS Q. 67, 81 (2009).

48 The waste proviso is applied here in retrospect, meaning after property was acquired, and is meant to resolve market failures and not to affect the ex-ante distribution of rights. It incorporated economic analysis of copyright to the Lockean approach. Under this approach, my analysis in Part II is relevant here as well. A different market analysis of the waste proviso in the context of copyright was suggested by Damstedt, who argued that intellectual works automatically create infinite copies of such works that could never be fully used by the owner thus violating the sufficiency proviso. *See* Damstedt, *supra* note 27, at 1182–3.

49 Simmons, *supra* note 22, at 285–6.

50 *See, e.g.*, Locke, *supra* note 21, at § 37; Simmons, *supra* note 21, at 285; Waldron, *supra* note 20, at 207.

51 Waldron, *supra* note 20, at 207–8.

52 Ernest J. Weinrib, CORRECTIVE JUSTICE 2 (2012).

53 *Id.* at 11. Weinrib explained this framework through the distinction between factual and normative gains and losses. *See* Ernst J. Weinrib, THE IDEA OF PRIVATE LAW 114–20 (2012).

54 *See* Weinrib, *supra* note 52, at 9.

55 Immanuel Kant, *The Metaphysics of Morals, in* PRACTICAL PHILOSOPHY 6:229 (Mary J. Gregor trans. & ed., 1996) (1797).

56 *Id.*, at 6:231. For elaboration on Kant's free will approach *see* Weinrib, *supra* note 52, at 87–95.

57 *Id.*, at 6:231, 6:261, 6:268.

58 Arthur Ripstein, FORCE AND FREEDOM: KANT'S LEGAL AND POLITICAL PHILOSOPHY 95 n.13 (2009). For a similar argument *see* Neil Netanel, *Copyright Alienability Restrictions and the Enhancement of Author Autonomy: A Normative Evaluation*, 24 RUTGERS L.J. 374, 374–5 (1993). According to Ripstein, in contrast to Locke and Hegel, Kant understood property as external to an individual's personhood and not a thing in which personhood is embedded. Here, I will discuss copyright as something external to the personhood of an individual. The discussion on Hegel below will be different. For another Kantian exploration of copyright *see* Kim Treiger-Bar-Am, *Kant on Copyright: Rights on Transformative Authorship*, 25 CARDOZO ARTS & ENT. L.J. 1059 (2008).

59 Merges, *supra* note 27, at 77–8.

60 Abraham Drassinower, *A Rights-Based View of the Idea/Expression Dichotomy in Copyright Law*, 16 CAN. J.L. & JURIS. 1, 10–17 (2003); Abraham Drassinower, *Taking User Rights Seriously, in* IN THE PUBLIC INTEREST: THE FUTURE OF CANADIAN COPYRIGHT LAW 462, 468–72 (2005).

61 Abraham Drassinower, WHAT'S WRONG WITH COPYING? 56 (2015).

62 *Id.*, at 111–15.

63 The understanding of copyright infringement as compelled speech was implicit in the court's decision in Salinger v. Random House, Inc., 811 F.2d 90 (2d Cir. 1987). One of the court's justifications to deny the defendant's fair use argument is that his

unauthorized biography of J.D. Salinger was giving the impression that Salinger did actually write the paraphrased texts included in it. *Id.*, at 23–5.

64 Drassinower, *supra* note 61, at 222–4.

65 In fact, Kant himself referred to this conclusion almost implicitly as follows: "But if someone so alters another's book (abridges it, adds to it, or revises it) that it would even be a wrong to pass it off any longer in the name of the author of the original, then the revision in the editor's own name is not unauthorized publication and therefore not impermissible. For here another author, through his publisher, carries on with the public a different affair from the first, and therefore does not interfere with him in his affair with the public." *See* Immanuel Kant, *On the Wrongfulness of Unauthorized Publication of Books, in* PRACTICAL PHILOSOPHY 8:86–8:87 (1785) (Mary J. Gregor trans. & ed., 1996). For criticism on attempts to rely solely on Kant's literal text in this regards *see* Merges, *supra* note 27, at 78 n. 40.

66 For elaboration on the full model and the cases of forced joint-ownership under corrective justice *see* Omri Rachum-Twaig & Ohad Somech, *The Right-Based View of the Cathedral: Liability Rules and Corrective Justice*, 2017 PEPPERDINE L. REV. 461 (2017). In short, the argument is that some actions which do not constitute wrongs may lead to situations of joint ownership or accession between the property rights of two individuals.

67 *See* also Ripstein, *supra* note 58, at 89–99.

68 This model could explain the decision of the German Constitutional Court regarding the "free use" (freie Benutzung) doctrine. The court decided that the second author's freedom to use parts of protected works is compatible with the first author's right in his work. Moreover, the court further suggested that a setting a fair compensation for such use conforms with the freedom of both authors. *See* BVerfG, 1 BvR 1585/13, §§ 78–80 Mai 31, 2016.

69 "Transformative use" was coined by Judge Leval in his Article Pierre N. Leval, *Toward a Fair Use Standard*, 103 HARV. L. REV. 1105 (1990). It was also adopted by the Supreme Court. *See* Campbell v. Acuff-Rose Music Inc., 510 U.S. 569, 576 (1994).

70 *Id.* at 579.

71 For discussion, *see* Rebecca Tushnet, *Content, Purpose, or Both*, 90 WASH. L. REV. 869 (2015). *See also* Pamela Samuelson, *Possible Futures of Fair Use*, 90 WASH. L. REV. 815, 843–50 (2015).

72 *See* Anthony R. Reese, *Transformativeness and the Derivative Work Right*, 31 COLUM. J. L. & ARTS 467, 484, 494 (2008); Tushnet, *supra* note 71, at 887; Samuelson, *supra* note 71, at 843–4.

73 Authors Guild v. Google, Inc., 2015 U.S. App. LEXIS 17988, *27 (2d Cir. 2015).

74 Georg Friedrich Hegel, PHILOSOPHY OF RIGHT ¶¶ 34–41 (1821) (T.M. Knok trans., 1967); Waldron, *supra* note 20, at 353–63; Peter G. Stillman, *Property, Contract, and Ethical Life in Hegel's Philosophy of Right, in* HEGEL AND LEGAL THEORY 205, 210 (Drucila Cornell, Michel Rosenfeld & David Gray Carlson eds, 1991).

75 Hegel, *supra* note 74, at ¶¶ 34–44.

76 Waldron, *supra* note 20, at 361–65.

77 *Id.*, at 370–4. It is important to note that this part of Hegel's theory was heavily criticized by Karl Marx. Marx argued that if private property is necessary to fulfill the manifestation of personhood, but at the same time limits other persons from obtaining property and fulfilling their own personhood, Hegel's justification collapses and leads to an unjust society. Karl Marx & Friedrich Engels, THE COMMUNIST MANIFESTO 33–4 (1848) (The Floating Press, 2008). Hegel was explicitly aware of this point, but explained that his doctrine of right does not include distributive considerations, but is always subject to other normative considerations of "ethical life" (sittlichkeit) that may trump private rights based on distributive considerations. *See* Waldron, *supra* note 20, at 387–8; Stillman, *supra* note 74 at 209.

78 Margaret Jane Radin, *Property and Personhood*, 34 STAN. L. REV. 957 (1982).

79 This interpretation was suggested by Neil Netanel. *See* Neil Netanel, *Copyright Alienability Restrictions*, 24 RUTGERS L.J. 374, 377 n. 132 (1993).
80 *Id.*, at 378–80.
81 Hughes, *supra* note 27, at 337–41.
82 Voegtli, *supra* note 7, at 1253–4.
83 For a similar criticism on modern interpretations of Hegel *see* Drahos, *supra* note 46, at 79–80.
84 Hegel, *supra* note 74, at 69. Hegel added that in his times no one spoke of plagiarism and implied (perhaps sarcastically) that the sense of honor was enough to eliminate plagiarism or that (more realistically) plagiarism ceased to be considered immoral since the use of intellectual products to make new intellectual works that change the originals are creative enough not to be considered plagiarism. *Id.* However, it must be noted that in Hegel's lifetime at the end of the eighteenth century German copyright laws only included prohibitions on reprinting of print editions. *See, e.g.*, Prussian Statute Book (ALR), Berlin (1794) §§ 996–1036, Primary Sources on Copyright (Lionel Bentley & Martin Kretschmer eds, 1450–1900), http://www.copyrighthistory.org/cam/tools/request/showRepresentation.php?id=representation_d_1794&pagenumber=1_3&imagesize=small#TranscriptionDisplay; Reprinting Regulation for the Grand Duchy of Baden, Karlsruhe (1806), Primary Sources on Copyright (Lionel Bentley & Martin Kretschmer eds, 1450–1900), http://www.copyrighthistory.org/cam/tools/request/showRepresentation?id=representation_d_1806, that granted authors and publishers the exclusive right to reprint book editions in the kingdom of Prussia and the Duchy of Baden, where Hegel lived (in the cities of Berlin and Heidelberg respectively).
85 Hans-Georg Gadamer, TRUTH AND METHOD 306 (2nd edn, Joel Weinsheimer and Donald G. Marshall trans. & revs., 2004).
86 Roberta Rosenthal Kwall, THE SOUL OF CREATIVITY 2–3 (2010).
87 Zohar Efroni, ACCESS-RIGHT: THE FUTURE OF DIGITAL COPYRIGHT LAW 11–13 (2010).
88 Gadamer, *supra* note 85, at 291, 298, 305–306. For elaboration on Gadamer's notion of understanding *see* Jean Grondin, *Gadamer's Basic Understanding of Understanding, in* THE CAMBRIDGE COMPANION TO GADAMER 36 (Robert J. Dostal ed., 2002).
89 Gadamer, *supra* note 85, at 307–308, 320–21.
90 *Id.*, at 390.

4 The derivative works right

A critical review

I. Introduction

Most copyright laws afford first owners an extensive right to control the creation of derivative products of their work, meaning the right to make works that are based substantially on the first work. In most cases, this is an exclusive right that prohibits others from making such derivative works without the consent of the first author, subject to general rights and defenses such as fair use. In Chapter 3 we saw that the justifications to grant such an extensive right to control derivative works are weak, when considering the main theoretical approaches to copyright law, while such theories do justify a more limited right of the first owner in such derivative works. Thus, I argued that the right to make derivative works must be adjusted to allow second authors to use expressions from first works more freely in comparison to the creation of mere reproductions. The purpose of this chapter is to critically review the current right to make derivative works and explain why it should be adjusted to fit its underlying justifications, and which aspects of the right should be adjusted. The following chapter will propose the way to make such adjustments in order to resolve the current difficulties.

I am not the first to review the difficulties raised by the derivative works right in its current form. However, despite the current treatment of such difficulties, I believe that the current criticism does not sufficiently address the ways to resolve such difficulties. This is because most commentators depart from the viewpoint that the derivative works right is overbroad. Most critical literature is based on the historical development of the derivative works right as an extension to the reproduction right and its vague statutory definition. The historical expansion process and the broad statutory definition led to the fear that first owners will receive too much control over first works and limit the ability of second authors to engage in creative activities. Such fear led commentators to focus on the scope of the right – meaning, when will a specific work be considered a derivative, both with respect to the relationship between derivative works and reproduction and with respect to the extent such right expands the reproductions right to control abstract components of the first work (or protecting ideas and not expressions).

I argue that although current literature has properly reviewed the question of the scope of the right, meaning the extent to which it should (or not) expand the reproduction right, the current debate only focusses on the intersection between the two rights but has not properly reviewed the justifications for an independent right to make derivative works separate from the reproduction right. A by-product of the focus of the current literature is that insufficient discussion has been dedicated to the appropriate remedies that should be afforded when the derivative works right is infringed, separately and without regard to the reproduction right. In other words, I believe that current literature lacks a proper discussion on the scope of the right to make derivative works in light of its independent justifications, as well as of its proper corresponding remedies. This chapter seeks to fill this gap.

To show the existing gap in the literature, I will address the historical development of the derivative works right alongside the expansion of the reproduction right in United States and English laws. Such parallel development of the two rights has led, as I will show, to a *de facto* overlap between the two. Such overlap, I argue, does not allow the independent existence of the derivative works right due to the fact that almost every action that amounts to the making of a derivative work will be considered as a reproduction under current law. In addition, the overlap between the two rights does not allow courts to legally differentiate between them, both in terms of scope and available remedies. Therefore, to the extent that there is a justification for the independent existence of the derivative works right, and to the extent that such justification supports a weaker formulation of the right in terms of remedies, discussing the scope of the derivative works right alone cannot be sufficient.

In the previous chapter I argued that each of the main theoretical approaches to copyright law in general, and the derivative works right in particular, support an independent derivative works right which is separate from the reproduction right. This is because it would create a space in which first authors could enjoy the fruits of the first work and remain somewhat connected to it, while at the same time second authors would be free to engage in creative activity also based on protected expressions from existing works. According to the economic analysis of copyright law we saw that it is unclear why an exclusive right to make derivative works is necessary to incentivize authors to create *ex ante* due to the other exclusive rights in the copyright bundle. However, we saw that there is value in allowing first authors to enjoy some of the gains from the second work to maximize the incentives to create in the first place. In addition, we saw that granting an exclusive right to make derivative works causes significant costs and burdens; inhibiting access to existing works for the purpose of enriching the creative world by making new derivative works. Thus, absent clear empirical evidence, the economic approach will support an independent right to make derivative works which grants the first author a portion of the gains from future derivative works while allowing second authors to make such works without the former's consent. Other right-based approaches to copyright law support the independent existence of a derivative works right. Under the Lockean approach, it seems that granting an exclusive right to make derivative works will lead, in many cases, to the violation of the sufficiency proviso as well as the non-waste proviso, which contradicts the Lockean justification for private property altogether. However, we saw that limiting the first author's right does not necessarily mean revoking it altogether, rather contracting it in a manner that will preserve the connection between the first author and the derivative work even if not granting her full control over it. According to corrective justice as well, even if a derivative works right could be justified at all, it does not need to be an exclusive right affording its owner a right for injunctive relief. This is because the second author's freedom to act in the world as an author must be equal to that of the first author, even when considering expressions included in the first work. However, it is difficult, under this approach, to ignore the first author's right in derivative works based on expressions from her first work.

The key to adjusting the derivative works right to its underlying justifications, therefore, lies in two main features. The first, separating between the right and the reproduction right and setting a clear border between them. Such a separation is required both theoretically and practically to avoid the current discussion which entangles the reproduction right and the derivative works right in an inseparable way as I will explain below. The second is the strength of remedies afforded to the right's owner. These two aspects are interrelated and the difficulties of the derivative works right cannot be resolved without treating both aspects for several reasons. First, the strength of the derivative works right, like every other legal right, is dependent both on its scope of applicability and on the strength of its accompanying remedies, and these two aspects are important criteria for its proper design. Second, limiting the remedies afforded to the right's owner without separating them from the reproduction right is useless, since this would leave the applicability of the reproduction right unchanged in almost every case of derivative works, together with the strong remedies for the reproduction right. Limiting the scope of the right alone would be insufficient too, because changing only this aspect will effectively bring about the elimination of the derivative works right. Therefore, my argument is that the derivative works right could only be adjusted to fit its underlying justification by limiting its remedies on the one hand while completely separating it from the reproduction right on the other. The discussion on how to design such an adjustment will appear in Chapter 5 below.

This chapter too will demonstrate how finding a match between the positive right to make derivative works and its underlying justifications could relieve the tension between the right and non-legal approaches to creativity as depicted in Chapters 1 and 2. We saw that using prior domain-relevant knowledge (including protected expressions) is an inseparable part of the cognitive process of creation and that the ability to use common building blocks from existing works and identify them in new works enables and establishes creative patterns and is a cornerstone for attaching meaning to creative products. Separating the derivative works right from the reproduction right well aligns with these non-legal approaches that show a qualitative difference between mere reproduction, which is generally not creative, and the making of derivative works which is a creative act in its essence. Separating the two rights will give effect to such qualitative difference between the two underlying activities as far as creativity is concerned, and limiting the respective remedies will support a wider use of preexisting expressions for creative activities that enrich the creative world. In this sense, the principles I suggest for adjusting the derivative works right with its underlying justifications fit with non-legal approaches for creativity, even if they do not result from them.

This chapter will progress as follows: Part II will present the historical development of the derivative works right alongside the expansion of the reproduction right in the United States and England, in order to lay the foundations for the discussion of the overlap between the two rights and explain its origin; Part III will explain the existing overlap between the two rights, whether by statute or by judicial interpretation, and will demonstrate the need to separate them; Part IV will present and characterize the existing literature on the scope of the derivative works right and discuss its deficiencies and their implications; Part V will explain why adjusting the derivative works right to fit its underlying justification (as discussed in Chapter 3), requires limiting its remedies and completely separating it from the reproduction right. The following chapter will propose and outline the just and most efficient way to make such adjustment and resolve the difficulties raised by the current formulation of the right.

II. The development of the derivative works right

The development of the derivative works right to its current formulation is interrelated to the development and expansion of the reproduction right. I will explore such parallel development, *inter alia*, based on prior literature on this subject, in order to lay the foundation for the discussion below and to clarify certain necessary terms.

1) The reproduction right

The reproduction right is the most basic and oldest right in copyright law. The origin of the right is in the beginning of copyright law when it was meant to protect the print industry and publishers from manual copying of their published books.[1] The first statute to include the reproduction right in its most basic sense was the English Statute of Anne of 1709, that granted authors the exclusive right to "print, reprint or import their books."[2] Similarly, the United States first copyright act of 1790 granted the authors of books, tables and maps the exclusive right to "print, reprint, publish and sell" their works.[3] In this basic sense, the reproduction right protected authors only from photocopying or from literal copying of their works, meaning only the re-making or reprinting of the work in its entirety and in a manner identical to the original copy would be considered copyright infringement in that time.[4]

Over time, the reproduction right in United States law was expanded in a line of court decisions. It was first expanded to protect the copying of only parts of the original work.[5] Later, in a famous case, the Supreme Court decided that the motion picture "Ben Hur" was based on a similar literary work thus infringing the author's right to transform the work between different media.[6] A further significant expansion of the reproduction right was in the protection granted by United States courts to fictional characters from cinematographic, visual or literary works independently from the entire protected work. Thus, Judge Learned Hand determined that, as a matter of principle, a character could be protected independent of the general plot to the extent that it could be considered original standing alone.[7] And indeed, courts often ruled that fictional characters are standalone protected works.[8]

Today, the reproduction right in United States law is defined as the right "to reproduce the copyrighted work in copies or phonorecords."[9] To show that the reproduction right was infringed, a plaintiff must first show that the work was copied as a matter of fact.[10] But mere copying is not enough to prove copyright infringement. The main condition developed in United States case law is that an infringement must show *substantial similarity* to the protected work.[11] To establish an infringement of the reproduction right the plaintiff could prove literal copying, meaning that the entire work was copied verbatim, or substantial similarity, meaning that a substantial part of the first work was copied, quantitatively or qualitatively.[12] Although the substantial similarity requirement clarifies that the reproduction right does not protect insignificant parts of the protected expression, it is an expansion of the reproduction right in that partial reproduction still constitutes infringement.

English law reveals a similar development. At first, as noted, the Statue of Anne of 1709 granted authors only the exclusive right to print and import their books. This was the main protection afforded by English copyright laws in the nineteenth century, which expanded the protection to dramatic works, even if unprinted, and granted authors the exclusive right to publically display them.[13] Thus, much like the United States, at that period translating a literary work did not infringe copyright and that was the case also for dramatization of literary works.[14] However, at the turn of the century, courts in England began expanding the reproduction right and ruled that in some cases incorporating partial reproduction of works in new works did infringe copyright.

With the enactment of the Copyright Law of 1911, the legislator adopted an expansion of the reproduction right to substantial parts of the protected work.[15] Such expansion included two main types of uses of preexisting expressions – taking a substantial part of the work and using it independently and using substantial parts of the original work to change such work or to make a new work – or a combination of both.[16] The expansion of the reproduction right to partial reproduction was preserved under the current English Copyright Act. The Act grants the copyright owner the exclusive right to copy the work and determines that such right applies to substantial parts of the work as well.[17] Much like United States law, English law requires that copying would be established as a matter of fact, and that the copying would be of a substantial part, qualitatively and quantitatively.[18]

2) The right to make derivative works

The right to make derivative works is a far newer right in comparison to the reproduction right and is a direct continuation of the gradual expansion of the latter. From an international perspective, the original language of the Berne Convention, as well as several following amendments, did not include any reference to the derivative works right and only referred to the right of the author to translate a work or transfer it to another medium, to the extent that it does not amount to a new work.[19] The Berne Convention first mentioned a broader right to make adaptations of a work only in the Brussels Protocol of 1948.[20] In its current and very expansive definition, the right to make derivative works was first legislated as an independent right in 1976 as part of the new United States Copyright Act.[21] But a more limited right to make derivative work existed earlier in conjunction with the expanded reproduction right.[22] First, in 1870, the exclusive right of the author to translate her work or to dramatize it was acknowledged.[23] Then, in the United States Copyright Act of 1909, the author's exclusive right to make abridgements and adapt it if it is a musical work were also legislated.[24] Today, the right to make derivative works under United States law is defined as the right to make a work based on one or more preexisting works, with a list of exemplars.[25]

American case law adopted standards for determining whether a specific work amounts to a derivative work, an independent original work or mere reproduction. To constitute a derivative work, the work must include the preexisting work in its entirety or a significant part thereof, meaning that basing on trivial elements from the first work or on unprotected components such as ideas or facts is insufficient.[26] In addition, to meet the definition of a derivative work, the work utilizing preexisting expressions must show additional originality. The degree of originality required was discussed in several cases and the established rule determines that substantial additional originality is required in contrast to trivial originality.[27] Nimmer explained that the test for the degree of originality is that the second work would present distinguishable variation from the first work.[28]

The case in England is somewhat different. In contrast to United States law, England did not statutorily determine a wide and independent derivative works right. Instead, the author is granted an exclusive right to make adaptations of the first work, but this right specifies explicit uses that amount to adaptations. The right to make adaptations was introduced in the 1911 Act that determined, on top of the reproduction right, specific right for translations, dramatization and adaptation of dramatic works to non-dramatic media.[29] Later, in the 1956 Copyright Act, and in today's Copyright, Designs and Patents Act, these explicit rights were specifically included in addition to other rights, under the adaptation category.[30] The literature is divided as to whether the adaptation right is indeed an independent right or rather explicit examples for an extension of the reproduction right.[31] This discussion is related to the overlap between the two rights which will be discussed in the following part, but for this part of the discussion it is relevant to mention that the adaptation right under English law does not necessarily exhaust all potential rights of the author with respect to derivative works, as part of the general reproduction right, even if not explicitly mentioned in the Act.[32] Thus, for example, the owner of a literary work under English law will have the exclusive right to make a sequel of such work, although this right is not included in the adaptation right. Therefore, English law does, *de facto*, recognize an exclusive right to make derivative works, even if not explicitly legislated as an independent right.

III. Derivative works and reproduction under current law

1) Overlapping or separate rights

We saw that the derivative works right developed in parallel to the systematic expansion of the reproduction right. This raises the question of the interrelations between the two and whether the first is completely absorbed by the second. For example, with respect to United States law, Nimmer argued that the right to make derivative works is superfluous because for a work to be considered derivative it must be substantially based on preexisting work, meaning that it must always infringe the reproduction right as it included parts that are substantially similar to the first work.[33] Other commentators attempted to show that the overlap is not full since in some cases under positive law some derivative works would not constitute a reproduction of the first work.[34] One example is using a lawful physical copy of the first work to make a derivative work. Such an act does not meet the basic requirements of the reproduction right since no copy of the work was created by the second author.

There are three distinct options with respect to the interrelation between the derivative works right and the reproduction right. First, is that a full overlap exists between the two and the first is fully absorbed by the second. Second, is that partial overlap exists and each right may have independent applicability without triggering the other in some cases. Third, is that the rights are completely independent and no overlap exists. This part will examine United States and English laws and will argue that a full or almost-full overlap exists between the two rights, meaning that almost every derivative work is a reproduction but not all reproductions are derivative works.

2) English law – explicit statutory overlap

As explained, the Copyright, Designs and Patents Act treats the adaptation right separately. Section 21 of the Act determines that an adaptation is exclusively reserved to the owner of the first work and defines which acts amount to adaptations.[35] In addition, the Act explicitly addresses the relationship between the adaptation right and the reproduction right and determines that "no inference shall be drawn from this section as to what does or does not amount to copying a work".[36] It may be inferred by this that an overlap exists between the two rights in the sense that all in cases where adaptations infringe the reproduction right, the existence of an adaptation will not absorb the infringement of the reproduction right.

The statutory language led to two varying opinions in the literature with respect to the overlap between the right. Copinger & Skone James opined that all the exemplars of the adaptation right are in fact an infringement of the reproduction right as well and there is no reason that both rights cannot be infringed by the same act.[37] A different opinion by Laddie, Prescott & Vitoria is that the exemplars for adaptations are mere examples of the expansion of the reproduction right and therefore adaptation under English law is included in the reproduction right and completely overlaps it.[38] Despite the differences between the two opinions, both concur that the making of an adaptation amounts to an infringement of the reproduction right and therefore full overlap exists between the two.

English case law, in the few cases that addressed this issue, identified an overlap as well and acknowledged both approaches to the nature of such overlap. Thus, in Hodgson v. Isaac, the plaintiff argued that his copyright in the autobiography he wrote was infringed by the defendant who wrote and published a script based on it. The plaintiff asserted that the allegedly infringing work was an adaptation of his autobiography. The court specifically addressed the relationship between adaptations and reproduction. The court determined that although the borderline between reproductions and adaptations is unclear, there is no practical importance to the question since an adaptation is in fact a more specific and explicit definition for cases of partial reproduction of a protected work.[39] The court clarified that in order to determine whether copyright was infringed in adaptation cases, the general tests for unlawful reproduction and copying should be used.[40] This is in line with Laddie, Prescott & Vitoria since the practical meaning of this ruling is that there is no separate right of adaptation, rather it is completely absorbed by the reproduction right.

A slightly different approach was adopted in Abraham Moon & Sons Ltd. v. Thornber. There, the plaintiff argued that her copyright in fabric prints for furniture she created was infringed. The print was defined by a stamp depicting the characters of the print patterns and enabled its reproduction on fabrics. The plaintiff argued that the copyright in the stamp was infringed by the defendants who printed fabrics based on the stamp and marketed them. The specific action was for infringement of the reproduction right but the court raised the question of the interrelations with the adaptation right. The court clarified that according to the tests adopted by the case law, the defendants' print copied a substantial part of the stamp, and that additionally, it constituted an adaptation.[41] The court concluded that the defendants' prints infringed the copyrighted work. This is in line with Copinger & Skone James' approach, since even though the court did not explicitly determine that the adaptation is an independent right, it did acknowledge that a certain act could constitute both an adaptation and a reproduction. In any event, this approach too identifies a full overlap between the rights.

The overlap between adaptations and reproductions in English law is also evident in the identical tests for determining whether such actions actually occurred. Thus, the guiding cases for copyright infringement explicitly determined that to show such infringement the plaintiff must prove substantial similarity between the first and second work resulting from copying or adaptation of the first.[42] Determining a unified test for proving both reproduction and adaptation leads, *de facto*, to an overlap between the two.

3) United States law – overlap by case law

In contrast to English law, United States law does treat the reproduction and derivative work rights separately, and at least from the statutory language it appears that the two are separate rights. Section 106 of the Copyright Act defines the two rights in separate subsections.[43] However, a review of the derivative works right case law reveals that the overlap between it and the reproduction right is almost full, and that Nimmer's claim that the derivative works right is superfluous is not far from the truth.

The overlap between the two rights in United States law results from the tests adopted by courts for proving infringement of each right. Similar to English law, in the United States too courts determined in various cases that an infringement of the derivative works right occurs only when substantial parts are taken from the first work under the substantial similarity test. One example is found in the case of Midway Mfg. Co. v. Artic Int'l, Inc. There, the plaintiff argues that the defendant infringed its copyright in a video game by creating a faster version. The court reviews the claim under the derivative works right and clarified that the allegedly infringing work should contain expressions that are substantially similar to the first work in order to prove infringement.[44]

In a later case, the court of appeals for the ninth circuit reviewed the claim that the movie E.T., produced by the defendant, infringed the plaintiffs copyright in a musical she created. In that case, the plaintiff argued that both reproduction and derivative works rights were infringed. The court rejected the plaintiff's argument that a derivative work should include every work that is based on a preexisting work and explained that the legal standard for infringement is that the second work must be substantially similar to the first work under the terms of the reproduction substantial similarity test.[45]

This decision echoed in further decisions throughout the years and was repeated in the second circuit in Twin Peaks Prods. v. Publ'ns Int'l, Ltd. There, the plaintiffs argued that a book published by the defendants infringed their copyright in screenplays of several episodes of a television series they created. There too, the court addressed the derivative works right after reviewing the infringement of the reproduction right using the substantial similarity test. The court explicitly agreed with Nimmer's claim that discussing an infringement of the derivative works right is unnecessary when the infringement of the reproduction right is claimed due to the similar tests for the infringement of both rights. In addition, the court determined that since the defendants' book included substantially similar parts to the plaintiffs' screenplays, while transferring them to another medium, the derivative works right was infringed under existing doctrine.[46]

The most explicit reference to the overlap between the two rights exists in the decision of the court of appeals for the second circuit in Well-Made Toy Mfg. Corp. v. Goffa Int'l Corp., as part of reviewing the plaintiff's claim that its copyright in a doll created by it was infringed by the defendant's similar and larger doll. The court addressed the claim for infringement of the derivative work right and referred to its prior ruling in Castle Rock Entm't, Inc., and explained that the plaintiff there also claimed that both rights were infringed. The court explained that "we drew no distinction between the two forms of infringement and addressed both by asking whether the book was substantially similar to the television program."[47]

IV. Existing criticism on the derivative works right

Thus far we have seen that the right to make derivative works and the reproduction right overlap under positive law in the United States and England; almost every infringement of the derivative works right is an infringement of the reproduction right. In this part I will present the criticism of the derivative works right and the suggestions to resolve the difficulties it raises in existing literature, and will point out the deficiencies in such literature. The common approach under current literature is that the derivative works right is overbroad.[48] This is based on two types of justifications. Some commentators argued that the derivative works right excessively limits freedom of speech and therefore must be limited.[49] Others argued that the right is unjustified economically and that it burdens the benefits of creativity more than it contributes to it.[50] This general approach has led to various suggestions to resolve the difficulties raised by the right.

My main argument in this part is that although the literature has addressed the difficulties of the derivative works right theoretically, the question of its proper scope of applicability, and at times the proper scope of its afforded remedies, it has not offered sufficient solutions to such difficulties that address both the positive overlap between the derivative works right and the reproduction right and the independent justifications for a separate derivative works right.

1) Suggestions to limit the scope of the right

One example for a proposal to limit the scope of the derivative works right on an economic basis is found in Glynn Lunney's research. In his research asking to re-evaluate the economic justifications for copyright under the incentive-access paradigm (explained in Chapter 3) based on empirical data, Lunney suggested to contract the reproduction right to apply only to literal or almost-literal copyright of protected expressions.[51] Later, he argued that it is necessary to further limit the derivative works right to apply only to cases where an exact or near-exact transfer of the first work to another medium or language was made.[52] This is perhaps the most limiting suggestion in the literature today and it is based on Lunney's formulation of copyright's economic analysis which did not echo in further copyright literature. According to the economic approach to copyright, even if the derivative works right in its current form is too broad, it is still justified to allow the owner of the first work to gain some revenues from derivative works. Lunney's suggestion does not align with other theoretical approaches to copyright as well, since all main approaches justify the independent existence of a derivative works right separately from the reproduction right, even if in a more limited formulation compared to existing law.

Another suggestion for a significant limitation of the right's scope by changing its definition was brought by Naomi Voegtli. Based on economic, freedom of speech and right-based justifications to copyright, Voegtli suggested the following definition for a derivative work: a work would be considered derivative (1) if it is substantially based on a preexisting work while showing limited originality of its own or if it unjustly diminishes the value of the first works; or (2) if it is a translation, recording, reconstruction or abridgement of the first work.[53] This is a slightly more expansive definition than the one proposed by Lunney as it acknowledges that derivative works may exist even if there was no near-exact transformation of the first work to a different medium. Voegli did not, however, address the effects of her suggestion on the reproduction right.

A similar suggestion was brought by Christina Bohannan. Based on freedom of speech justifications, Bohannan suggested demystifying the definition of derivative works and limiting it to apply only to cases where the expression of the first work was converted to other types of media and not to cases in which the second work is constructed mainly of new content.[54] The value in that, according to her, is that such limitation of the derivative works right will create more certainty as to the interrelations between derivative works and the fair use doctrine in that derivative works will not apply to cases of transformative uses of protected expressions.[55] Bohannan's suggestion is similar to Lunney's and is limiting the derivative works right in a way that does not fit its underlying justifications as discussed in Chapter 3.

The suggestions discussed thus far raise two main concerns. First, they limit the right's scope as an independent right in a manner that does not fir its underlying theoretical justifications. As explained in Chapter 3, the various justifications for the derivative works right support its independent existence. Second, and perhaps more importantly, it is doubtful whether such suggestions could actually achieve their goals – limiting the broad right granted to the first author. Under positive law, these suggestions will indeed limit the cases in which derivative works apply. However, due to the almost complete overlap between the derivative works right and the reproduction right, all actions that are removed from the scope of the derivative works right remain in the scope of the broad and strong reproduction right and in fact grant the first author the same extensive rights under a different name instead of properly designing all rights granted to the author. This point emphasizes why one cannot speak of limiting the scope of the derivative works right without discussing the scope of the reproduction right as well.

In contrast to the above approaches, that depict the common understanding that the derivative works right is overbroad, two commentators purported the opposite, at least to the extent that the expansion of the reproduction right is concerned. Abramowicz argued, based on the economic justification he formulated for the derivative works right, as discussed in Chapter 3, that the rent seeking and rent dissipation expected by authors seeking to develop secondary markets to work justifies the centralized control over such markets by the first author.[56] Samuelson concurred, based on her interpretation of the current definition of the right. She discussed the difficulties raised by the right from a different angle and chose to examine how stable and clear is the definition of the right under current law, and whether it is in line with the historical and constitutional origins of the right as well as with statutory language.[57]

After thoroughly discussing the legislative history of the United States Copyright Act of 1976, Samuelson showed that the birth of the separate derivative works right resulted from the wish to simplify the language of the previous 1909 Act, granting an exclusive right for a long list of uses, on the one hand, and the will to explain in what circumstances and to what extent will a derivative work be considered an independent copyrightable work on the other hand.[58] Therefore, Samuelson argued that in order to interpret the scope of the derivative works right, its broad definition should be read in light of the nine exemplars provided in the statutory text, as well as close analogies to them.[59]

With respect to the explicit statutory exemplars, Samuelson offered three main characteristics. The first is short versions of the first work, the second is faithful renditions such as translations, and the third is transformations of the work from one medium or genre to another.[60] With respect to close analogies to the nine exemplars, Samuelson suggested to include sequels, prequels and works which are direct continuations of the first work, works that express the first work from a different viewpoint (such as criticism or parody) and several other examples from the case law.[61]

Samuelson argued that such interpretation will assist in contracting the borders of the derivative works right and prevent it from applying to a too wide array of cases for which the legislator did not intend to afford copyright protection. She continued to explain what types of works or uses will not amount to a derivative work under her suggested interpretation. First, Samuelson addressed uses explicitly allowed by the Act such as making useful articles based on copyrighted drawings,[62] changes and compatibility modifications to computer software or fair uses.[63] Second, Samuelson explains that works adding parts to existing works also do not infringe the derivative works right.[64] Software add-ons or compatibility features do not infringe the right according to Samuelson.[65]

Samuelson's suggestions examine the scope of the right to make derivative works and limit it to a certain extent. However, these observations discuss the higher end of the right, meaning the extent it expands the reproduction right. It is undoubtedly important to discuss such contraction of the right as it relaxes the concerns regarding its overbreadth. The uses mentioned by Samuelson will become allowed and will expand the array of expressions that second users could use as part of their creative process. Due to the fact that Samuelson's starting point was that there is no flaw in the current definition of the right it is not surprising (and there can be no criticism on that) that she did not address the scope of the reproduction right and its interrelations with the derivative works right, nor the scope of afforded remedies. I argue that the positive overlap between the two rights calls for a review of the borderline between the two rights, and the theoretical justifications for the derivative works right call for a review of the scope of afforded remedies. In addition, I argue that these two aspects are inevitably interrelated, as will be explained below.

After reviewing the suggestions brought thus far, we can see that except for Lunney's suggestion, none could limit the overall strength of the derivative works right. This is because limiting the right's scope of applicability without addressing its interrelations with the reproduction right cannot fully account for the overall strength of the right. Therefore, I argue that in order to discuss the limitation of the derivative works right, its interrelations with the reproduction right must be addressed as well. I will next discuss suggestions that indeed have addressed such interrelation.

2) Suggestions to clarify the interrelations between the two rights

One of the first commentators to challenge the overlap between the reproduction and derivative works right was Jed Rubenfeld. Rubenfeld reviewed the development of the derivative works right and showed, as was explained above, that at the beginning the reproduction right only protected from literal copying and not from partial reproductions of substantial parts.[66] After thoroughly discussing the parallel development of the two rights, Rubenfeld argued that the expanded reproduction right is in contrast to copyright's underlying principles, to the statutory language and obliterates the derivative works right.[67]

Rubenfeld argued that the key to adjusting copyright law to its underlying constitutional principles is contracting the reproduction right and reviving the distinction between it and the derivative works right. This is due to the fact that a derivative work always includes new additional expressions that cannot be limited under the first amendment to the United States constitution.[68] He suggested to differentiate between the two rights as follows: it must be reviewed if, independent of public domain elements or elements from previous works, the derivative work meets the originality requirement and whether it is considered an original work on its own account despite the fact that it uses preexisting expressions. Rubenfeld added that trivial additions or changes will not be sufficient to determine that a work is derivative, especially when these were added intentional to circumvent the reproduction right.[69] He used Campbell v. Acuff-Rose Music, Inc. as a case study for his proposal, because the first author there ended up without a valid copyright infringement claim,[70] and therefore suggested that the court in this case should have granted a portion of the revenues of the second work to the first author.[71]

Rubenfeld's suggestion was directly criticized by Abramowicz. Abramowicz agreed that an almost complete overlap exists between the two rights due to the substantial similarity test. He also agreed that a doctrine which will better differentiate between the rights will improve the current state.[72] However, he disagreed to the test suggested by Rubenfeld.

Abramowicz's main criticism on Rubenfeld's suggestion focusses on the inability to differentiate between a trivial addition to the first work intended to circumvent the reproduction right and a significant creative addition the exceeds reproduction and amounts to a derivative work. Rubenfeld's suggestion not to acknowledge trivial additions did not satisfy Abramowicz who argued that the threshold of creativity required under such a test is too low. This is also because the originality requirement with respect to derivative works is low and allows for minor changes to be considered independently original works and thus circumvent the reproduction right.[73]

Abramowicz argued that to the extent that Rubenfeld himself supports the basic approach that some uses of existing expressions must be limited and reserved for the first author, there must be a rule that will determine the scope of cases in which such expressions could be used for second works without the consent of the first author. Abramowicz argued that copyright law adopted such rule – the idea/expression dichotomy, as well as the fair use doctrine.[74]

I disagree with Abramowicz due to the fact that the idea/expression dichotomy does not reflect all the balances that copyright law offers to fit its underlying principles. As explained in Chapter 3, the derivative works right has independent justifications from the reproduction right, and these justify the former's separate and independent existence to fulfill a different purpose that the idea/expression dichotomy cannot fulfill alone. In addition, relying on fair use as the main tool to allow creativity based on previous expressions is very problematic since the purpose of this doctrine is different from the purposes of the derivative works right, despite a certain overlap, and cannot hold the entire normative load of the derivative works right. Putting the burden of allowing free uses of preexisting expressions on the fair use doctrine would lead to an "all or nothing" result which will damage the functionality of the doctrine. In addition, under the normative analysis presented in Chapter 3, one could certainly think of cases in which prohibiting a certain use would not be justified on the one hand while denying any gain from the first author would be unjustified on the other hand, and therefore a full permission use will not be adequate. For example, if an author decides to make a sequel to the Harry Potter book series, even if such action should not be prohibited, it is equally unjustified to withhold any interest in such new book from J.K. Rowling.

I discussed the justifications to the derivative works right suggested by Abramowicz, which stem from the product differentiation and rent dissipation economic theories in Chapter 3. Based on these justifications, which I attempted to refute, Abramowicz suggested a new definition to the derivative works and reproduction rights based on the effect that the infringing use has on the first work.[75] According to him, when a use of the first work directly competed with that same work, the right infringed is the reproduction right. Thus, for example, adapting the motion picture "Harry Potter and the Chamber of Secrets" to a black and white version may divert the demand for the first work and will therefore infringe the reproduction right.[76] In contrast, when a use of the first work competes in the secondary market for such work, it is an infringement of the derivative works right. Thus, the making of a sequel to the Harry Potter motion picture will most likely not divert demand for the first work but will clearly compete with other potential sequels and therefore will infringe the derivative works right.[77]

Abramowicz's definition is problematic in several ways. First, as recognized by Abramowicz himself, it may well be that a work utilizing the first work will compete with both the primary and secondary markets of the work at the same time and will therefore infringe both rights.[78] It is unclear that such an overlap is justified. Second, the test suggested by him does not account for the possibility that the use of the first work includes significant additional creativity and originality. Such cases, according to Abramowicz, will infringe the reproduction right without any textual or historical basis and in a manner that contradicts the non-legal understanding of creativity as discussed in the first chapters. Third, and similar to the limitations of the discussions of other commentators due to the overlap between the derivative works right and the reproduction right, the tests suggested by him do not explain the positive difference between this proposal and existing law with respect to the scope of the first author's rights and their strength.

Daniel Gervais also discussed the scope of the derivative works right and its interrelations with the reproduction right. He asked to first define the basic undisputed elements of the derivative works right. He first assumed that when a work fits one of the statutory exemplars in various jurisdictions it is a derivative work.[79] He further assumed that a derivative work transfers or changes a protected expression from the first work to the second work in that it changes it or adds to it. he also assumed that there must be some relativity between the first and second works for the latter to be derivative. In this context the difference between a reproduction and a derivative work, as per Gervais, is that while a reproduction takes a part of the first work, a derivative work takes and transfers or changes what made the first work original in the first place. From all the above, Gervais concluded that the first work must be original and the derivative work should include an additional originality of the second author. Such additional originality, and it alone, will be considered a derivative work and will be copyrightable.

Gervais emphasized that many cases of reproductions do not amount to derivative works (such as citations). An opposite example suggested by Gervais, is using a legal copy of the first work to create a new work without copying the first work, which does not amount to a reproduction.[80]

Beyond the basic principles of the right, Gervais asked to suggest additional defining principles for the derivative works right. First, he suggested that the derivative works right is not a direct continuation of the reproduction right, and despite the overlap between the two, they are based on different justifications.[81] Second, he argued that the derivative work includes a transformation of or an addition to a protection expression from the first work, which makes it copyrightable on its own account. Third, he added that the derivative work must be closely related enough to the first work. Gervais noted that such relativity could be learned from looking at the uses made of the elements that made the first work original in the first place.[82]

The distinction between the two rights suggested by Gervais is that while derivative works transfer and change original parts of the first work, reproduction only transfers expressions from the first work. According to Gervais, this distinction is important since it leads to a different review of the derivative works right in comparison to the reproduction right, which asks whether the original parts of the first work were indeed taken, transferred and changed as part of the derivative work.[83] I find this distinction problematic. It is undoubtedly important to review whether the second work utilized original parts from the first work (i.e., protected expressions). But the same review is conducted as part of the reproduction right when we consider whether a substantial part of the first work was taken, which must always be an original part of the first work.

Gervais suggested the following formula for the existence of a derivative work:

> the application of the derivative right is an equation that reflects the amount of originality of the primary work, the quality and quantity of the originality transferred from the primary work to the derivative work, and the amount of originality added by the author of the derivative work.[84]

Despite Gervais' objection to the argument that a derivative work is in fact a reproduction with additional creativity, it appears that his formula supports the exact same claim. The first part of the formula, reviewing the amount of originality transferred from the first to the second work is in fact the standard for reviewing reproduction, focussing on whether a substantial part of the first work was taken granted that such part must be a protected original expression. The second part of the formula addresses the additional originality of the second author. Therefore, there is no substantial difference between Gervais' approach and those of Goldstein and Rubenfeld, although Gervais did more deeply treat the question of the additional originality required from the second author. However, Gervais too did not explain how his distinctions change the positive legal status due to the almost complete overlap between the reproduction and derivative works rights, and therefore his suggestion is insufficient for the purpose of limiting the scope and strength of the derivative works right.

One more commentator that explicitly discussed the scope of the derivative works right, and implicitly addressed its interrelations with the reproduction right is Chris Newman. Newman suggested to understand copyright as prohibiting the unauthorized use aimed at transferring the same expressive experience of the first work to other media or language.[85] Therefore, "copying" expressions from previous works to make new works that do not repeat the expressive experience of the first work does not infringe copyright. In this definition, Neman actually contracts the reproduction right without explicitly discussing it. although I disagree with the basis Newman offered for the interrelations between the two rights and their scope, his suggestion is clear and analytically consistent to the extent it is understood as contracting the reproduction right to apply merely to literal or near-literal copying and limiting the derivative works right to transfers of the expressive experience of the first work to other media.

The discussion thus far helps gather several conclusions with respect to the scope of the derivative works right. First, it is important to discuss the scope of the derivative works right together with the scope of the reproduction right and their interrelations, if the goal is to limit the overall strength of the derivative works right. Second, and to the extent we believe that the two rights have different purposes, in light of their almost complete overlap in positive law, the two rights must be separated because as long as they overlap the right to make derivative works could not be discussed and designed independently. Third, and as I will later show in further detail, to the extent that there is a justification for an independent derivative works right, its overall scope should be discussed together with its accompanying remedies. This is mainly because in order to limit the strength of the right without addressing its remedies, it should be contracted significantly to the point where it has no effective independent existence. In the next part, I will explain what are the necessary main features of the right that should be discussed and changed to fit its underlying justifications.

V. Separation from reproduction and limiting remedies – adjusting the derivative works right to its underlying justifications

The basic assumption of this chapter is that the current right to make derivative work raises significant difficulties in light of its underlying justifications and that it must be adjusted to fit such justification. The previous part explained why the suggestions brought in the current literature were insufficient to make such an adjustment. I will now explain the main aspects of the right that must be redesigned and why. In short, I argue that the derivative works right must be fully separated from the reproduction right, and that its accompanying remedies should be limited, and that only by addressing these two aspects together could we provide a full resolution to the difficulties of the current right. These two aspects are interdependent for two main reasons. First, much like any legal right, the strength of the derivative works right is affected not only by its scope of applicability but also by the remedies it affords the owner, and these two features are interrelated. Second, due to the theoretical justifications for the right, as discussed in Chapter 3, it should exist independently of the reproduction right on the one hand, but the current control it grants the right owner is unjustified and must be limited. Therefore, addressing only the scope of applicability will not be enough and we must also address the strength of the right's remedies and find the proper balance between the two.

1) The interrelations between the right's scope and remedies

To fully explain the interdependency between the scope of the derivative works right and its remedies, I will dedicate a short discussion to the general interrelations of rights and remedies.

The discussion of rights and remedies customarily divides into three main approaches: the superiority of remedies approach, the superiority of rights approach and the unity of rights and remedies approach.[86] The first approach is evident in the Roman expression, and the respective common law rule, of *ubi remedium ibi ius*, which was resurrected in the writing of Oliver Wendel Holmes. Holmes suggested that one cannot speak of a right without a remedy since rights are only predictions of legal outcomes, which eventually come down to remedies only.[87]

The second approach of rights superiority is the complete opposite. Under this approach, rights are completely independent of their remedies and could exist without remedies at all. In addition, the remedies should result from their respective right and be in line with it. This approach resulted from the historical effort to organize the common law that was based on rights and causes of action in a systematic manner, and is related to formalistic approaches to the law which see rights as absolute entitlements.[88]

The third approach of rights and remedies' unity sees the remedy as an inseparable component of the right, much like other components that constitute it. This approach is a result of criticism of the right superiority approach, without falling back to the other extreme. One of the main commentators that offered a theoretical basis for this approach was Carl Llewellyn. According to Llewellyn, rights are important because they provide the underlying normative purpose for remedies. However, he explained that rights should not be unlimited and that an important way to limit and design them is their respective remedies. Therefore, remedies should be conceived as inseparable elements of rights, and rights as designed by their remedies.[89]

It appears that the third approach is mostly echoed in private law jurisprudence. One significant adoption of this approach is in the economic analysis of Guido Calabresi and Douglas Melamed, who offer the distinction between liability rules and property rules. Under this approach, rights (or entitlements) are defined by their respective protection rules – the remedies.[90] Another example for the adoption of this approach in private law is in the concept of the bundle of rights. According to the bundle of rights approach to private property, developed by Hoefeld and Honore, the property right consists of various events that define different types of ownership in property. Such events also refer to the various remedies afforded to the right's owner such as the right to exclude, the right to transfer ownership, the right to manage, the right to revenues and the right to prevent expropriation.[91] Waldron, for example, explained that such events should not be understood as necessary elements for ownership or for rights. He suggested to think of ownership and property as a concept, and the various rights in the bundle as potential conceptions for a specific ownership regime.[92] This approach is also in line with the pluralistic approach to property suggested by Hanoch Dagan, according to which property should be conceived as various institutions constituted by specific aggregations of rights according to their underlying normative justifications, which are designed by their respective remedies.[93]

It appears, if so, that remedies have a significant effect on the design and strength of rights. This is true to rights in general and to the derivative works right in particular. Therefore, I argue that the overall strength of the derivative works right could not be fully addressed and designed without considering its respective remedies.[94]

2) The underlying justifications require limiting the right's remedies and separating it from the reproduction right

Thus far we have seen that under current law the derivative works right almost completely overlaps the reproduction right. I further argued that the full strength of the right could not be understood without addressing its respective remedies. The current literature does not sufficiently treat these matters in its attempts to adjust the right to its normative justifications. I will now turn to explain why the adjustment of the right to its underlying justifications requires both its full separation from the reproduction right and limiting its respective remedies, and why only adjusting its scope of applicability cannot suffice.

Despite the strong interrelations between rights and remedies, the overall strength of the right could be, as a matter of principle, limited by adjusting the scope of applicability alone. However, for such limitation to have actual effect, the derivative works right should be almost completely limited, leaving a very narrow independent derivative works right. This was, in fact, the approach of Lunney, Bohannan and Newman, each in her or his turn suggesting limitation of the right's scope to the extent that it is almost completely eliminated. This is a plausible approach based on an inner logic. However, as I explained, such significant limitation of the right does not fit its underlying justifications. The main approaches to copyright law justify the existence of an independent derivative works right, separate from the reproduction right, that grants the first author some interest in second works significantly based on the first work. Thus, focussing on the scope of the right alone to adjust it to its underlying justifications cannot resolve the difficulties it raises.

Similarly, it is possible, in principle, to limit the right's strength only by limiting its respective remedies, for example by switching from a property rule protection to a liability rule protection that allows second authors to use prior expressions more freely. However, the remedies afforded to the right's owner are not the sole component affecting its strength and it will always be required to review its scope of applicability to determine if it meets the underlying justifications. Given the overlap between the rights in positive law, addressing the derivative works right's remedies alone cannot resolve the difficulties either, because the reproduction right will always apply in parallel and will afford its owner a wider array of remedies that undercuts the limitation of the remedies afforded to the derivative works right.

Therefore, the separation of the derivative works right from the reproduction right together with limiting its respective remedies is required for two main reasons. First, addressing both these aspects is required due to the discussion on the underlying justifications of the right as explained in Chapter 3. As we say there, the theoretical approaches to copyright law justify an independent existence of the derivative works right, separately from the reproduction right. The almost complete overlap between the rights under current law does not allow such independent existence and hence a more precise definition for the derivative works right, which will set the borderline between the two rights, is required. In addition, all approaches justify a wider freedom for second authors to use preexisting expressions while maintaining some interest of the first author in such works. Therefore, there is a direct justification to limit the respective remedies of the right and to switch from a full control regime to a more relaxed regime that affords more freedom to second authors. Addressing both these aspects – scope and remedies – is also in line with the theoretical approaches explaining the interrelations between rights and remedies.

Second, the full separation between the two rights in positive law is required, as a practical matter, due to the need to limit the strength of the remedies afforded to the derivative works right. The current full overlap between the two rights cannot allow limiting the respective remedies of the derivative works right, because as long as the reproduction right has overlapping applicability, all cases of derivative works will also be governed by the remedies regime offered for the reproduction right. Therefore, if the underlying justifications for the derivative works right require the limitation of its respective remedies as a normative matter, it must first be fully separated from the reproduction right in a positive manner so that each right will have its respective proper remedies model. It is important to note that this purpose could be fulfilled without formally separating the two rights, if it would be determined that in overlapping cases, the only remedies afforded will be those attached to the derivative works right and not the reproduction right.

3) Adjusting the derivative works right to its underlying justifications resolves the tension with non-legal approaches to creativity

Separating the derivative works right from the reproduction right and limiting its respective remedies is required due to the underlying normative justifications for the right. However, it is interesting to see that adjusting these two features of the right to match their underlying justifications also resolved the tension with the non-legal approaches to creativity explained in Chapters 1and 2.

One of the conclusions from the discussion of the cognitive process of creation in Chapter 2 was that this field of knowledge does not support the legal distinction between creative uses of ideas and creative uses of prior expressions, due to the centrality of both components as part of the use of prior domain-relevant knowledge and memory in the creative process. Another conclusion was that there is a material difference between creative and non-creative activities. The suggested separation between the rights resolves a significant part of this tension. First, it is well in line with the understanding that the actions underlying both rights are qualitatively different. Thus, the reproduction right will apply (in general) to non-creative activities and the derivative works right will apply to creative activities. Second, the separation is one step of a larger plan to remodel the derivative works right to allow more uses of preexisting expressions for the making of new works. Such remodeling of the derivative works right is well in line with the importance and centrality of using prior expressions in the creative process.

Accordingly, changing the remedies model of the derivative works right to fit its underlying justifications and to allow second authors to more freely use prior expressions, will also resolve the described tension. A new remedies model that allows second authors to use preexisting expressions for the making of new works would be much in line with the conclusions from the cognitive psychology discussion according to which there is no qualitative difference between creative uses of ideas or expressions. Even if such a new derivative works right would still lead to material distinctions between original works based on ideas and derivative works based on expressions, at least to the extent that remedies are concerned, such a new model would fit the conclusions from the creative studies discussion better than existing law.

The adjustment of the derivative works right to its underlying justifications also relaxes the tensions raised in the discussion on genre theories in Chapter 2. Genre theories show that the use of common building blocks is essential both for the establishment and development of genres and for the meaning-making process to texts and rule systems from the audience point of view. The importance of using common building blocks is based both on existing rules and conventions (derivation) and the development of the existing rules (originality). Genre theories are indifferent to the question whether such use of common building blocks relies on ideas or expressions, so long as it is accompanied by the development and expansion of existing genres or the creation of new genres. In contrast, the use of common building blocks (of any kind) without additional development of the creative discourse does not contribute to the creative world and has no significant role in the eyes of genre theories. Therefore, genre theories too are in line with the suggested separation between the two rights which will establish the qualitative difference between uses of common building blocks that enrich the creative discourse, and those that do not.

We further saw that the main clash between the existing derivative works right and genre theories is in the ability of the first author to prevent second authors from using expressions as common building blocks. Limiting the remedies afforded to the derivative works right and shifting to a model under which a second author could more freely use preexisting expressions will resolve this tension and will be in line with the conclusions from the genre theories discussion.

As explained, although the non-legal discussion does not constitute a standalone normative justification to adjust the current derivative works right, it is well in line with the conclusions based on the right's underlying normative justifications. Although this match does not necessarily create a normative link between the non-legal approaches and legal doctrine, I do not believe that it is merely a happy coincidence, rather another indication that copyright law, when properly adjusted to its underlying normative justifications and fulfilling its overarching goal of supporting creativity, is well in line with a deeper understanding of the creative process and creativity under non-legal fields of knowledge.

V. Conclusion

The aim of this chapter was to establish the argument that in order to adjust the derivative works right to its underlying normative justifications, we must address its two main aspects. First, it must be fully separated from the reproduction right and the borderline between the two must be set. Second, its respective remedies must be limited.

To establish this argument, I reviewed the historical development of the derivative works right alongside the gradual expansion of the reproduction right and showed that as a matter of positive law the two rights almost completely overlap. Based on this conclusion I reviewed the critical literature on the derivative works right and the suggestions brought for its remodeling. We saw that although existing literature does review the question of the right's scope vis-à-vis the reproduction right, it does not sufficiently discuss the borderline between the two in light of their positive overlap and the question of adjusting the derivative right, both in terms of remedies, to its underlying justifications as an independent and separate right.

Finally, we saw why these two aspects – the scope of the right and its remedies – are essential components for the design of the right. I discussed the general interdependency of rights and remedies and explained why the theoretical approaches to copyright law, as discussed in Chapter 3, require the right's separation from the reproduction right as well as limiting its remedies. In addition, we saw that separating the right to make derivative works is also required due to practical reasons involving the said overlap and the normative justification for a different remedies model for each of the rights. The next chapter will focus on outlining the proper, most efficient and just way to implement the principles presented in this chapter.

Notes

1 *See, e.g.*, Brad Sherman & Lionel Bently, THE MAKING OF MODERN INTELLECTUAL PROPERTY LAW: THE BRITISH EXPERIENCE, 1760–1911, 11–13 (1999), arguing that copyright legislation was a direct continuance of the privileges regime that granted full monopolies over printing presses to certain publishers.
2 8 Ann. Ch. 19 (1709).
3 Act of May 31, 1790, Ch. 15, § 1, 1 Stat. 124 (repealed 1831).
4 The protection afforded by the early reproduction right was narrow. *See, e.g.*, Burnett v. Chetwood, 2 Mer. 441, 35 Eng. Rep. 1008 (Ch. 1720). In that case the court rejected a claim that an English translation of a Latin book infringes copyright while ruling that translation does not constitute a reprint of the original work. A similar famous American case was Stowe v. Thomas, 23 Fed. Cas. 201 (C.C.E.D. Pa. 1853), in which the court denied a claim arguing that a German translation of *Uncle Tom's Cabin* infringes copyright. For a review of the early development of the reproduction right *see* Paul Goldstein, *Derivative Rights and Derivative Works in Copyright*, 30 J. COPYRIGHT SOC'Y U.S.A. 209, 211–15 (1983).
5 *See, e.g.*, Daly v. Palmer, 6 F. Cas. 1132 (C.C.S.D.N.Y 1868), in which the court determined that a play depicting identifiable scenes from a previous work infringes copyright, and the famous ruling in Metro-Goldwyn Pictures Corp., 81 F.2d 49, 56 (2d Cir. 1936), according to which "it is enough that substantial parts were lifted; no plagiarist can excuse the wrong by showing how much of his work he did not pirate."
6 Kalem Co. v. Harper Bros., 222 U.S. 55 (1911).
7 Nichols v. Universal Pictures Corp., 45 F.2d 119 (2d Cir. 1930).
8 *See* Melville B. Nimmer & David Nimmer, 1 NIMMER ON COPYRIGHT § 2.12, note 6 (2016) and the references id (hereinafter: NIMMER ON COPYRIGHT).
9 17 U.S.C. § 106(1).
10 The main way to prove copying as a matter of fact is to show that the alleged infringer had access to the work and that the alleged infringing work is similar enough to indicate copying. This is considered probative similarity. *See* Alan Latman, *"Probative Similarity" as Proof of Copying: Toward Dispelling Some Myths in Copyright Infringement*, 90 COLUM. L. REV. 1187, 1204 (1990). *See also* 4 NIMMER ON COPYRIGHT, *supra* note 8, at § 13.02[B].
11 *See, e.g.*, Feist Publications, Inc. v. Rural Tel. Serv. Co., 499 U.S. 340, 361 (1991); Newton v. Diamond, 388 F.3d 1189, 1193 (9th Cir. 2004). For further elaboration *see* 4 NIMMER ON COPYRIGHT, *supra* note 8, at § 13.03.
12 *See, e.g.*, Ringgold v. Black Entertainment Television, Inc., 126 F.3d 70, 75 (2d Cir. 1997). For further elaboration *see* 4 NIMMER ON COPYRIGHT, *supra* note 8, at § 13.03.
13 *See* Dramatic Literary Property Act, 3 & 4 Will.IV, Ch. 15 (1833) which was later incorporated in Section 20 of the English Copyright Act of 1842. *See* Copyright Law Amendment Act, 5 & 6 Vict., Ch. 45 (1842). *See also* 1 Kevin Garnett, Gillian Davies & Gwilym Harbotlle, COPINGER & SKONE JAMES ON COPYRIGHT § 7–26 (16th edn 2011) (hereinafter: COPINGER & SKONE JAMES ON COPYRIGHT). *See also* Ronan Deazley, *Commentary on Dramatic Literary Property Act 1833, in* PRIMARY SOURCES ON COPYRIGHT (1450–1900) (Lionel Bentley & Martin Kretschmer eds, 2008), http://www.copyrighthistory.org/cam/tools/request/showRecord?id=commentary_uk_1833.
14 COPINGER & SKONE JAMES ON COPYRIGHT, *id.*, at §§ 7-123-7-124 and fn. 21, 25 id; 1 Hugh Laddie, Peter Prescott & Mary Vitoria, THE MODERN LAW OF COPYRIGHT AND DESIGNS § 3.154 (3rd edn 2000). In general, before the Copyright Law of 1911 courts in England consistently ruled that a change of medium does not infringe copyright. *See* Laddie, Prescott & Vitoria, id., at § 3.78 and the cases brought there.
15 Section 1(2) of the 1911 Copyright Act determined that "for the purposes of this Act, 'copyright' means the sole right to produce or reproduce the work or any substantial part thereof in any material form whatsoever." The language of the Berne Convention

(that the United Kingdom signed), at the time, meaning the version including the Berlin Protocol of 1908, included a certain expansion of the reproduction right as well and referred to "indirect appropriation" of protected works such as medium shifting as part of the author's rights. However, this version of the Berne Convention explicitly determined that such protection is only for mere copying which does not lead to the making of a new work. *See* Revised Berne Convention for the Protection of Literary and Artistic Works art. 12, Nov. 13, 1908 (hereinafter: Berne Convention, Berlin Version).

16 *See* COPINGER & SKONE JAMES ON COPYRIGHT, *supra* note 14, at § 7–23; Laddie, Prescott & Vitoria, *supra* note 14, at § 3.130

17 *See*, respectively, Copyright, Designs and Patents Act, 1988 s. 16(1)(a), 16(3)(a).

18 *See* COPINGER & SKONE JAMES ON COPYRIGHT, *supra* note 14, at §§ 7–12–7-17, 7–27–7-25; Laddie, Prescott & Vitoria, *supra* note 14, at §§ 3.125–3.126, 3.130–3.131.

19 *See* Articles 8 and 12 of the Berne Convention, Berlin Version.

20 Berne Convention for the Protection of Literary and Artistic Works art. 12, Jun. 26, 1948.

21 17 U.S.C. §§ 101, 106(2).

22 For a review of the development of the derivative works right in comparison to the reproduction right under United States law *see* Goldstein, *supra* note 4, at 211–15; Oren Bracha, *The Ideology of Authorship Revisited: Authors, Markets, and Liberal Values in Early American Copyright*, 118 YALE L.J. 186, 224–33 (2008); Jed Rubenfeld, *Freedom of Imagination: Copyright's Constitutionality*, 112 YALE L.J. 1, 49–52 (2002)

23 Act of July 8, 1870, Ch. 230 § 86, 16 Stat. 212 (repealed 1909).

24 Act of March 4, 1909, Ch. 320, § 1(b), 35 Stat. 1075 (repealed 1976).

25 17 U.S.C. § 101. The open exemplars list is as follows: "translation, musical arrangement, dramatization, fictionalization, motion picture version, sound recording, art reproduction, abridgment, condensation, or any other form in which a work may be recast, transformed, or adapted."

26 *See, e.g.*, Castle Rock Ent. v. Carol Pub. Group, Inc., 150 F.3d 132, 143 n.9 (2d Cir. 1998); Well-Made Toy Mfg. Corp v. Goffa Int'l Corp., 354 F.3d 112, 117 (2d Cir. 2003). *See also* 1 NIMMER ON COPYRIGHT, *supra* note 8, at § 3.01.

27 *See, e.g.*, Sherry Mfg. Co. v. Towel King of Fla. Inc., 753 F.2d 1565 (11th Cir. 1985).

28 1 NIMMER ON COPYRIGHT, *supra* note 8, at § 3.03[A].

29 Copyright Act, 1911 s. 1(2)(a)-(d).

30 The explicit examples under the adaptation rights are the making of a translation, dramatizing a non-dramatic work, making a non-dramatic version of a dramatic work, making a visualized version of a literary work, making adaptations, changes and translations of computer software and making arrangements and transcripts of musical works. *See* Copyright, Designs and Patents Act, 1988 s. 21(3).

31 Laddie, Prescott & Vitoria argued that the separate treatment of the adaptation right is rooted in historical reasons and only clarifies that certain uses infringe the general reproduction right. *See* Laddie, Prescott & Vitoria, *supra* note 14, at §§ 3.154–3.155.

32 This argument was raised by Laddie, Prescott & Vitoria based on the fact that the reproduction right under English law applies to any use of a substantial part of the first work, including other forms of adaptations and making of derivative works which are not specifically included in Section 21 of the Act. *See id.*, at § 3.157.

33 2 NIMMER ON COPYRIGHT, *supra* note 8, at § 8.09[A][1].

34 Daniel Gervais, *The Derivative Right: Or Why Copyright Law Protects Foxes Better Than Hedgehogs*, 15 VAN. J. ENT. & TECH. L. 785, 844 (2013).

35 Copyright, Designs and Patents act, 1988 s. 21.

36 Copyright, Designs and Patents Act, 1988 s. 21(5).

37 COPINGER & SKONE JAMES ON COPYRIGHT, *supra* note 14, at § 7–137.

38 Laddie, Prescott & Vitoria, *supra* note 14, at §§ 3.155–3.259.

39 Hodgson v Isaac [2010] EWPCC 37, p. 21.

40 *Id.*, at p. 22.
41 Abraham Moon & Sons Ltd v. Thornber [2012] EWPCC 37, p. 92.
42 *See, e.g.*, Francis Day & Hunter Ltd. v. Bron [1963] Ch. 587, 610; Designers Guild Ltd v. Russell Williams (Textiles) Ltd [2000] 1 W.L.R. 2416, 2432.
43 17 U.S.C. § 106(1), (2). It must be noted that the House Report for the Act explicitly addressed the overlap between the rights as follows: "The exclusive right to prepare derivative works, specified separately in clause (2) of section 106, overlaps the exclusive right of reproduction to some extent. It is broader than that right, however, in the sense that reproduction requires fixation in copies or phonorecords, where as the preparation of a derivative work, such as a ballet, pantomime, or improvised performance, may be an infringement even though nothing is ever fixed in tangible form." *See* H.R. REP. NO. 94–1476, at 62 (1976).
44 Midway Mfg. Co. v. Artic Int'l, Inc., 1981 U.S. Dist. LEXIS 16881, 24 (N.D. Ill. June 2, 1981).
45 Litchfield v. Spielberg, 736 F.2d 1352, 1357 (9th Cir. 1984).
46 Twin Peaks Prods. v. Publ'ns Int'l, Ltd., 996 F.2d 1366, 1373 (2d Cir. 1993). The court of appeals for the second circuit applied this decision in Castle Rock Entm't, Inc. v. Carol Publ'g Grp., Inc., 150 F.3d 132 (2d Cir. 1998), where it found that the making of trivia cards based on the television series *Seinfeld* infringed the copyright of the producers of the show. The court addressed both the reproduction and derivative works rights under the same discussion and applied the substantial similarity test to both. *See, id.*, at fn. 9 ("Indeed, if the secondary work sufficiently transforms the expression of the original work such that the two works cease to be substantially similar, then the secondary work is not a derivative work and, for that matter, does not infringe the copyright of the original work").
47 Well-Made Toy Mfg. Corp. v. Goffa Int'l Corp., 354 F.3d 112, 117 (2d Cir. 2003). *See also* Mulcahy v. Cheetah Learning LLC, 386 F.3d 849, 853 (8th Cir. 2004) ("While substantial similarity is the test we use in determining copyright infringement, here the issue is whether Mulcahy's book is a derivative work. In general, the two tests are similar. In the words of a leading copyright treatise, 'Unless sufficient of the pre-existing work is contained in the later work so as to constitute the latter an infringement of the former, the latter by definition is not a derivative work'"); and Kumar v. Inst. of Elec. & Elecs. Eng'rs, 2013 U.S. Dist. LEXIS 140989 (D.N.J. Sept. 30, 2013) ("... the right to prepare derivative works is simply one of the rights accorded every copyright owner under 17 U.S.C. § 106, and the infringement test described above applies where the derivative-works right is allegedly implicated, just as it applies when the right invoked is, for example, the exclusive right to reproduce the work in copies".)
48 This was argued by Samuelson. *See* Pamela Samuelson, *The Quest for a Sound Conception of Copyright's Derivative Work Right*, 101 GEO. L.J. 1505, 1510 (2013), and the literature brought in fn. 24 there which I will discuss below.
49 *See, e.g.*, Christina Bohannan, *Taming the Derivative Work Right: A Modest Proposal for Reducing Overbreadth and Vagueness in Copyright*, 12 VAND. J. ENT. & TECH. L. 669, 688 (2010); Neil W. Netanel, *Copyright and a Democratic Civil Society*, 106 YALE L.J. 283, 347–64 (1996); Niva Elkin-Koren, *Cyberlaw and Social Change: A Democratic Approach to Copyright Law in Cyberspace*, 14 CARDOZO ARTS & ENT. L.J. 215, 277–83 (1996).
50 *See, e.g.*, Stewart Sterk, *Rhetoric and Reality in Copyright Law*, 94 MICH. L. REV. 1197, 1215–17 (1996); Shubha Ghosh, *Market Entry and the Proper Scope of Copyright*, 12 INT'L J. ECON. & BUS. 347, 351 (2005); Shyamkrishna Balganesh, *Foreseeability and Copyright Incentives*, 122 HARV. L. REV. 1569 (2009); Glynn S. Lunney, *Reexamining Copyright's Incentives-Access Paradigm*, 49 VAND. L. REV. 483, 650–3 (1996); Goldstein, *supra* note 4, at 227.
51 Lunney, *id.*, at 628–9.
52 *Id.*, at 650–3.
53 Naomi Abe Voegtli, *Rethinking Derivative Rights*, 63 BROOK. L. REV. 1213, 1267 (1997).

54 Bohannan, *supra* note 49, at 697.
55 *Id.*, at 697–8.
56 Michael Abramowicz, *A Theory of Copyright's Derivative Work Right*, 90 MINN. L. REV. 317 (2005). I will further discuss Abramowicz's approach below with respect to the interrelations with the reproduction right.
57 Samuelson, *supra* note 48, at 1509–11.
58 *Id.*, at 1511–17.
59 *Id.*, at 1517–18. The nine exemplars are: translation, musical arrangement, dramatization, fictionalization, motion picture version, sound recording, art reproduction, abridgment, condensation.
60 *Id.*, at 1518–20.
61 *Id.*, at 1523–5.
62 *See* Baker v. Selden, 101 U.S. 99 (1879).
63 Samuelson, *supra* note 48, at 1534–8.
64 *Id.*, at 1539–41.
65 *Id.*, at 1552–4. With respect to add-ons, this is the rule under current case law. *See* Galoob Inc. v. Nintendo of America Inc., 964 F. 2d 965 (9th Cir. 1992). *See also*, Tim Wu, *Tolerated Uses*, 31 COLUM. J.L. & ARTS 617, 631 (2008). A similar suggestion to Samuelson's was proposed by Tylor Ochoa. Ochoa discussed the lack of clarity with respect to the derivative works right in light of case law inconsistency, mainly due to the lack of a fixation requirement for derivative works. *See* Tyler Ochoa, Copyright, *Derivative Works, and Fixation: Is Galoob a Mirage or Does the Form(Gen) of the Alleged Derivative Work Matter?*, 20 SANTA CLARA COMP. & HIGH TECH. L.J. 991, 1020 (2004).
66 Rubenfeld, *supra* note 22, at 49–50.
67 *Id.*, at 50.
68 *Id.*, at 53.
69 *Id.*, at 54–55.
70 Campbell v. Acuff-Rose Music, Inc., 510 U.S. 569 (1994).
71 Rubenfeld, *supra* note 22, at 56.
72 Abramowicz, *supra* note 56, at 332–35. Abramowicz mentioned the case of Anderson v. Stallone, 1989 U.S. Dist. LEXIS 11109 (C.D. Cal. Apr. 25, 1989) in which the court decided that a script for a sequel to the *Rocky* movie series that was written without the authorization of the first author infringes both the derivative works right and the reproduction right.
73 *Id.*, at 337–38.
74 *Id.*, at 339.
75 *Id.*, at 372–3.
76 *Id.*, at 374.
77 *Id.*
78 *Id.*, at 373.
79 Gervais, *supra* note 34, at 801–7.
80 *Id.*, at 839. *See also* Mirage Editions, Inc. v. Albuquerque A.R.T. Co., 856 F.2d 1341 (9th Cir. 1988); Lee v. A.R.T. Co., 125 F.3d 580 (7th Cir. 1997); Muñoz v. Albuquerque A.R.T. Co., 829 F. Supp. 309 (D. Ala. 1993), *aff'd* 38 F.3d 1218 (9th Cir. 1994).
81 *Id.*, at 805.
82 *Id.*, at 806.
83 *Id.*, at 806–7.
84 *Id.*, at 837.
85 Chris Newman, *Transformation in Property and Copyright*, 56 VILL. L. REV. 251, 304 (2011).
86 For a full review of these approaches *see* Daniel Friedman, *Rights and Remedies, in* COMPARATIVE REMEDIES FOR BREACH OF CONTRACT 3 (Nili Cohen & Ewan Mckendrick eds 2005).

87 Oliver W. Holmes, *The Path of Law*, 10 HARV. L. REV. 457, 458 (1897).

88 In United States law, the right superiority is specifically evident in constitutional law and the discussion on constitutional rights and the protection they afford individuals. For a critical discussion on this approach in constitutional law *see* Owen M. Fiss, *Foreword: The Forms of Justice*, 93 HARV. L. REV. 1, 46–52 (1979); Daryl J. Levinson, *Rights Essentialism and Remedial Equilibration*, 99 COLUM. L. REV. 857, 870–2 (1999). This is directly related to Dworkin's approach that differentiates between policy-based arguments and right-based arguments and sees rights as trump cards over policy-based arguments. *See* Ronald Dworkin, *Rights as Trumps, in* THEORIES OF RIGHTS 153, 153–4 (Jeremy Wadron ed., 1984); Ronald Dworkin, TAKING RIGHTS SERIOUSLY 82–4 (1977).

89 Karl L. Llewellyn, *A Realistic Jurisprudence, in* JURISPRUDENCE: REALISM IN THEORY AND PRACTICE 3, 8–18, 21–3 (1962); Karl L. Llewellyn, *Some Realism about Realism*, in JURISPRUDENCE: REALISM IN THEORY AND PRACTICE 42, 63 (1962). For a discussion on the effect of remedies on constitutional rights *see* Fiss, *supra* note 88; Levinson, *supra* note 88; Richard H. Fallon, Jr.; Daniel J. Meltzer, *New Law, Non-Retroactivity, and Constitutional Remedies*, 104 HARV. L. REV. 1731, 1777–1806 (1990).

90 Guido Calabresi & Douglas A. Melamed, *Property Rules, Liability Rules and Inalienability Rules: One View of the Cathedral*, 85 HARV. L. REV. 1089 (1972).

91 A.M. Honorè, *Ownership, in* OXFORD ESSAYS IN JURISPRUDENCE 370 (A.G. Guest ed., 1961). *See also* Honorè, *Property, Title and Redistribution, in* PHILOSOPHY OF LAW: CLASSIC AND CONTEMPORARY READINGS 263 (1977) (Larry May & Jeff Brow eds, 2010); Wesley Newcomb Hohfeld, *Fundamental Legal Conceptions as Applied in Judicial Reasoning*, 26 YALE L.J. 710, 720, 733–4, 746–7 (1917).

92 Jeremy Waldron, THE RIGHT TO PRIVATE PROPERTY 49–53 (1988).

93 Hanoch Dagan, *Property and the Public Domain*, 18 YALE J.L. & HUMAN. 84, 85–6 (2006).

94 For a similar argument with respect to patent law *see* Bernard Chao, *The Infringement Continuum*, 35 CARDOZO L. REV. 1359, 1404–17 (2014). For a discussion on the many features of a right that determine its overall scope in intellectual property law *see* Mark A. Lemley & Mark P. Mckenna, *Scope*, 57 WILLIAM & MARY L. REV. 2197 (2016).

5 A new model for the derivative works right

I. Introduction

How should we design the right to make derivative works? In the previous chapter, we saw that in order to adjust the right to make derivative works to fit both its underlying normative justifications and the non-legal understanding of creativity, two aspects of the right must be addressed. First, the derivative works right must be separated from the reproduction right and the border line between the two must be articulated. Second, the right's scope of remedies must be limited. The purpose of this chapter is to portray the way to redesign the right to make derivative works according to these principles. In other words, whereas Chapter 4 showed what should be done to resolve the difficulties raised by the derivative works right, this chapter suggests the best way to do so.

I will first address the scope of applicability of the derivative works right. To fully separate it from the reproduction right, I argue that a clearer definition for the right must be adopted. My main argument is that cases in which substantial parts of preexisting expressions are used, in addition to a significant creative contribution (quantitatively), which cannot be separated from the used expressions without undermining the purpose of the second work, and cannot be substituted with non-protected preexisting expressions, should be considered as the making of a derivative work and should not fall under the reproduction right. Thus, the right to make derivative works should be adjusted to apply to such cases, even if they fall under the reproduction right under current law. To illustrate the suggested definition, I will give examples for typical creative activities that should be considered derivative works. The main novelty in this definition is that, unlike the current definition, it diverts the focal point from reviewing the use of preexisting expressions and the substantial similarity between the second and first works, to the additional originality and creativity of the second work and its relationship to the preexisting expressions. This will allow the review to continue past the threshold of substantial similarity, and fully separate the derivative works right from the reproduction right.

After discussing the suggested definition and the typical cases associated with it, this chapter will review its implications on positive law as well as its pros and cons. It will show how the definition for the derivative works right could establish a separate independent discourse on the right, which will focus on analyzing its boundaries and underlying justifications. It will also allow reviewing cases that fall under the reproduction right today, under the derivative works right which more accurately fits their normative basis. In addition, I will explain how the suggested definition, which separates the derivative works right from the reproduction right, establishes an independent discussion on the scope of each of these rights' remedies.

In the remainder of this chapter, I will discuss the second significant aspect of the derivative works right – its remedies. Building on the argument from Chapter 4, which justified the separation of the derivative works right from the reproduction right and the limitation of its remedies, I will explain that the normative justifications for the derivative works right (as discussed in Chapter 3), require limiting the scope of its remedies, and in fact, shifting from a property rule protection to a liability rule that allows second authors to use expressions from first works without the owner's consent. I will also review various suggestions to remedies models for the derivative works right (and copyright in general) suggested in existing literature, and explain their shortcomings. Following this discussion, I will argue that the best remedies model for the derivative works right is compulsory licenses.

Finally, this chapter will portray the compulsory licenses model for derivative works, and respond to potential criticism. In short, I argue that the most desirable model allows second authors to use expressions from the first work for the making of derivative works without the owner's consent, subject to paying reasonable royalties from future revenues. If the parties will not reach an agreement, the second author could initiate judicial proceedings to determine the fair royalties rate, provided that she will pay an initial lump sum to cover the procedural costs and the expected goodwill and reputation revenues from using the existing expressions. The model will be subject to a blocking period which will allow the first author to exclusively make derivative works or allow others to do so in her stead. I will conclude by examining the model's relationship with other copyright and intellectual property doctrines, namely fair use, moral rights of attribution and trademark law.

The chapter will proceed as follows: Part II will suggest a new definition for the derivative works right which will completely separate it from the reproduction right. It will discuss the positive implications of the definition and its practical advantages. Part III will focus on the scope of the right's remedies, explain why they should be substituted for a new model based on liability rules and discuss the difficulties of remedies models suggested in the literature. Part IV will portray the suggested model of compulsory licenses for the making of derivative works, its advantages over alternative models and will deal with potential criticism. It will also discuss the relationship between the suggested model and other copyright and intellectual property doctrines.

II. Separate but not equal: separating the derivative works right from the reproduction right

As was previously explained in Chapter 4, the normative justifications for the derivative works right require its separation from the reproduction right. Such separation is also required due to the overlap between the two rights under current case law and due to the practical implications of that overlap. I will now turn to a more nuanced definition for the derivative works right which, as I argue, better fits its normative justifications and allows for its coherent separation from the reproduction right. For this I will also use the non-legal understanding of creativity, as was discussed in Chapters 1 and 2, to achieve a better match between the definition and the various phenomena of derivative works and the use of preexisting expressions.

1) The basis for the suggested definition

To separate between the derivative works right and the reproduction right, it is first necessary to establish a definition that will be the basis for the distinction between the two rights – i.e., what the conditions are under which a certain use of the first work will be defined as a derivative work. Clearly, this definition cannot be solely based on the main condition for the existence of reproduction – substantial similarity between the first and second works – because, as explained in Chapter 4, this cannot help us distinguish between a mere reproduction and a derivative work. This is due to the fact that absent substantial similarity, no copyright infringement would exist and therefore no derivative work would exist, and *vice versa*, when a derivative work is made there will always be substantial similarity between the first and second works.

One necessary component for the separating definition, which seems to be accepted by a significant part of the commentators on derivative works, is that the second work should include a substantial original contribution in excess of the first work.[1] This component is necessary for two reasons. First, without requiring substantial additional originality in comparison to the first work, the right to make derivative work will allow to circumvent the reproduction right (assuming no overlap between the two). Second, I believe that this component is the best basis for adjusting the derivative works right to its underlying normative justifications, as well as to the non-legal understanding of creativity as discussed in Chapters 1 and 2. Recall that originality is a prerequisite for copyright protection, and absent substantial additional originality it would be difficult to perceive the second work as creative, and its creator an author. The mirror image of this is that, in general, a reproduction that does not include additional originality is not a creative act.[2] In addition, in order to determine that the substantial additional originality removes the use from the scope of reproduction and into the scope of a derivative work, I argue that the use of preexisting expressions should meet two additional cumulative conditions. First, that the taken expression constitutes an inseparable part of the second work,[3] and second, that the taken expressions could not be substituted with a different existing non-protected expression without undermining the purpose of the second work.[4] These two conditions – inseparability and non-fungibility – derive from the definition of the derivative work as a work that is "based on one or more preexisting work" and elaborate such requirement. Note that the inseparability condition does not focus on whether expressions from the first and second work could be distinguished and recognized (i.e., whether expressions could be clearly attributed to the first or second authors), rather on whether the two expressions could be separated without undermining the purpose of the second work.

The definition itself is insufficient. It presents a preliminary basis for the separation, and although more detailed than the current definition of the right, it is still too general and requires further elaboration. A second component for the definition should be based on exemplars or typical representative uses which cover the array of circumstances in which an act will constitute a derivative work rather than a reproduction. This is also the approach of the United States Copyright Act. In the American context, Pamela Samuelson argued that acts which fall under the nine statutory exemplars, or similar acts, should be considered derivative works.[5] However, in contrast to the current definition, the exemplars I suggest do not only describe a list of types of derivative works, rather portray the normative stance embedded in the first component, and, as I will show, extend the current scope of acts that constitute derivative works.

Samuelson suggested three main characterizations for the nine statutory exemplars. The first is short versions of the first works, the second is faithful renditions (such as translations) and the third is transformation of expression from one medium or genre to another. In addition, she suggested that sequels or prequels as well as criticism should also be considered as derivative works. I suggest a characterization that is different from Samuelson's, albeit relying on her distinctions, expanding the scope of uses which will be considered as derivative works and not as reproductions. In addition, the types of uses I suggest, while based on the normative justifications for the derivative works right, fit the non-legal understanding of creativity.

The first category of uses is short versions of the first work, its editing and annotations. To the extent that these constitute original works and are inseparable from the expressions of the first work, they should not be considered as reproductions, rather as derivative works. In the case of abridgements for example, to the extent original (i.e., there is distinct originality in the selection and arrangement of the various abridged parts from the first work), it is easy to see why these would be inseparable from the expressions of the first work and why they constitute a derivative work. As far as annotations are concerned, there are cases in which these could be completely separated from the first work, and in such cases they should be considered an independent work and not a derivative. However, to the extent that the annotations include expressions from the first work that could not be separated, they should be considered derivative works.

The second and important category of uses is translations of the first work and its communication to new audiences (that requires a change in the work).[6] This category includes a large variety of uses of preexisting works. The most basic example for this category is a translation of a literary work to a different language. To the extent that the translation is original in its own account, it will be considered a derivative work as explicitly stated in the statutory language.[7] But translation does not necessarily have to be between languages. Translation could occur between genres (as in a shift in musical genre),[8] or between media (as in the cinematographic version of a literary work),[9] and even when the first work is adapted to fit a new platform (as often happens with computer software and compatibility between programming languages).[10] The common ground for these uses is that the changes and additions to the first work are mainly intended to communicate it to a different audience (even if some overlap may exist between the original and new audiences) and not to significantly change the expressions of the first work.

This type of use fits well with the way cognitive psychology understands creativity, because although the transfer of a work to a new language, medium or genre requires the use of domain-relevant knowledge such as expressions, which is part of the creative process, it also requires additional creativity originating in the individual thought of the second author and fulfills all components of the cognitive process of creativity. According to genre theories, too, this type of use fits the understanding of the development and enrichment of the creative world, since common building blocks are used for the purpose of establishing a new genre or developing an existing one. According to Fishelov, for example, a translation is an explicit example of secondary generic productivity which contributes to the development of genres.[11] Fowler, too, believed that the transfer of subjects from one genre to another, or the mixture of generic characters from two genres are main ways to develop the creative world, and the act of translation and transfer of a work from one medium or genre to another are classic examples of that.[12]

A third category of uses focuses on improvement and developments of first works. This category includes, for example, sequels and prequels in the context of literary, artistic and dramatic works,[13] but also version updates and improvements to computer software.[14] The common feature of these cases is that the changes and additions to the first work were meant to preserve a certain core of expressions, develop, and improve it, usually in the same genre of the first work.

This type of use is in line with the understanding of creativity under cognitive psychology, because while the second author uses domain-relevant previous knowledge (expressions) from the first work, new expressions that originate in the second author are added too. Under genre theories, this type of use develops and enriches the creative world since the second author uses common building blocks from the first work to develop the genre and the ability of the audience to evaluate and generate meaning for both the first and second works, as well as other works to be created as part of the genre. This type of use fits with both parts of generic productivity described by Fishelov, according to which new texts that are perceived as belonging to the same genre establish the predominance of the genre and enable the secondary generic productivity – the making of other texts according to the generic pattern by, for example, "copying" which is the preservation of the form of the first work while changing its content.[15] When the additional original part of the second work is not dependent on the expressions of the first work, the second work will not constitute a derivative work as it does not use preexisting expressions from the first work. A clear example of this, referred to by Samuelson, is add-ons to computer programs.[16]

The fourth category of uses is the disassembly and reconstruction of the first work. Examples for this type of use will be mainly from the artistic fields of postmodern and appropriation arts. One clear example for this type of uses from the field of musical works is the making of a remix or a mashup.[17] The common feature of this category is the way in which expressions from the first work are used, in contrast to the purpose of the use. The disassembly of the first work and its reconstruction, for example by remix, could be an arrangement of the expressions from the first work which preserves the form of the first work. A mashup work, however, could transfer the expressions from the first work from one genre to another and even change the underlying expressions completely, for example, by parody.

The fifth and last category of uses is the taking of parts from the first work in order to make a new, different work. The difference between this category and the third one is that here, the second work does not preserve a core of expressions from the first work and the purpose of use is to make a completely different work. This category includes a wide array of uses and overlaps, to a certain extent, with the fair use doctrine. Thus, for example, making a parody or satire based on expressions from a first work could significantly change the first work and may, in many cases, constitute transformative use which will be considered fair.[18] In contrast, taking a substantial part of a chorus of a song in order to make a different song with new lyrics does not necessarily change the first expression in a way which will be considered transformative, and therefore fair use will not apply.[19] Both cases should, however, be considered derivative works to the extent that the second work is sufficiently original.

The fifth category of uses is the most extensive one in comparison to existing law and therefore fully reflects the purpose of the first component. It also raises an important question – when substantial parts are taken from first works in order to create works that have no apparent connection to the first work, should such acts be considered the making of a derivative work, an infringing reproduction or a non-infringing use? Chris Newman believes that in these cases there is no derivative work on the one hand and no reproduction on the other hand, and therefore they should be considered non-infringing uses.[20] Some courts have obviously determined that these instances constitute infringing reproduction, while ignoring the question of derivative works. While I believe that the freedom that the derivative works right should grant second authors shall not be misused in order to circumvent the reproduction right, I argue that these cases, in general, should be reviewed as derivative works, and not reproductions. This is because these circumstances are at the heart of the type of creative activities that copyright law should foster, facilitate and allow. The two conditions suggested here are sufficient to remove the concern of misuse of the derivative works right. The inseparability condition is a good tool to examine the substantiality of the use and the importance of the taken expression to the second work. In addition, it will exclude from the derivative works right cases that could be defined as "reproduction *plus* original work", meaning linking a protected expression to a new original work which is not dependent on the previous expression. The non-fungibility condition is meant to guarantee that the derivative works right shall not be overused. Thus, to the extent that the second author could replace the protected expression used with a different unprotected expression, without derogating from the purpose of the new work, she ought to do so and not misuse the tools that copyright law provides her.[21]

In addition, the derivative works right should apply to cases in which the second work uses preexisting expressions due to an inspiration from a specific existing work or cases in which the use of preexisting expressions could be considered a creative "shortcut." An example would be the use of sound samples from preexisting sound recordings and combining them in new musical works.[22] Another example is the use of existing software code in order to combine parts of the previous software in a new one. The reason for this lies in the notions from the discussion on cognitive psychology and genre theories. With respect to cognitive psychology, the creative process, even when the work of authorship is highly original and innovative, includes the use of previous domain-relevant knowledge. Such knowledge can include explicit expressions from preexisting works stored in the author's memory and is not restricted to the making of sequel works or works in the same genre. Therefore, the use of expressions from the first work for the purpose of creating a second original work which is not a sequence of the first work is a creative activity, and is therefore more suitable to the derivative works right than to the reproduction right. This is also true with respect to genre theories. Chapter 2 showed that the enrichment of the creative world includes the use of common building blocks that consist of explicit protected expressions. One way to develop a genre and the creative world in general, as suggested by Fowler, is generic mixture, meaning the addition of characteristics from one genre to another or the mixture of components from one text with those of another.[23] This description fits well with the fifth category of uses that includes cases in which expressions from the first work are taken for the purpose of combining them with different expressions in order to create a different work, sometimes in the genre, in order to develop the creative world. However, in contrast to Newman, I argue that the uses included in the fifth category should be considered part of the first author's copyright. As explained in Chapter 3, the theoretical justifications to copyright law will favor a situation in which the taking of expressions from the first work will not be prohibited but will afford the first author some consideration. Thus, the uses included in the fifth category should be part of the derivative works right in order to grant the first author some interest in them.

The five categories described above do not exclude each other. It may well be that in some cases a specific use will fit various categories. This will be the case where the second work is a translation of the first into a new medium and at the same time improves the first work or continues it. an example would be the adaptation of a classical novel to a motion picture while changing some of the main plotlines and adapting them to a modern time period. Another example, in the context of computer software, could be the compatibility of a software to a new platform or technological medium while adding new and improved features.[24] In both cases, the derivative work will fit both the second and third categories. Combining all of them, however, should cover all the circumstances which will be considered as derivative works under the first component of the definition.

The definition here is not free of concerns. First, it changes the current law significantly in a way that will require conducting a new discourse on the derivative works right, and, at least at the beginning, create some uncertainty. Second, the definition significantly expands the derivative works right, mainly at the expense of the reproduction right. Such expansion could be opposed due to the argument that it allows the relatively easy circumvention of the reproduction right. I dealt with this concern above and explained that the proposed conditions of the definition (inseparability of the first expression from the second work and non-fungibility of the first expression) should resolve this difficulty. However, this is indeed a significant expansion that will contract the reproduction right considerably. Third, while I believe that the proposed definition is more accurate, normatively desirable and contributes to the clarity and certainty of existing law, it will require setting new rules and applying them in practice. Thus, even under the proposed definition, courts will have to determine what is the threshold of required additional creativity for the second work to be considered derivative, when will the additional creativity be considered inseparable from the preexisting expressions and under what circumstances will such combination be necessary for the purpose of the second work.

Despite these concerns, the adoption of the proposed definition is required in order to fit the right to make derivative works with its underlying normative justifications and is well in line with the non-legal understanding of creativity, therefore relieving the tension between these fields and the law. In addition, it is important to note that this could be achieved without statutory change which will create the *de facto* separation. This could be done by deciding that when an act constitutes both the making of a derivative work and a reproduction, the remedies available to the owner will only be those accompanying the derivative works right since this is the more particular right that applies to such acts and their normative basis in comparison to the reproduction right.

To conclude this part, in order to distinguish between the derivative works right and the reproduction right, and to separate between the two rights, on the basis of the justifications discussed in Chapter 4, I proposed a basis for a definition including two components (see Figure 5.1). The first component is the conditions under which an act will be considered the making of a derivative work and not a reproduction. The definition focusses on the use of preexisting works which is accompanied by substantial additional originality, when the preexisting expressions are inseparable from the second work and could not be replaced by unprotected expressions. The basis for this definition is normative and results from the normative justifications for the derivative works right and the need to distinguish and separate between it and the reproduction right. The main contribution of this definition is that it shifts the discussion from the question of similarity to the first work to the additional originality and the relationship between the preexisting expressions and the new work. It goes without saying that in order to fall under the definition of a derivative work the taken preexisting expressions must be substantially similar to the first work. However, in contrast to the reproduction right for which the review stops at similarity and the act of copying (as opposed to original creation), the main question here is whether the use of a preexisting work is accompanied by inseparable additional creativity under the conditions set forth above.[25] Such a change of the existing law is meant to align the derivative works right with its underlying normative basis, and for that, it must be separated from the reproduction right in a mutually-exclusive way. Any review which stops at the threshold of substantial similarity will be undermining such purpose and will create, *de facto*, an overlap between the reproduction right and the derivative works right.

The second suggested component includes categories of typical uses that should be considered derivative works according to the proposed definition. This component is, in part, prescriptive-pedagogic and is meant to exemplify how the proposed definition should be applied to different cases. Additionally, the second component is also normative since it reflects the differences between the proposed definition and existing law and captures the full array of uses that should be considered derivative works. Thus, the fifth category of uses, which is a residual category, shows how according to the new definition, many uses will be considered derivative works and not reproduction in light of the independent normative justifications of the derivative works right that focus on the originality (and creativity) of the second author and its relationship with the taken preexisting expressions. In the next part, I will demonstrate how this category of uses includes uses that are reviewed under the reproduction right under existing law.

2) *Implications of the new definition*

a) Establishing a separate discourse and independent development of the derivative works right

One of the most important implications of the suggested definition for the derivative works right, which separates it from the reproduction right, is the establishment of a separate discourse on the derivative works right that mandates its independent development. As discussed in Chapter 4, there is an almost complete overlap between the derivative works right and reproduction right under current law. Such overlap may cause the discourse to be incomplete and allows courts to conclude the discussion on the derivative works right by focussing on substantial

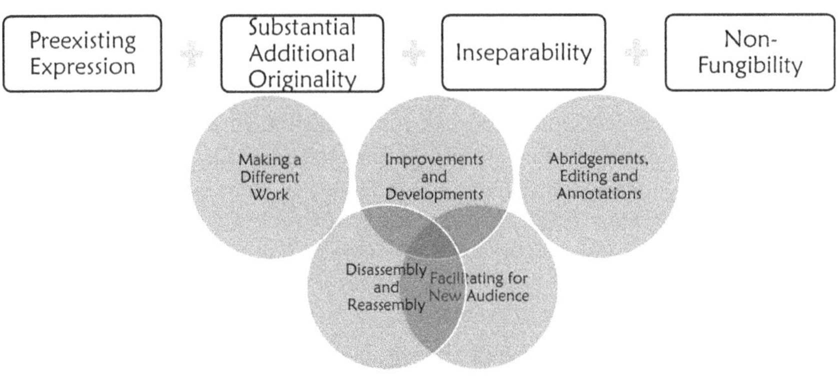

Figure 5.1 Two components of the definition of derivative works

similarity alone, which is, as explained, the basis of the reproduction right. The proposed separating definition will require courts, in the right cases, to discuss the derivative works right and not the reproduction right, and by doing so, determine whether the conditions for the existence of a derivative work are fulfilled, a question which is not reviewed by courts today due to the overlap between the rights.

This implication will expectedly be evident in case law, in cases that were reviewed under both rights in the past, and under the new definition will be reviewed only under the derivative works right and its new set of remedies as will be described below.[26] Another manifestation of the new definition will be in cases which were previously reviewed by courts under the reproduction right alone, without resorting to the derivative works right, but under the new definition will be considered solely as derivative works or will at least require such classification.

One typical example is the decision in Elvis Presley Enterprises, Inc. v. Passport Video.[27] In this case, the plaintiffs, who owned copyrights in videos and photographs of Elvis Presley, argued that the defendants infringed their copyright by creating a documentary motion picture on the singer. The documentary was 16 hours-long and included photographs of Presley which appeared on screen for a maximum of 30 seconds as well as videos from the singer's shows which were included in the documentary lasting up to one full minute. The court decided that five to ten percent of the defendants' documentary included materials belonging to the plaintiffs. However, the court emphasized that the documentary was "extensive" and included over 200 in-depth interviews covering every aspect of the singer's life. In its decision, the court did not once refer to the term "derivative work" and sufficed with the fact that substantial parts of the plaintiffs' works were included almost identically in the defendants' documentary as a basis for copyright infringement. Under the proposed definition, however, this case will be classified under the fifth category of uses described above and will require determining whether due to the defendants' substantial additional originality, and due to the integration of both materials in a new work, the outcome should be considered a derivative work or merely a reproduction.[28]

A different characteristic case is Swirsky v. Carey.[29] In this case, the court reviewed a claim against singer Mariah Carey arguing that her song "Thank God I Found You" infringes the plaintiffs' copyright in their song due to substantial similarity between the choruses of the two songs, in the lyrics, rhythm and melody. The court determined that substantial similarity exists between the two choruses due to expert opinions brought by the plaintiffs. It emphasized that in order to prove that copyrights were infringed the plaintiffs have to show that Carey *copied* protected parts of their work.[30] However, there was no disagreement that the two songs differ in lyrics and melody of the various verses.[31] According to the factual determinations of the court, it seems that in this case too, under the proposed definition, Carey's song would be considered a derivative work of the plaintiffs' song, since it included substantial additional originality combined with the preexisting expression. At least, this case raises the question whether the preexisting expression was inseparable from the new work created by Carey and whether indeed substantial additional originality existed.[32]

Staying with the context of musical works, another example would be second works sampling parts of the first work. In the case of TufAmerica Inc., v. Diamond, the court reviewed a claim against the Beastie Boys for copyright infringement of four songs owned by the plaintiff.[33] The plaintiff argued that five Beastie Boys' songs contained six digital samples from four of her songs. In this case too, the court decided that in order to prove copyright infringement, the plaintiff must show that substantial parts of her works were *copied*. After reviewing the infringement claims under the substantial similarity doctrine, the court decided that two out of six alleged infringements indeed constitute copyright infringement, while one infringement appears for nine seconds and the other for 51 seconds in Beastie Boys' songs. Here too, according to the proposed definition, and since there was no disagreement that Beastie Boys' songs included substantial additional originality, an analysis of derivative works is in place.[34] It is important to note that my argument here extends the scope of the derivative works right in comparison to existing law, in the sense that the review does not stop at the question of what was taken from the first work, rather continues an examines how the taken parts are integrated in the new work. I argue that this extension is required due to the normative justifications for the derivative works right.

Cases in which courts did not consider derivative works, but under the proposed definition will most likely have to, are evident in the field of computer software as well. One important case is the tech giants dispute between Google and Oracle which was reviewed by the Court of Appeals for the Federal Circuit.[35] This dispute revolved around two software development platforms created by the two companies. Oracle is the owner of the Java platform which allows software developers to use a consistent language for the development of software that could be run on various operating systems without further adaptations. The specific version of Java included 166 application programming interfaces (API) including two parts of code – declarative code and implementation code – which could be used for the creation of Java-based software. Google, which first attempted to obtain a license from Oracle to use the Java platform and adapt it for smartphone interfaces, developed its own platform named Dalvik which it used for its smartphone operating system Android. Google's platform included 168 APIs and the dispute between the two companies revolved on Oracles allegations that 37 of Java's APIs were included in Google's platform.

The parties agreed that Google did independently develop the rest of its platform APIs. The court's decision dedicated a long discussion to the question of copyrightability of Oracle's APIs due to the fact that a jury decision already determined that substantial similarity exists, and the district court denied Oracle's claim only because it decided that the APIs are not copyrightable. However, despite the fact that Google's software included many original parts in addition to its use of Oracle's APIs, the court did not consider the question of derivative works. According to the proposed definition, this case is a potential example for a case in which computer software could be considered a derivative work of previous software. This is because, in contrast to existing law which reviews such circumstances as reproduction (plus additional originality), the proposed definition does not stop at substantial similarity and asks whether the expressions from the first work are inseparably combined with the second work.

b) Implications on third parties

The separation between the derivative works right and the reproduction right is expected to have an implication on third parties acting with respect to the first and second works as well as on issues arising from the granting of licenses to make derivative works.

With respect to the effect on third parties, the separation between the rights is significant. The separation affects the relationship between the second author, which is not the owner of the first work, and a third party acting with respect to the second work. In many cases, act with respect to the second work will include use of expression from the first work. To the extent that the second work is merely a reproduction, there is no rivalry between the second author and the third party, since the second author has no claim to the second work. However, to the extent that the second work is a derivative work (or an original work completely detached from the first work), rivalry between the second author and the third party exists.

In the same context, the question who has the right to enforce copyrights with respect to derivative works against third parties – the first or second author – was raised in United States case law. When the third party uses expressions which originated from the second author alone, meaning new expressions that only exist in the second work, the answer is simple, and the right to enforce is with the second author.[36] Things become more complex when the third party uses expressions from the first work which are also included in the second work for the purpose of making yet another derivative work. The answer to these cases under existing law depends on the type of license that the second author received from the first author, and the purpose for which the third party used the expressions. To the extent that the second author received an exclusive license from the first author and the third party used expressions from the first work to make yet another derivative work, only the second author will be allowed to bring suit against the third party.[37] To the extent that the second author only received a non-exclusive license or if the third party used the underlying expressions for reproduction and not derivative work purposes, or to make derivative works outside the scope of the license granted to the second author, the right to enforce will remain with the first author.[38] Thus, it is important to determine whether a specific use is merely a reproduction or rather a derivative work, both with respect to the second author and with respect to third parties.

To conclude this part, the proposed definition separating between the derivative works right and the reproduction right is expected to have two important implications. First, if adopted, the new definition will lead to the establishment of an independent and distinct discourse on the derivative works right and will require a judicial review of its scope in many cases which, under existing law, are reviewed under the reproduction right alone. A dedicated discussion on the derivative works right is expected to make the boundaries between this right and the reproduction right clearer and to focus on the independent normative justifications of the derivative works right that look at the original contribution of the second author and not merely at the substantial similarity to the first work. Second, the separation between the rights may affect the relationship between the first and second authors and third parties, specifically in cases where third parties act with respect to the derivative work and it must be decided against whom legal rivalry arises.

III. Alternative remedies for the derivative works right

1) The need for weaker remedies

In addition to the need for a normative and conceptual separation between the derivative works right and the reproduction right, there is a strong normative justification for a change in the remedies model of the derivative works right. Under existing law, the remedies for the reproduction right are identical to those of the derivative works right. This means that the owner of the first work has the exclusive right to make derivative works, to decide whether derivative works will indeed be created and by whom. To the extent that a different person will make an unauthorized derivative work, the owner will have various monetary remedies, but mainly the right for an injunctive relief preventing the second author from making or distributing the second work.[39]

Chapter 3 showed that under each of the normative justifications for copyright in general and the derivative works right in particular, the current remedy model for the derivative works right is inappropriate. As the discussion in Chapter 4 showed, aligning the derivative works right with its underlying normative justifications requires limiting its remedies to allow second authors to use preexisting expressions more freely. In fact, the basis for the discussion in this part is that there is a strong normative justification to change the remedies model for the derivative works right from a property rule protection to a liability rule protection.[40] The purpose of the discussion here is to examine which alternative remedies model will be the best, most efficient and fair way to fulfill the right's underlying purpose. The discussion will be based on the assumption that all such alternative remedies models can, at least potentially, fit the underlying normative justifications of the right, and while considering their deficiencies on one hand and the outweighing benefits of the proposed model on the other hand I will focus on secondary criteria such as efficiency, political plausibility and just distribution of powers between first and second authors. I am not the first to argue that weaker remedies for the derivative works right are called for. This part discusses the main alternative remedies models proposed in the literature for copyright in general and derivative works in particular, and the deficiencies of each of them. In the next part I will present my suggested model and explain its advantages.

2) No injunctive relief and distribution of profits

The most acceptable proposal for an alternative remedies model in the context of derivative works focusses on refraining from granting injunctive relief to the first author and granting a remedy of distribution of profits or ongoing royalties instead. Orit Fischman Afori suggested that this remedies model be adopted only in certain cases and that courts should be left the discretion to decide when injunctive relief should be granted and when a monetary remedy would suffice.[41] Other authors such as Paul Edward Geller and Lydia Pallas Loren suggested that in the case of derivative works injunctive relief should never be granted and the first author should only be entitled to monetary remedies.[42] In any event, if injunctive relief is not granted, the court should grant the first author a monetary remedy in the form of distribution of profits arising from the second work, or a fixed rate of ongoing royalties that the second author must pay the first owner for use of the derivative work.[43]

The main advantage of this remedies model is that it does not require any legislative change for its application. In many jurisdictions, including the United States, copyright laws grant the copyright owner the right to seek injunctive relief for copyright infringement. However, the court has discretion whether to grant such relief.[44] In fact, courts sometimes consider refraining from granting injunctive reliefs. For example, in the case of Abend v. MCA, Inc., the court decided that although the defendant infringed the plaintiffs' copyright, no injunction should be granted and monetary damages will suffice due to the damage that may be caused to the public if injunctive relief is granted.[45] However, despite the courts' willingness to refrain from granting injunctive relief, as far as copyright is concerned (and specifically the derivative works right), courts, at least in the United States, generally grant injunctive reliefs in most cases.[46]

The most significant deficiency of this remedies model lies in the uncertainty that it causes on two different levels, which may offset the social benefit underlying such model and the incentive for second authors to make derivative works. On the first level, to the extent that courts have full discretion to decide whether injunctive relief will be granted in each and every case, the second author will always remain uncertain as to whether she could exploit the second work without the first author's consent. This uncertainty puts the second author in a similar situation as the current model does. Thus, a rational second author will decide, in many cases, not to make the derivative work without the first author's consent, in order to avoid the risk of losing her entire investment.

On the second level, even if the no-injunctive-relief rule will always apply, additional uncertainty is created since the second author has no way of knowing what portion of the future profits from the second work she will be entitled to. This is because this remedies model is subject to judicial review and the decision will always be made after the second work was already created (and even distributed), and after the first author has filed an infringement claim. In addition, under this model, the first author will have full control over the timing of the infringement claim and will be able to act strategically and wait for the distribution of the second work and its market impact before seeking distribution of profits. This uncertainty also offsets much of the social benefits underlying this model, since the incentive for rational second authors to make derivative works will diminish significantly due to the uncertainty with respect to future profits.

3) Blocking copyright

Another alternative remedies model is a doctrine named "blocking copyright," which is based on a parallel doctrine in patent law. The blocking patent doctrine refers to a parallel issue to derivative works – improvement patents – which are patents based on preexisting patent protected technology for the purpose of significantly improving it. According to the blocking patent doctrine, the inventor of an improvement patent may register a patent on her improvement, and thus, while she cannot use the product protected by such patent (as it infringes the first patent), so is the first inventor barred from using the improved product (as it will infringe the second patent). In this case, the deadlock created between the parties is expected to lead them to a rational deal for a cross-license in cases in where significant value is created by the second patent.[47] In other words, according to the blocking patent doctrine, the state refrains from using its power to set the royalties rate to which each of the investors is entitled, and instead prohibits the use of the improvement patent until the parties themselves reach an agreement.

A parallel copyright law doctrine does not exist. Thus, in United States case law, when the second author makes an infringing derivative work, she will not be entitled to copyright protection for her original contribution, and the first author will be free to use the second work without her consent.[48] Therefore, the second author is deprived from the leverage that patent law offers second inventors who create improvement patents, and the bargaining power of the second author is significantly lower in comparison to that of the patent improver.

Mark Lemley compared the way in which patent law treats improvement to the way copyright law does, and reached the conclusion that with respect to derivative works, there is a strong economic justification to change existing law and shift to a blocking copyright model.[49] He argued that blocking copyright will benefit second authors in two main ways and thus benefit the making of sequential works which in turn will benefit society. First, in contrast to existing law, blocking copyright will afford second authors a bargaining tool against first authors. Such change in bargaining power, according to Lemley, will lead to a larger number of deals for the making of derivative works. Second, Lemley argued that blocking copyright will slightly diminish the fear of second authors from infringement claims, since the first authors will have a lower incentive to sue as they will not be expected to gain ownership over the second work even if they win.[50]

The main advantage of the blocking copyright doctrine is that it only requires a slight change to existing law. All that needs to be done is to grant the second author's rights in her additional original contributions included in the second work even if created without the first author's consent. The positive economic effect of the doctrine will be coordinated by the market and the parties will reach efficient rational deals. However, the blocking copyright doctrine has two significant deficiencies.

First, as extensively argued by Robert Merges with respect to blocking patents, there will be many cases in which the deadlock between the first and second authors will not lead to a deal at all, thus creating a significant deadweight loss. For example, many deals will not happen due to inconsistent valuation of the derivative work between the parties in comparison to the value of the first work.[51] In addition, irrational behavior of the parties for reasons of ego and anger may also lead to the failure of potential deals. One additional case in which no deal will be made is when the derivative work was not yet created and its value to society is not high enough to reward both authors.[52]

Second, in contrast to patent law that affords strong and full protection from the unauthorized exploitation of the idea underlying the patent, copyright law only protects the expression and not the underlying idea of the work. Thus, when the second author will create a derivative work and turn to the first author for a license, to the extent that the first author deems the second work successful, she will be able to make a substitute derivative work without infringing the right of the second author. Therefore, in cases where the cost of making the second work is insignificant, the second author may fear to expose her work to the first author, thus preventing an efficient deal.[53]

Finally, from a distributive perspective, the state's refusal to impose a deal on the parties, preventing the use of the derivative work until the parties reach an agreement, will give additional weight to the proportionate bargaining power of the parties in setting the royalties rate. The stronger party will likely be the first author whose financial situation is not dependent on the profits from the second work and is thus freer not to reach a deal. In contrast, under the previous model and under the compulsory license model which will be presented below, in which without the parties' consent the court will determine the royalties rate, it is more likely that the original bargaining power of the parties will be less significant.

4) Taxes and levies

One last alternative model, although less accepted in the literature, is a model based on a taxation or levies system supporting the grant of free access to existing work for users (and second authors), and offering fair remuneration to first authors.

This extensive remedies model in copyright law was first suggested by William (Terry) Fisher. He suggested to shift to a system in which authors will register their works in a registry and receive a digital code that could be embedded in digital copies of their works for tracking purposes. The state, on its part, will raise money through taxes in order to remunerate the authors so registering their works. By digitally tracking the use of works and by rating samples, the state will determine the proper remuneration method and the sum to which each author is entitled for the use of her works. At the same time, the exclusive rights granted to authors under copyright will be revoked and users will be allowed to freely use existing works.[54] In the context of the derivative works right, Fisher explained that this model will have a significant contribution in light of new creative patterns which systematically use preexisting works, such as digital sampling and mash-up. In addition, according to Fisher, the suggested model will facilitate the establishment of further new creative patterns characterized by the making of derivative works.

A similar alternative would be a system of levies for certain types of uses of works. In contrast to a general taxation model, a levies model only imposes payment obligations on specific groups that use works in specific ways. Different mechanisms of levies as an alternative remedies model for private uses of copyrighted works exist throughout the world, but these focus mainly on the reproduction right (or similar rights), and determine that the personal use of works is allowed while determining a mechanism for the payment of levies and distribution of revenues between the authors.[55] Neil Netanel suggested, with respect to derivative works, that such levies mechanisms should be extended to allow both private and commercial uses of works for making derivative works.[56]

The main advantage of these remedies models is that they allow the free making of derivative works without the intervention of a judicial or administrative body that has to approve the use *ex ante* or *ex post*, as well as without any direct relationship between the first and second authors. However, this remedies model has significant shortcomings which make it almost completely impossible politically. First, this model creates significant costs of establishing a centralized taxation mechanism, the identification of works and their use and distribution of profits. These costs may offset a significant part of the benefits underlying this model. Second, and perhaps more importantly, this model requires significant governmental intervention (both legislative and administrative), both with respect to the tax collection and with respect to the distribution of profits. These decisions have significant distributive effects, and making the right decisions in this context is a difficult and perhaps impossible task politically, both for the legislature and for the relevant administrative authority, the legitimacy of which as a discretionary decision maker is highly doubted.

IV. The proposed remedies model – compulsory licenses for the making of derivative works

1) Compulsory licenses in copyright law

A compulsory license model refers to cases in which the law allows a specific use of the property of another, subject to a predefined license agreement or under terms set forth in adjudication, if the parties themselves do not reach an agreement. In intellectual property law, some mechanisms of compulsory licenses exist. One prominent example is the statutory license for the making of sound recordings based on existing musical work (the "cover version" license) in the United States (and other jurisdictions). Section 115 of the United States Copyright Act determines that the recording of a cover version of a previously recorded musical work, and its distribution, is allowed subject to a statutory fee.[57] Although the Act determines that the parties are free to negotiate a deal for such a license, it also established a committee whose purpose is to determine the fair royalties rate for non-consensual use of such works, and, *de facto*, creates a statutory license – meaning that the fee for the license is statutorily predetermined.[58] This part will focus on compulsory licenses (meaning, that the terms of the license and the fee are not statutorily predetermined) and not on statutory licenses.

I am not the first to suggest a shift to a compulsory license model for the making of derivative works. Several commentators suggested that a compulsory (or statutory) license model be adopted for the making of specific types of derivative works only. Jane Ginsburg suggested that statutory licenses for the making of derivative works based on work of low creative nature (such as databases) be adopted.[59] Peter Menell suggested to shift to a statutory license model for the making of mash-up works.[60] Kembrew McLeod and Peter DiCola suggested a compulsory license model for musical works based on digital sampling is justified.[61] Other commentators suggested shifting to an extensive compulsory license model for derivative works. Naomi Voegtli, for example, explained that one way to deal with the many difficulties of the derivative works right is a compulsory license model.[62] Robert Morrison suggested that a full statutory license model for derivative works is justified under some normative grounds.[63]

Although such general suggestions for a shift to a compulsory license model for the making of derivative works exist, none of them outlined a model for implementing this idea in a way that resolves the difficulties underlying this model,[64] and none explained why a compulsory license model is better than the alternative remedies models. In the remainder of this part I suggest a model for compulsory licenses for making derivative works, explain its advantages in comparison to the alternative model discussed above and address several parallel doctrines resolving a significant part of the shortcomings of the model.

2) The suggested model and its advantages

As already explained, my main argument is that a compulsory license model for the making of derivative works is the best, most efficient and fairest remedies model for the derivative works right. Now, I will outline the general model for its implementation and explain how its different characteristics overcome the main difficulties underlying compulsory licenses in general and their application to derivative works in particular. This discussion will focus on the main principles required for the operation of the model. Naturally, I will not address all procedural and technical aspects related to this model. When I will address procedural and technical aspects, I will explain why these are necessary and why they are required to resolve substantial difficulties in the suggested model. In addition, I will address potential shortcomings of the model. This discussion is based on the assumption that a change in the current remedies model for the derivative works right is required, as previously discussed in Chapter 4, and that a shift from a property rule protection to a liability rule protection is justified. Therefore, the discussion will focus on choosing the best, most efficient and fairest way to do so, and thus will focus on the advantages of the suggested model in comparison to the previously described models and not in comparison to current law.

The basic principle in a compulsory license model for the making of derivative works is that the making of such works should be allowed even absent the first author's consent, provided that due royalties will be paid for the use of protected expressions.[65] This is a relatively simple rule that overcomes one of the most significant difficulties in the context of compulsory licenses – the cost of establishing and maintaining a statutory framework for the various types of works, the cost of the license and its terms.[66] This rule overcomes another difficulty, which is the fear of setting a high price for a specific use and limiting the contractual freedom of the parties, since the setting of a statutory maximum price leads to a fixation of this price for all relevant bargains.[67] An open rule of compulsory (as opposed to statutory) licenses allows the parties to freely negotiate the terms of the license and its price.[68] If the parties will reach an agreement, the social benefits of the deal will be high since transaction costs will be lower in comparison to current law or to the statutory license model, the derivative work will be created and distributed, and both parties, the first and second authors, will be rewarded under terms acceptable to them.

Further to the basic rule, if the parties cannot reach an agreement with respect to the terms of the license and its price, the second author could file a claim to a judicial tribunal to determine the appropriate rate of royalties. This has two main difficulties. First, the ability of judges to determine the appropriate royalties rate may be put in doubt, and there may be concern that the price determined will be higher (or lower) than the price that could be achieved through an arms-length transaction.[69] Second, the mechanism creates significant adjudication costs that may offset the social benefits of the model and have certain distributive effects on the parties. While these difficulties must be addressed, I argue that they do not pose a significant obstacle to the adoption of this model and do not significantly undermine its efficiency. I will suggest possible responses to these difficulties without ruling out other ways to mitigate these concerns or the possibility that some of these difficulties cannot be fully eliminated and will have to be taken into account as a structured cost.

As for the first difficulty, judges' competence to determine an appropriate royalty rate is not different to their competence to determine the appropriate damages in any other legal field. Much like other fields, the court (or a dedicated tribunal for royalties) can rely on expert witnesses to determine the appropriate royalties.[70] The royalties should be based on a percentage from the future revenues of the derivative work and not on a fixed price for the use of the preexisting expressions or for each copy of the work. This is beneficial in two ways. First, it will facilitate the task of setting the appropriate royalties rate. The court (with the assistance of expert witnesses) will have to determine what is the contribution of the first work (or the protected expressions thereof) to the second work. This determination must be both quantitative and qualitative and the result will be set as a percentage. Second, this rule does not excessively burden second authors in that it does not impose significant costs before any revenues have been made from the second work, and thus does not have significant distributive effects other than the cost of adjudication.[71] A rule which sets the royalties rate based on the percentage of revenues from the second work must, however, take into account the reputation and goodwill benefits for the second author when making a derivative work, since these are not dependent on the revenues from the distribution of the second work.[72] To deal with this issue, a preliminary lump sum for the making of the derivative work must be determined, which will reward the first author for such reputation and goodwill. This fixed sum also responds to the second difficulty elaborated below.

As for the second difficulty, it must first be noted that the costs of adjudication in this model will not be different than the current costs of litigation in copyright infringement cases. In addition, it seems that several rules could be adopted to significantly limit the number of adjudications in the context of infringements of the derivative works right which will significantly reduce the overall costs for several reasons. First, it could be determined that the fixed sum paid by the second author for the making of the derivative work (regardless of the royalty rate) will also fund the future adjudication to the extent that it only relates to the rate of royalties. This will effectively cause the second author to internalize the costs of the model and will impose an "entry fee" for the making of the derivative work which will prevent misuse of the model. Second, the compulsory license model creates strong incentives, for both parties, to reach an agreement with respect to the royalty rate in most cases. From the viewpoint of the second author, judicial adjudication is tied with a payment of the fixed fee and with the risk that the outcome of the procedure would be that the making of the derivative work was in fact a wrongful reproduction. From the viewpoint of the first author, the procedure may result in a decision that the making of the derivative work was in fact fair use and thus allowed without any payment, or that no protected expressions from the first work were used at all.[73] Therefore, both the first and second authors are subject to an "all or nothing" risk in such adjudication. In addition, both are under uncertainty with respect to the royalty rate to be determined in such adjudication, which could be lower or higher than their expectations. Therefore, an *ex ante* consensual license provides insurance for both sides and will be preferred by them over adjudication in most cases.[74] In addition, it could be expected that market forces will establish various mechanisms facilitating consensual deals between the parties with respect to the license terms and fees. One example could be existing or new collecting societies, that will aggregate the rights to make derivative works of various authors and will predefine specific licenses for the making of such derivative works.[75] It is important to note that the discussion here assumes that such secondary rules, dealing mainly with procedural aspects, could be adopted. Different jurisdictions have different procedural rules and different treatment of the question whether these could be deviated from for specific purposes, which may pose a difficulty both normatively and from the perspective of political feasibility. The suggestion to adopt such a system of rules is brought here as one theoretical alternative to implement the suggested model in the most efficient way, but it is of course not the only alternative that could achieve such purpose.

If the above complementary rules are adopted, the adjudication with respect to derivative works will focus on three main cases. The first type refers to cases where the first author is convinced that the derivative work is in fact a wrongful reproduction while the second author is convinced that it is indeed a derivative work. The second type refers to cases where the second author is convinced that the derivative work is in fact fair use (or a completely original work) and is therefore allowed for free and the first author is convinced that it is not. The third type refers to cases where the difference between the parties' estimations of the value of the contribution of the first work for the derivative work is extremely high. The costs related to these types of cases cannot be considered as offsetting the social benefits of the suggested model. Focussing the legal adjudication on the borderline cases discussing the difference between the reproduction right and the derivative works case on one hand, and the difference between the derivative works right and fair use on the other hand, is of great social benefit. Due to the discussion on the overlap between the derivative works right and the reproduction right, a remedies model leading to the clarification of the scope of each of these rights is efficient because it diverts the current costs of litigation to the review of legal questions contributing to the certainty of the parties with respect to the borders of such rights and doctrines. Therefore, these litigation costs cannot be seen as an excessive social cost. The third type of case is of social benefit too. Cases in which significant differences in evaluation between the parties will assist the court, with the aid of expert witnesses, to determine guideline rules for calculating the appropriate rate of royalties for compulsory licenses, and to signal to the market what would be a fair rate of royalties thus reducing the uncertainty, and eventually leading to a greater number of consensual deals.[76]

An additional difficulty results from the need of the first author, who is interested in making derivative works on her own, for due preparation time to make and market the work. The most significant economic justification for the derivative works right is affording the first author due time to make a derivative work.[77] For the suggested model to meet this need, the model should only apply following a certain blocking period, meaning, that the first author will have an exclusive right to make the derivative work for a limited time.[78] The blocking period will, most likely, have to vary with respect to different types of works. Making a motion picture version of a book requires greater time than making a sequel book, while both require a different amount of time than making new and improved versions of computer software. The discussion here does not suggest determining such periods, but the intention is for short time periods measured in months or several years depending on each type of work.[79]

The most significant advantage of the suggested model is that it creates higher certainty for second authors with respect to the feasibility of making derivative works and allows them control over the process and timing for determining the terms of such licenses and the amount of royalties. This is in contrast to models that refrain from injunctive reliefs which leaves the parties in uncertainty and grants such control to the first author, thus "punishing" the authors of successful derivative works. In addition, in comparison to the injunctive relief-based model, in which the first author initiates the proceedings only after the second author created the second work and distributed it, under the compulsory license model the second author could, *ex-ante*, find out whether the making of the derivative work, or at least its marketing and distribution, are efficient and thus save the cost of making inefficient derivative works and the costs created by not making efficient works. Moreover, the suggested model does not impose high legislative costs tied with statutory licenses, and reduces the general litigation costs in copyright law and channels them to the review of socially important questions. Finally, in contrast to the blocking copyright model, the suggested model allows for the making of almost all derivative works that second authors wish to make without resulting in deadlocks and deadweight loss.[80]

The suggested model also has several shortcomings. First, a complex set of secondary procedural rules must be established to prevent adjudication costs and adverse distributive effects. Second, a full adoption of the model requires legislative change. Third, the model raises a certain tension between the derivative works right and other copyright and intellectual property doctrines. I have suggested several ways to mitigate the first shortcoming and will suggest ways to address the third shortcoming below. However, not all such shortcomings could necessarily be eliminated, and the suggested model may have certain costs. I believe that even given such costs the suggested model is significantly better than the existing law and the alternative models discussed above, and that its adoption is justified based on the normative justifications for the derivative works right.

To conclude this part, the suggested compulsory licenses model includes a basic rule according to which the making of derivative works will be prohibited without the first author's consent for a limited time period, and following such period the second author could make derivative works absent the first author's consent, subject to the payment of appropriate royalties. To the extent that the parties will not reach an agreement, the second author could initiate legal proceedings to determine the rate of royalties, which should also take into account goodwill and reputation gains of the second author. Now it remains to discuss the parallel applicability of other copyright and intellectual property doctrines, and address several additional difficulties that may arise.

3) Parallel applicability of additional doctrines

a) Moral rights

The right to make derivative works has some overlap with the right of attribution and the right of integrity included in the moral right granted to authors in some jurisdictions. Therefore, under a compulsory license model for derivative works, some cases may contradict with the right of integrity, and even with the right of attribution. Even in the United States, in which the author's moral rights are very limited,[81] the right to make derivative works functions as a *de facto* protection on the moral rights of the first author.[82] Thus, the compulsory license may, in many cases, limit the first author's moral rights.

This concern is unjustified. With respect to the integrity right, under which the first author can prevent changes to her work which adversely affect her dignity, in most cases the second work will not have such effect. Moreover, to the extent that the integrity right is limited to adversely affect the goodwill and dignity of the first author, there is no reason that such right will not have parallel applicability to the compulsory license model, so that a use of such license will not be a defense for a violation of the integrity right. In addition, a strong right of integrity, prohibiting any change of the first work absent the author's consent, is unjustified exactly for the same reason for which the strong derivative works right is unjustified.

With respect to the attribution right, the concern is somewhat more substantiated. The right of attribution grants the first author the right that her work will be attributed to her. This aspect of the moral right does not pose a specific difficulty and could easily apply in parallel to the compulsory license model. The more difficult question is how to deal with cases in which the first author is not interested that the derivative work will be attributed to her. To resolve this concern, the compulsory license model must allow the first author to demand that the derivative work will not be attributed to her, both to protect her attribution right and to prevent the second author from making excessive reputation benefits from such use. This will remove any concern arising from the existence of moral rights.

b) Trademarks

An additional difficulty that may arise from the compulsory license model is a misuse of the license by the second author to exploit the reputation of the first author and to mislead the public as to the origins of the derivative work. A solution to this difficulty lies in two parallel sets of laws in the field of intellectual property – trademark law, preventing consumer misleading, and commercial torts law and passing off in particular, protecting the reputation and goodwill of the owner of a product or a service.

Trademark law prohibits the use of a registered or well-known trademark for the publication, manufacturing or marketing of goods without the trademark's owner's consent.[83] The passing off tort prohibits the appropriation of a person's reputation by causing consumers to believe that a specific product is manufactured or associated with such person.[84] Thus, if the second author markets the second work made under a compulsory license using the first owner's trademarks, or if she markets it in a way that causes the audience to believe that the first author created it or endorsed its creation, she will infringe the trademark of the first author or will commit a passing off.[85] As an illustration, if a second author will choose to make an eighth book in the Harry Potter series and market it under the name "Harry Potter 8" (assuming that "Harry Potter" is a registered trademark), she will violate J.K. Rowling's or her publisher's rights. In addition, to the extent that such author will choose to market the sequel book in a manner causing the audience to believe that Rowling was part of its writing or endorsed it, she will violate her rights as well.

These sets of laws merge, to a certain extent, with the first author's right that the second author's work will not be attributed to her without her consent and give an additional response to the concern raised due to potential misuse of the compulsory license model to ride the reputation of the first author. They eliminate a significant difficulty of the model and limit the ability of the second author to gain reputation on the expense of the first author.

c) Fair use

One final difficulty arises from the opposite direction – the interest of second authors (and users) to fairly use preexisting protected expressions. The fair use doctrine allows a wide range of uses of preexisting protected expressions without the need for a license or any payment duties to the first author. The adoption of a compulsory license for derivative works may contradict this.

The fair use doctrine in the United States determines that some uses of protected expressions (such as criticism, news reporting, teaching, academic research and similar uses) are not considered copyright infringement under certain conditions. The question whether a specific use of a protected expression infringes copyright is reviewed by (at least) four factors: (1) the purpose and character of use; (2) the type of work from which the expression was taken; (3) the scope and quality of the used expression in relation to the protected work from which it was taken; and (4) the effect of the use on the potential market of the protected work or its value.[86]

Empirical studies have shown that even though the fourth factor is most frequently mentioned as an important factor for the determination of the fairness of the use, the first factor is in fact the most influential on the courts' decisions.[87] United States case law clarified that in weighing the first factor, the most prominent question is whether the use is transformative.[88] Transformative use was defined as adding something new, creating an additional purpose or character which alters the first expression in creating a new expression, meaning or message.[89] A use of an expression could be transformative in two main ways – in the purpose of expression and in the meaning of the expression.[90] The transformativeness of the purpose of expression can exist, for example, when a certain work is embedded in a news reporting or when a different work is fully displayed in a parodic manner.[91] Transformativeness of the content of expression can exist when a change of the content of a work (while using protected expressions) significantly changes the overall meaning of the first work so that it is no longer intended for the first communicative purpose of the first work.[92] It is apparent that some overlap exists between the fair use doctrine and the making of derivative works, in that in some cases the making of a derivative work will constitute fair use.[93] A good example for this will be the making of the sequel book, "Harry Potter in Space". Such a book will be considered a derivative work and may also constitute transformative use which will be considered fair.

A first response to this difficulty is that the fair use doctrine may fully apply in parallel to the compulsory license model. Thus, when the second author makes a derivative work that also constitutes fair use, she will not have to obtain a compulsory license and will be free to do so for no consideration. The more complex aspect of the relationship between the compulsory license model and fair use is the potential effect that such a model may have on the way courts interpret the fair use doctrine. Today, given a strong right to make derivative works, courts may be more open to the possibility that some derivative works should be considered fair use. This is because the current regime is an "all or nothing" model under which a decision to the contrary will effectively mean a strong prohibition on the making of socially valuable derivative works. Under a compulsory license model, courts may misperceive the making of a derivative work absent a compulsory license as unfair use and thus limit the scope of the fair use doctrine.[94] This difficulty has no magic solution, since it results from the individual perception of judges and their understanding of the creative world and the role of the fair use doctrine in it. However, it may be possible to begin overcoming this difficulty by explicitly determining that the possibility of the user to obtain a license for a specific use does not affect the consideration of the fairness of such use.

V. Conclusion

The purpose of this chapter was to outline the path to align the right to make derivative works with its underlying normative justification in order to remove the difficulties raised by its application in existing law. The discussion here is based on the general conclusion from Chapter 4 according to which aligning the derivative works right with its underlying justification requires both its separation from the reproduction right and its independent definition, as well as limiting its remedies model. Therefore, outlining the optimal way to make such alignment has also included secondary factors such as efficiency, political feasibility and fairness, and absorbed from the non-legal understanding of creativity and the creative process.

As for the first aspect, in order to fully separate between derivative works and reproductions, I suggested a definition that will distinguish between the two, based mainly on the fact that a derivative work, as opposed to a reproduction, has significant additional originality which is inseparable from the first expression and cannot be substituted for a non-protected expression without derogating from the purpose of the second work. In addition, I offered several categories of uses as exemplars for derivative works and not reproductions, including works that summarize the first work, translate it and make it accessible to new audiences, improve and develop it, disassemble and reassemble it as well as using it for the making of a completely different work. With respect to the last residual category, I explained why it is the most extensive one in comparison to existing law and why it best reflects the underlying normative purpose of the suggested definition. Moreover, we saw the implications of this separation both in the establishment of independent discourse on derivative works and in different outcomes in comparison to existing law.

As for the right's remedies model, in light of the need to limit such remedies due to the normative justifications for the right as discussed in Chapter 3 and the further elaboration in Chapter 4, I outlined the most appropriate remedies model. Several alternative remedies models were discussed – refraining from injunctive relief, blocking copyright and taxes and levies – and I explained their main shortcomings. My main argument was that the most appropriate, efficient and fair remedies model for the derivative works right is a compulsory license model. Accordingly, I suggested a detailed model for compulsory licenses while responding to significant difficulties that may arise, and explained how it fits with other parallel doctrines such as moral rights, trademarks and commercial torts, and the fair use doctrine, in a manner that leads to an efficient outcome which will contribute to the development of the creative world and enrich the world of expressions. In short, the appropriate model relies on a rule allowing the second author to use expressions from the first work for the making of a derivative work without the first author's consent, subject to the payment of reasonable royalties derived from the future revenues of the work. To the extent that the parties do not reach an agreement, the second author could initiate proceedings to determine the rate of royalties, subject to the payment of a fixed price for the cost of proceedings and the expected reputation gains. The entire model is subject to a blocking period which will allow the first author to exclusively make derivative works for a limited time period.

Notes

1 *See, e.g.* Jed Rubenfeld, *Freedom of Imagination: Copyright's Constitutionality*, 112 YALE L.J. 1, 54–5 (2002); Daniel Gervais, *The Derivative Right: Or Why Copyright Law Protects Foxes Better Than Hedgehogs*, 15 VAN. J. ENT. & TECH. L. 785, 837 (2013).

2 There are some acts of reproduction that, at least prima facie do not include additional originality, which could definitely be defined as creative acts. Such actions will often be considered fair use because although they use the preexisting expression in its entirety, they change the purpose or meaning of the expression in a way that arises to transformative use which is often allowed under the fair use doctrine. An example for this would be presenting the original work in a context that changes its meaning, for example placing the character of Harry Potter in the Tate Gallery to express dissatisfaction in the quality of modern fictional literature. Patrick Ogilvy argued that this type of use will not be considered derivative rather as an allowed reproduction. *See* Patrick W. Ogilvy, *Frozen in Time? New Technologies, Fixation, and the Derivative Work Right*, 8 VAND. J. ENT. & TECH. L. 687, 694–5 (2006). However, this is obviously not the only option. If we take the notions from cognitive psychology on the creative process and the notions from genre theories on the way in which the creative work develops seriously, we can reach the conclusion that changing the method of presentation of a work in a way that changed its expression or meaning could amount to substantial additional originality which could constitute a derivative work. In fact, in one case the court for the south district of New York emphasized that in order to determine that substantial originality exists in the second work, one should focus on the creative process leading to its creation and not only on the final creative product: *see* Tempo Music v. Famous Music Corp., 838 F. Supp. 162 (S.D.N.Y. 1993) ("Once it is understood that originality, for copyright purposes, looks to creative process rather than novel outcomes or results, it becomes clear that harmony can, as a matter of law, be the subject of copyright").

3 The condition that the preexisting expression be inseparable from the second work is quite similar to the idea of accession in property law. For elaboration *see* Omri Rachum-Twaig & Ohad Somech, 2017 *The Right-Based View of the Cathedral: Liability Rules and Corrective Justice*, PEPPERDINE L. REV. (2017). Thus, there is a direct link between the act of the second author, mixing part of the first work with the second work in an inseparable way, and the legal outcome of the act which in our case is the definition of a derivative work and a compulsory license model. For elaboration on this link *see supra* Chapter 3.IV.

4 It is important to note that requiring that the taken expression be non-fungible does not mean that the second author cannot choose a preexisting work to incorporate in the second work. For example, a second author who chooses to make a sequel to the Harry Potter book series will be allowed to use expressions from the first work and still meet this condition. This is because in the context of a sequel to the book series, there are necessary preexisting expressions (such as characters and main plot lines) which cannot be substituted without derogating from the essence of the work.

5 Pamela Samuelson, *The Quest for a Sound Conception of Copyright's Derivative Work Right*, 101 GEO. L.J. 1505, 1518–27 (2013).

6 This is in contrast to communication to new audiences which is only based on new technologies but maintains the first work in its entirety without change. These should be considered as public display or communication to the public.

7 *See* 17 U.S.C. § 101. Much like the discussion on annotations as part of the first category of uses, not every translation will necessarily constitute a derivative work and the author of a translation will have to show that it is original in its own account. Thus, some translations may be entirely (or partly) functional and dictated by the rules and constraints of language. These types of translations will not constitute original works and therefore will not be considered derivative works. To the extent that such

translations will make unauthorized use of protected expressions from the first work, they will infringe the reproduction right, even if literal copying is unrecognizable due to the language change. I do not *see* the difficulty in understanding a non-original translation as the copying of expressions from one language to another. An example would be the translation of instructions of use or legal documents which purpose is to preserve, to the fullest extent possible, the meaning of the original document. This could also be true to the translations of short artistic literary works which content does not allow for much translation gap.

8 The famous case of Campbell v. Acuff-Rose Music, Inc., 510 U.S. 569 (U.S. 1994) is a good example for such use, in which the plaintiffs arranged the famous song "Pretty Woman" to the hip-hop genre and significantly changed the lyrics. The court decided the case on the basis of the fair use doctrine because the second work was considered a parody of the first. However, Justice Kennedy's opinion in this case stated that when a musical arrangement changes the genre of the first work and does not constitute a parody, it would be considered an infringing derivative work. *See id.*, at 599 ("Almost any revamped modern version of a familiar composition can be construed as a 'comment on the naivete of the original,' ante, at 583, because of the difference in style and because it will be amusing to hear how the old tune sounds in the new genre").

9 Adapting a literary work to a motion picture requires substantial additional originality from the second author, but such addition does not aim at changing the original expression rather at preserving it and communicating it in a different medium. A motion picture adaptation of a literary work is a statutory exemplar. Samuelson suggested in this context that the transfer of a two-dimensional work to a three-dimensional form will also constitute a derivative work. *See* Samuelson, *supra* note 5, at 1525. *See* in this context the case of King Features Syndicate v. Fleischer, 299 F. 533 (2d Cir. N.Y. 1924) in which the court decided that making a horse shaped doll based on a horse drawing from a children's book infringes the copyright of the first author. In the same case, which was decided before the enacting of the 1976 Copyright Act, the court ruled that this act constitutes a reproduction of the first work. I believe that in many cases the making of a three-dimensional work based on a two-dimensional work, and vice versa, will amount to reproduction and not to the making of a derivative work due to the lack of originality in such actions.

10 *See, e.g.*, Oracle Am., Inc. v. Google Inc., 750 F.3d 1339 (Fed. Cir. 2014), which will be discussed in length below.

11 David Fishelov, METAPHORS OF GENRE 35–9 (1993).

12 Alastir Fowler, KINDS OF LITERATURE 181–8 (1982).

13 A good example for this is the case in which the scriptwriter created a script for a sequel to the Rocky motion picture series (Rocky IV, to be exact), without the authorization of the owner of the previous scripts, Silvester Stallone. The court decided in this case that the new script infringed the derivative works right and that the rights to the infringing script are Stallone's. *See* Anderson v. Stallone, 1989 U.S. Dist. LEXIS 11109 (C.D. Cal. Apr. 25, 1989). Another example for this type of uses is the case of Salinger v. Colting, 607 F.3d 68 (2d Cir. 2010), in which an author created a sequel to the book "The Catcher in the Rye" which tells the story of the main character, Holden Caulfield, 60 years after the first book.

14 One example would be the case of Midway Mfg. Co. v. Artic Int'l, Inc., 704 F.2d 1009 (7th Cir. 1983), in which the court decided that an add-on to a video game which uses the existing code through a chip that substitutes part of the existing hardware to make the game faster and hence more challenging, is an infringing derivative work. Another example is the case of Oracle Am., *supra* note 10, which revolved around Google's Android operating system which was developed based upon Oracle's Java platform. Google's use does not only constitute a change of medium (PC to mobile) rather an improvement of the existing platform which includes several important additions. This last use will probably fall also under the previous category sine its main purpose was

creating compatibility between the Java and Android platforms in order to make the platform available for mobile applications developers.

15 Fishelov, *supra* note 11.

16 An example would be the case of Galoob Inc. v. Nintendo of America Inc., 964 F. 2d 965 (9th Cir. 1992), in which the court decided that an add-on to a video game which adds code that makes the game faster, does not constitute a derivative work and is not infringing. *See* Samuelson, *supra* note 5, at 1539–41.

17 Remix is the disassembly of a work (usually musical work) to its substantial components and reconstructing them in a way that enriches the first work, changes its character of adapts it to a different style. It is in fact an arrangement that uses a sample of the original sound of the first work instead or performing it. for a discussion on the definition of remix *see* Eduardo Navas, *Regressive and Reflexive Mashups in Sampling Culture, in* MASHUP CULTURES 157, 159 (Stefan Sonvilla-Weiss ed., 2010). Mashup is the connection of two (usually musical or audio-visual) works merging them to one work that could be continuously displayed. *See* Ragnhild Brøvig-Hanssen, *Justin Bieber Featuring Slipknot, in* THE OXFORD HANDBOOK OF MUSIC AND VIRTUALITY ch. 15 (Sheila Whiteley & Shara Rambarran eds, 2016); Ragnhild Brøvig-Hanssen & Paul Harkins, *Contextual Incongruity and Musical Congruity: The Aesthetics and Humour of Mash-Ups*, 31 POPULAR MUSIC 87, 89 (2012).

18 One famous example is the decision in SunTrust Bank v. Houghton Mifflin Co., 268 F.3d 1257, 1265–7 (11th Cir. 2001), in which the plaintiff published a book that included part of the famous book "Gone with the Wind" in order to criticize the way in which the first book presented the slavery in southern United States during the civil war. The court decided that although this was a derivative work of the first book, it should be considered parody which is protected under fair use. In a different case, the court decided that a commercial for a motion picture which used a famous photography of the plaintiff, in which a nude pregnant woman is displayed in a position resembling Botticelli's famous Birth of Venus, while substituting the head of the woman with the picture of the lead actress in the motion picture, is a derivative work which amounts to parody and therefore considered fair use. *See also* Leibovitz v. Paramount Pictures Corp., 137 F.3d 109 (2d Cir. 1998) but *cf.* Dr. Seuss Enters., L.P. v. Penguin Books USA, Inc., 109 F.3d 1394 (9th Cir. 1997), in which the court decided that the defendants, who created a literary work based on Dr. Seuss' "The Cat in the Hat" in order to critically portray the O.J. Simpson case, made an infringing derivative work which is considered a satire and is not protected under fair use. *See also* New Line Cinema Corp. v. Bertlesman Music Group, Inc., 693 F. Supp. 1517 (S.D.N.Y. 1988), in which the video clip produced by the defendants, combining the character of Freddy Kruger in "A Nightmare on Elm Street" in the video accompanying their song, was decided to be infringing derivative work.

19 Clear examples for this type of uses are the abovementioned cases dealing with the use of a song's chorus or another part of a musical work, or alternatively the digital sampling of previous works, in order to create new musical works. *See* Swirsky v. Carey, 376 F.3d 841 (9th Cir. 2004); Newton v. Diamond, 388 F.3d 1189, 1193 (9th Cir. 2004); Bridgeport Music, Inc. v. UMG Recordings, Inc., 585 F.3d 267 (6th Cir. 2009); Copeland v. Bieber, 789 F.3d 484, 492–93 (4th Cir. 2015); TufAmerica Inc. v. Diamond, 968 F. Supp. 2d 588 (S.D.N.Y. 2013); Mayimba Music, Inc. v. Sony Corp. of Am., 2014 U.S. Dist. LEXIS 152051 (S.D.N.Y. Aug. 19, 2014).

20 Chris Newman, *Transformation in Property and Copyright*, 56 VILL. L. REV. 251, 304–7 (2011).

21 While this condition fulfills the internal purposes of copyright law and the derivative works right, it does not impede the freedom of expression of the second author. This is because the condition does not limit the second author at the stage of selecting the essence of the work she chooses to create. The meaning of this condition is that after freely choosing the essence of the second work, the author must remain committed to

such essence when using previous protected expressions for its creation, and only such uses that are connected to the essence of the work will be considered derivative works and not reproductions.

22 It is important to note that in many cases the use of sound samples should not be considered a shortcut. Often, the use of sound samples results from an artistic approach of gestures to previous authors or the will to create in the form of collage. However, the use of sound samples can be considered a shortcut when it is functional in its nature (e.g., sampling a specific musical instrument in order to create the illusion that the new sound recording included many musical instruments).

23 Fowler, *supra* note 12.

24 The case of Oracle Am., Inc. is a good example since in this case Google made a compatible version of Java for mobile phones; effectively translating it to a new medium, and at the same time significantly improved the work in a manner that constitutes an additional original work.

25 This is in explicit contrast to the famous ruling of Judge Learned Hand according to which "... it is enough that substantial parts were lifted; no plagiarist can excuse the wrong by showing how much of his work he did not pirate." *See* Sheldon v. Metro-Goldwyn Pictures Corp., 81 F.2d 49, 56 (2d Cir. 1936). *See also* Nichols v. Universal Pictures Corp., 45 F.2d 119, 121 (2d Cir. 1930). I argue that while this ruling is true for the review of an infringement of the reproduction right, it does not fit the derivative works right to the extent that it is a separate and independent right with different underlying purposes in comparison to the reproduction right.

26 For a discussion on these cases *see* Chapter 4.III above.

27 Elvis Presley Enterprises, Inc. v. Passport Video, 357 F.3d 896 (9th Cir. 2003).

28 It is important to note that under the proposed definition, the question is not whether the preexisting expressions from the first work are identifiable in the second work, rather whether they could be separated (meaning, removing the preexisting expressions from the second work without damaging it). A different case also dealing with documentary work is Jacobsen v. Desert Book Co., 287 F.3d 936 (10th Cir. 2002). The plaintiff, which was held captive in the Philippines and Japan during the second world war, wrote a memoir. The defendant published a series of five fictional books focussing on the like of a family during the war while the story of one family member is substantially similar to the plaintiff's memoir. *Id.*, at 940–1. The court of appeal remanded the case for further hearing after determining that substantial similarity exists between the two works and therefore the defendant copies the plaintiff's memoir. The court also determined that "We realize the five-volume *Children of the Promise* series contains much material not taken from the single-volume *Who Refused to Die*". *Id.*, at 945. According to the court's determination that the two works are substantially similar, it seems that here too, under the proposed definition, the second work would constitute a derivative work based on the plaintiff's work.

29 Swirsky v. Carey, *supra* note 19.

30 "To establish a successful copyright infringement claim, Swirsky must show that (1) he owns the copyright in *One* and (2) Carey copied protected elements of *One*". *Id.*, at 844.

31 *Id.* ("*One* and *Thank God* have generally dissimilar lyrics and verse melodies").

32 For a different case in which the substantial similarity in the choruses of two songs led the court to the decide that the reproduction right was infringed, without resorting to derivative works although the rest of the "infringing" song was original *see* Mayimba Music, Inc., *supra* note 19. *See* also Bridgeport Music, Inc., *supra* note 19. in another case, the court of appeals overturned a lower court's decision that several songs by Usher and Justin Bieber are not substantially similar to a song composed by the plaintiff. The court determined that according to the intrinsic similarity test the songs are sufficiently similar although they are in different genres and "that difference is striking upon first listen, and at least as a linguistic matter, the very fact of these different genres might be thought to make the songs different in 'concept and feel'" and that "taken

numerically, the points of dissimilarity may well exceed the points of similarity". *See* Copeland *supra* note 19. in fact, the only similarity between the songs was a sequence of three words from the chorus of the first song (with same lyrics and rhythm), and as the court determined "It is not simply that both choruses contain the lyric 'somebody to love'; it is that the lyric is delivered in what seems to be an almost identical rhythm and a strikingly similar melody". In this case too, under the new definition, an analysis of derivative works would be required.

33 TufAmerica, *supra* note 19.

34 For additional cases focussing on copyright infringement by digital sampling without resorting to derivative works *see* Fisher v. Dees, 794 F.2d 432 (9th Cir. 1986); Newton v. Diamond, *supra* note 19.

35 Oracle Am., Inc., *supra* note 10.

36 Melville B. Nimmer & David Nimmer, 1 NIMMER ON COPYRIGHT § 3.05 (2017) (hereinafter: NIMMER ON COPYRIGHT).

37 *See, e.g.*, Gamma Audio & Video, Inc. v. Ean-Chea, 11 F.3d 1106, 1112 (1st Cir. 1993); Roy Export Co. Establishment v. Columbia Broadcasting Sys., Inc., 503 F. Supp. 1137 (S.D.N.Y. 1980). Nimmer on Copyright, *supra* note 36, at 3.05.

38 *Id.*, at 3.05.

39 *See* 17 U.S.C. § 502.

40 Guido Calabresi & A. Douglas Melamed, *Property Rules, Liability Rules and Inalienability: One View of the Cathedral*, 86 HARV. L. REV. 1089 (1972).

41 Orit Fischman Afori, *Flexible Remedies as a Means to Counteract Failures in Copyright Law*, 29 CARDOZO ARTS & ENT. L.J. 1 (2011). For similar suggestions to limit injunctive relief in copyright generally *see* Wendy J. Gordon, *Property Right in Self-Expression: Equality and Individualism in the Natural Law of Intellectual Property, A*, 102 YALE L.J. 1533, 1573–74 (1993); Benjamin Kaplan, AN UNHURRIED VIEW OF COPYRIGHT 110–11 (1967).

42 *See* Paul Edward Geller, *Hiroshige vs. Van Gogh: Resolving the Dilemma of Copyright Scope in Remedying Infringement*, 46 J. COPYRIGHT SOC'Y U.S.A. 39, 61 (1998); Lydia Pallas Loren, *Pope's Copyright – Aligning Incentives with Reality by Using Creative Motivation to Shape Copyright Protection, The*, 69 LA. L. REV. 1, 40 (2008). *See also* John Tehrainian, *Whither Copyright - Transformative Use, Free Speech, and an Intermediate Liability Proposal*, 2005 BYU L. REV. 1201, 1236–39 (2005); Thomas F. Cotter, *Fair use and Copyright Overenforcement*, 93 IOWA L. REV. 1271, 1295 (2008); Pamela Samuelson, *Possible Futures of Fair Use*, 90 WASH. L. REV. 815, 862–63 (2015). These approaches express, *de facto*, the transition from a property rule protection to a liability rule protection.

43 For a guiding Supreme Court decision with respect to distribution of profits in the case of copyright infringement *see* Sheldon v. Metro-Goldwyn Pictures Corp., 309 U.S. 390, 406 (1940). For the rule that, in some cases, ongoing royalties should be granted *see* Petrella v. MGM, 134 S. Ct. 1962 (U.S. 2014); Practice Mgmt. Info. Corp. v. AMA, 121 F.3d 516 (9th Cir. 1997). For an updated application of this rule in the case of a musical work based on a preexisting work, which effectively arises to a derivative work, *see* Williams v. Bridgeport Music, Inc., 2015 U.S. Dist. LEXIS 97262, 121–40 (C.D. Cal. July 14, 2015).

44 17 U.S.C. § 502 ("Any court having jurisdiction of a civil action arising under this title may… grant temporary and final injunctions on such terms as it may deem reasonable to prevent or restrain infringement of a copyright").

45 Abend v. MCA, Inc., 863 F.2d 1465, 1479 (9th Cir. 1988). However, the decision in this case was based on the fact that the derivative work was made under the first author's consent and became infringing only due to later circumstances. This may be the reason for this decision which does not align with prior and later decisions in the context of remedies for copyright infringement.

46 For example, the Supreme Court decided in eBay Inc. v. MercExchange, L.L.C., 547 U.S. 388 (U.S. 2006), that plaintiffs in copyright cases must meet four criteria in order

to be granted injunctive relief: (1) irreparable harm has been caused; (2) monetary damages will not cure such harm; (3) the balance of interests between the plaintiffs and defendants is weighed in favor of plaintiffs and (4) the public interest will not be adversely affected by the injunction. *Id.*, at 391. Despite the fact that the court decided in this case that the rule in copyright law is that injunctive relief is not automatic, *Id.*, at 392, a review of later case law shows that the most dominant remedy for copyright infringement is injunctive relief. *See* Jiarui Liu, *Copyright Injunctions after eBay: An Empirical Study*, 16 LEWIS & CLARK L. REV. 215 (2012).

47 For elaboration on the blocking patents doctrine *see* Robert P. Merges and Richard R. Nelson, *On the Complex Economics of Patent Scope*, 90 COLUM. L. REV. 839, 860–62 (1990); Robert P. Merges, *Intellectual Property Rights and Bargaining Breakdown: The Case of Blocking Patents*, 62 TENN. L. REV. 75, 78–81 (1994); Mark A. Lemley, *Economics of Improvement in Intellectual Property Law*, 75 TEX. L. REV. 989, 1008–9 (1997).

48 *See* Anderson v. Stallone, 1989 U.S. Dist. LEXIS 11109 (C.D. Cal. Apr. 25, 1989). This determination is not necessarily mandated by the language of the Copyright Act. Section 103(a) of the Copyright Act only determines that to the extent that a derivative work includes parts based on previous works without the first author's consent, the derivative works right will not apply to them. *See* 17 U.S.C. § 103(a). However, in *Anderson* the court reached the conclusion that the meaning of an exclusive right to make derivative works is that unauthorized derivative works will not be copyright protected with respect to the second author. *Id.*, at 31. *See also* Pickett v. Prince, 52 F. Supp. 2d 893, 906–7 (N.D. Ill. 1999); NIMMER ON COPYRIGHT, *supra* note 36, at 3.06. *Cf.* Kelly Casey Mullally, *Blocking Copyrights Revisited*, 37 COLUM. J.L. & ARTS 57, 73–80 (2013), suggesting an alternative interpretation of the Copyright Act which allows for blocking copyright.

49 Lemley, *supra* note 47, at 1074.

50 For similar approaches *see* Wendy J. Gordon, *Toward a Jurisprudence of Benefits: The Norms of Copyright and the Problem of Private Censorship*, 57 U. CHI. L. REV. 1009, 1019–20 (1990); Matthew A. Kaplan, *Rosencrantz and Guildenstern Are Dead, But Are They Copyrightable: Protection of Literary Characters with Respect to Secondary Works*, 30 RUTGERS L.J. 817, 841–2 (1999); Paul Goldstein, *Derivative Rights and Derivative Works in Copyright*, 30 J. COPYRIGHT SOC'Y U.S.A. 209, 211, 244 (1983); Kelly Casey Mullally, *Blocking Copyrights Revisited*, 37 COLUM. J.L. & ARTS 57, 80–92 (2013).

51 Merges, *supra* note 47, at 89–90.

52 For a similar argument with respect to patent law *see* Robert P. Merges, *A Brief Note on Blocking Patents and Reverse Equivalents: Biotechnology as an Example*, 73 J. PAT. & TRADEMARK OFF. SOC'Y 878, 885–6 (1991). To illustrate the argument, take the following example: a second author intends to create a derivative work which value is (regardless of the first work) 200. Assuming that both parties are equally positioned, the first author will ask for 100 to allow the second author to make the work. However, to the extent that the cost of creating the work for the second author is at least 101, there will be no positive surplus for her and she will not agree to the deal. This assumes that information gaps exist between the parties and the second author cannot make a reliable representation with respect to her cost of creation. For a discussion on the possibility that deals entailing positive surplus will not occur even under rational behavior, for example due to information asymmetry, *see* Robert Cooter, Stephen Marks & Robert Mnookin, *Bargaining in the Shadow of the Law: A Testable Model of Strategic Behavior*, 11 J. LEGAL STUD. 225, 226 (1982); Lucian Arye Bebchukm, *Litigation and Settlement under Imperfect Information*, 15 RAND J. ECON. 404 (1984).

53 This case resembles the paradox presented by Kenneth Arrow which refers to the market failure in deals for the sale of information. As per such paradox, in order to sell information one must disclose it, but once disclosed there is no need to purchase the information. *See* Kenneth J. Arrow, *Economic Welfare and the Allocation of Resources for Invention*, *in* THE RATE AND DIRECTION OF INVENTIVE ACTIVITY: ECONOMIC AND SOCIAL FACTORS

609, 615 (The National Bureau of Economic Research ed., 1962). For a discussion of this paradox in the context of blocking patents and a partial solution under trade secret law *see* Merges, *supra* note 47, at 81. Lemley was of course aware of this problem, but the basis for his support of the blocking copyright model was its comparison to existing law and not to alternative solutions. *See* Lemley, *supra* note 47, at 1075.

54 William W. Fischer III, PROMISES TO KEEP 202–3, 234–6 (2004).

55 Article 5 of the European Information Society Directive allows the member states in the European Union to determine that private copying is allowed subject to a fair remuneration model. *See* Directive 2001/29/EC of the European Parliament and of the Council of 22 May 2001. Twenty-two member states in the European Union adopted such a mechanism. *See* Martin Kretschmer, PRIVATE COPYING AND FAIR COMPENSATION: A COMPARATIVE STUDY OF COPYRIGHT LEVIES IN EUROPE (A Report to the UK Intellectual Property Office, 2011). The most extensive mechanism exists in Germany which allows various private uses subject to the payment of levies by producers of equipment that allows such uses. *See* Urheberrechtsgesetz [Copyright Act] Sept. 9, 1965, BGBL. I at 1273, §§ 53–54, as amended, Oct. 1, 2013, BGBL. I at 3728. *See also* William Patry, HOW TO FIX COPYRIGHT 180–1 (2011). For elaboration on the various levies imposed in the European Union *see* Stravoula Karapapa, PRIVATE COPYING 118–37 (2012).

56 Neil Weinstock Netanel, *Impose A Noncommercial Use Levy to Allow Free Peer-To-Peer File Sharing*, 17 HARV. J.L. & TECH. 1, 38–40 (2003).

57 17 U.S.C. § 115(a). For an historical description of the development of this mechanism *see* Howard B. Abrams, *Copyright's First Compulsory License*, 26 SANTA CLARA COMP. & HIGH TECH. L.J. 215, 217–20 (2010).

58 For example, as of today, the special committee determined that the fee for the making of a cover version and its recording is the higher of 9.1 cents per song or 1.75 cents per minute. *See* 74 F.R. 4510, 4515.

59 Jane C. Ginsburg, *Creation and Commercial Value: Copyright Protection of Works of Information*, 90 COLUM. L. REV. 1865, 1924–36 (1990).

60 Peter S. Menell, *Adapting Copyright for the Mashup Generation*, 164 U. PENN. L. REV. 441 (2016).

61 Kembrew McLeod & Peter DiCola, CREATIVE LICENSE: THE LAW AND CULTURE OF DIGITAL SAMPLING 226–29 (2011). Patry also suggested to shift to statutory licenses when the transaction costs for making of some derivative works is particularly high. PATRY, *supra* note 55, at 180–3.

62 Naomi Abe Voegtli, *Rethinking Derivative Rights*, 63 BROOK. L. REV. 1213, 1264–5 (1997).

63 Robert J. Morrison, *Derivers' Licenses: An Argument for Establishing a Statutory License for Derivative Works*, 6 CHI.-KENT J. INTELL. PROP. 87 (2006). For other commentators suggesting such a model (without further elaboration or normative discussion) *see* Kaplan, *supra* note 50, at 839–40; John Tehrainian, *Whither Copyright – Transformative Use, Free Speech, and an Intermediate Liability Proposal*, 2005 BYU L. REV. 1201, 1238–9 (2005).

64 Menell did suggest a comprehensive model for statutory licenses for mash-up works, but this model is essentially a statutory license model and not a compulsory license model. *See* Menell, *supra* note 61, at 49–59. Morrison too suggested a specific model for such licenses, but it too is in fact a statutory license model. *See* Morrison, *supra* note 63, at 104–7.

65 Recently, the constitutional court of Germany acknowledged that the use of pre-existing expressions for the making of a new work will be allowed, based on Section 24 of the German Copyright Act, subject to the payment of reasonable royalties based on the revenues of the second work. This was based on the assumption that such a decision will promote the freedoms of both the first and second authors to participate in the creative world equally. *See* BVerfG, 1 BvR 1585/13, §§ 66–80, Mai 31, 2016, https://www.bundesverfassungsgericht.de/SharedDocs/Entscheidungen/DE/2016/05/rs20160531_1bvr158513.html.

66 *See* Voegtli, *supra* note 62, at 1264.

67 Merges, *supra* note 47, at 99–100; Kaplan, *supra* note 50, at 840; Jason S. Rooks, *Constitutionality of Judicially-Imposed Compulsory Licenses in Copyright Infringement Cases*, 3 J. INTELL. PROP. L. 255, 271–2 (1995).

68 The mere existence of a compulsory license will of course limit the bargaining power of the first author in comparison to existing law in which it has full veto power with respect to the making of derivative works. However, this limitation is justified, as explained above, and therefore does not have to be addressed when considering the efficiency of the proposed compulsory license model in comparison to alternative remedies models.

69 *See, e.g.*, Rooks, *supra* note 67, at 271–72, who explained that this may pose a constitutional problem.

70 For a discussion on the role of experts in copyright infringement cases *see* NIMMER ON COPYRIGHT, *supra* note 36, at 13.03[E]. This discussion was raised in the early 50s of the previous century. *See* Paul W. Orth, *Use of Expert Witnesses in Musical Infringement Cases, The*, 16 U. PITT. L. REV. 232 (1955); Dana Bullen, *Role of Literary Experts in Plagiarism Trials, The*, 7 AM. U. L. REV. 55 (1958).

71 For the concern of the distributive effects of compulsory licenses *see* Diane Leenheer Zimmerman, *Is There a Right to Have Something to Say – One View of the Public Domain*, 73 FORDHAM L. REV. 297, 368 (2004); Tehranian, *supra* note 63, at 1239. *See also* C. Edwin Baker, *First Amendment Limits on Copyright*, 55 VAND. L. REV. 891, 903 (2002). For the argument that one of copyright law's goals is to lead to a just distribution between users and authors *see* Molly Shaffer Van Houweling, *Distributive Values in Copyright*, 83 TEX. L. REV. 1535, 1540–2, 1562–6 (2005); Oren Bracha & Talha Syed, *Beyond Efficiency: Consequence-Sensitive Theories of Copyright*, 29 BERKELEY TECH. L.J. 229, 289–99 (2014).

72 Thus, for example, the second author can choose to distribute the second work for free to gain reputation. In this case, royalties based on a percentage of the revenues will be meaningless and the second author will still gain from the making of the derivative work.

73 The relationship between the suggested model and the fair use doctrine will be further discussed *infra* in Part IV.3.

74 The two economic factors determining whether the parties will reach an agreement are the expectancy that each of them attributes to the legal procedure, and the cost of the procedure. Adding the possibility of an "all or nothing" outcome for both parties in a future adjudication, by arguing that the use is fair use on the one hand or a reproduction on the other hand, raises the risk associated with the legal proceedings. This risk is added to the cost of the proceedings (assuming that the parties are risk averse) and thus increases their potential to reach a consensual deal without affecting their relative bargaining power. The incentive of the parties to reach such agreement and refrain from hold-outs, may be further increased by adopting a more complex rule regarding the costs of the proceedings, if initiated. To the extent that during the proceedings one party will raise a reproduction or fair use claim, the party whose claim is denied will bear the costs of the proceedings. Osnat Jacobi and Avi Weiss argued that in order to overcome hold-outs resulting from legal rules granting excessive bargaining power to one of the parties, legal mechanisms should be adopted that determine how the parties will share the benefits of the negotiations and that the party deciding to deviate from such default mechanism and shift to adjudication should bear the costs of the proceedings. *See* Osnat Jacobi & Avi Weiss, *Law Design: Methodology* (working paper 2015), http://papers.ssrn.com/sol3/papers.cfm?abstract_id=2637899. According to the suggested model for compulsory license for the making of derivative works, it cannot be foreseen which party will "blow" the deal since, in contrast to statutory licenses, there is no default rule for the appropriate rate of royalties. Therefore, I argue that the costs of the legal proceedings should be borne by the party whose final proposal during negotiations was the furthest from the rate of royalties eventually determined by the court.

For example, if the first author demanded 100 for a license to make the derivative work and the second author only offered 50, to the extent that the court eventually determines that the rate of royalties is higher than 75, then the second author will bear the costs of the procedure, and *vice versa*. This suggested rule is meant to deal with a specific range of potential strategic games between the parties. Other games are of course possible and the parties are expected to behave strategically under any set of rules. Therefore, it is important to adopt the rule that best addresses such strategic behavior inherently, and which will lead the parties to behave fairly without damaging the public interest.

75 An example for this exists today. The United States Copyright Act determines a compulsory license for the public performance of musical works through music appliances. *See* 17 U.S.C. §§ 111(d)(4)(A), 116(b)(2). Lemley showed that under such compulsory licenses, the parties rarely turn to the court for setting the appropriate royalties rate, and in most cases the parties reach an agreement with respect to such rate. For this argument and for the argument that contractual agreements with respect to liability rules exist as often, if not more frequently, than with respect to property rules, *see* Mark A. Lemley, *Contracting around Liability Rules*, 100 CAL. L. REV. 463, 464–5, 476–83 (2012). For a discussion on the role of collecting societies in forming the market for licenses in the context of intellectual property *see* Mark A. Lemley, *Intellectual Property Rights and Standard-Setting Organizations*, 90 CAL. L. REV. 1889 (2002).

76 For a suggestion of rules for the determination of appropriate royalties in the context of patent law *see* Daralyn J. Durie & Mark A. Lemley, *A Structured Approach to Calculating Reasonable Royalties*, 14 LEWIS & CLARK L. REV. 627 (2010).

77 Michael Abramowicz, *A Theory of Copyright's Derivative Work Right*, 90 MINN. L. REV. 317, 319–21 (2005); Samuelson, *supra* note 42, at 1530–1.

78 This point is related to the discussion on Locke's waste proviso with respect to the derivative works right in Chapter 3.III(2) above, the result of which was the need to shorten the period of protection for this right.

79 This will of course result in higher adjudication costs if the determination will be on a case-by-case basis. The determination of the blocking periods will be cheaper if made by the legislator, but will be less dynamic and sensitive to the different types of works.

80 This argument must be reserved in that some derivative works, the profit expectancy of which will be so little that the fixed fee for their creation will not justify entering the compulsory license mechanism, and thus their making will not be possible. I do not believe that this reservation detracts from the justification of the suggested model. In order to allow the making of derivative works of extremely low profit expectancy, the current burden of the model must be flipped and the author of the second work should be allowed to make the second work without a license. The difficulty in this flip is that, in contrast to a use which constitutes fair use and the second author is at liberty to make for free, the case of making a derivative work is, at least to some extent, contradicting the right of the first author. Imposing the burden to detect the making of derivative works and initiate legal proceedings for a discussion of compulsory licenses on the first author, un-proportionately damages the right of the first author which is already limited by the suggested model.

81 *See* 17 U.S.C. § 106A which only applies to visual arts.

82 This argument must be understood in context. Since United States law does not include a general moral rights protection on the one hand, and the United States is subject to the Berne Conventions which includes a general protection of moral right on the other hand, it was suggested that the derivative works right (together with other rights from the fields of trademark and commercial torts laws) created a *de facto* moral right since it grants the author full control of the integrity of the work. *See* Roberta Rosenthal Kwall, *Copyright and the Moral Right: Is an American Marriage Possible*, 38 VAND. L. REV. 1, 39–47 (1985); Jane C. Ginsburg, *Have Moral Rights Come of (Digital) Age in the United States*, 19 CARDOZO ARTS & ENT. L.J. 9, 9 (2001); Lydia Pallas Loren, *The Changing Nature of Derivative Works in the Face of New Technologies*, 4 J. SMALL &

EMERGING BUS. L. 57, 83 (2000); NIMMER ON COPYRIGHT, *supra* note 36, at 8D.02(C). *See*, in this context, Gilliam v. American Broadcasting Cos., 538 F.2d 14 (2d Cir. 1976). In this case the entertainment group of Monty Python requested to prohibit the broadcasting of an adaptation of episodes from its television show by ABC network, arguing that it infringed their derivative works right. The substantial claim in this case was that these adaptations do not meet the standards of the originals, and in fact violate the right of integrity.

83 15 U.S.C. §§ 1114(1), 1125(c).

84 15 U.S.C. § 1125(a).

85 The Supreme Court addressed this situation in the context of derivative works and determined that the marketing of a motion picture based on a television series, in a manner causing the audience to believe that the motion picture was produced by or endorsed by the producer of the television series, may result in an infringement of the rights of the television series producer. *See* Dastar Corp. v. Twentieth Century Fox Film Corp., 539 U.S. 23, 36 (2003). For elaboration *see* Morrison, *supra* note 63, at 99–101.

86 17 U.S.C. § 107.

87 Barton Beebe, *An Empirical Study of U.S. Copyright Fair Use Opinions*, 1978–2005, 156 U. PENN. L. REV. 549 (2008); Neil Weinstock Netanel, *Making Sense of Fair Use*, 15 LEWIS & CLARK L. REV. 715 (2011). For an additional study reviewing fair use decisions *see* Matthew Sag, *Predicting Fair Use*, 73 OHIO ST. L.J. 47 (2012).

88 Transformative use is a phrase created by Judge Leval in his article Pierre N. Leval, *Toward a Fair Use Standard*, 103 HARV. L. REV. 1105 (1990). This phrase was later adopted by the Supreme Court in Campbell v. Acuff-Rose Music Inc., 510 U.S. 569, 576 (1994).

89 For elaboration *see* Netanel, *supra* note 87, at 724, 746.

90 For a discussion on both types of transformativeness *see* Leval, *supra* note 88, at 1111–16; Campbell, *supra* note 88, at 576. For a distinction between transformative of purpose and transformative of content *see* Tushnet, *Content, Purpose, or Both*, 90 WASH. L. REV. 869 (2015). *See also* Samuelson, *supra* note 42, at 843–50.

91 Tushnet, *id.*, at 869. Tushnet showed that his type of transformativeness most likely leads to a conclusion that the use is fair. *Id.*, at 875–83. *See also* Anthony R. Reese, *Transformativeness and the Derivative Work Right*, 31 COLUM. J.L. & ARTS 467, 493–4 (2008).

92 Tushnet, *supra* note 90, at 869–70.

93 For a discussion on the overlap between the derivative works right and fair use *see* Reese, *supra* note 91.

94 In this context, *see* Yafit Lev-Aretz's argument that the lack of possibility to obtain a license for a specific use could lead to the conclusion that the use is fair even absent consent. Yafit Lev-Aretz, *The Subtle Incentive Theory of Copyright Licensing*, 80 BROOK. L. REV. 1357 (2015). Gibson showed, in this context, that in weighing the fourth factor of the fair use doctrine – effect on the market of the work – courts often examine whether a market for licenses for the specific use exists, while if such market exists the chance to prove fair use reduces. James Gibson, *Risk Aversion and Rights Accretion in Intellectual Property Law*, 116 YALE L.J. 882, 887–98 (2007).

Conclusion

This book focussed on the derivative works right and the dual tension between it and non-legal understandings of creativity on the one hand and copyright's underlying normative justifications on the other hand. Due to this dual tension, prescriptions for the adjustment of the current derivative works right were suggested.

The discussion focussed on the derivative works right but it highlighted more extensive issues in copyright and intellectual property particularly, and perhaps in legal research at large. First, it emphasized the question: what should be the central focus of copyright law and intellectual property? Most research today focusses on the relationship between existing legal doctrines and the technological developments in the underlying subject matters, and the adjustment of the doctrines for such changes. The discussion in this book focussed on reexamining a basic copyright doctrine in light of its underlying normative justifications and related non-legal understandings. As it attempted to show, there is merit in revisiting, from time to time, basic copyright doctrines to review whether their positive application fits their underlying values and normative justifications. Second, this book reviewed the relationship between non-legal understandings of creativity and the legal doctrine that focusses on creativity. In this sense, it raised the broader question of the interrelations between the law and the behavioral and sociological norms it applies to. On top of the contribution to the specific discussion on derivative works, this book is at the heart of these broader questions and could be used as a test case for more general conclusions.

As far as derivative works are concerned, this book had two main goals. The first was to show that the current derivative works right does not fit both the non-legal understandings of creativity and its underlying normative justifications. From the non-legal part, creativity studies show that the use of preexisting expressions is an inseparable part of the creative process. Additionally, genre theories show that the development of the creative world, from both the author and audience perspectives, is based on the use of common building blocks, that include expressions, as tools that enable creativity as well as meaning-making. From the normative part, we saw that under all main justifications to copyright – economic analysis, Lockean theory, corrective justice and personality approaches – the current derivative works right does not reflect its basic justifications.

The second goal of this book was to explain what aspects of the derivative works right require adjustment to resolve the aforementioned tension, and what is the optimal way to do so. This was based on the premise that a broad derivative works right granting full control over derivative works is unjustified based on the normative justifications discussed. Analyzing the development of the right alongside the reproduction right revealed an almost complete overlap between the two, that does not allow an independent existence for the derivative works right. Therefore, I suggested that two conditions are necessary for the adjustment of the derivative works right to fit its underlying justifications. First, it must be fully separated from the reproduction right and the borderline between the two must be clarified. Second, its remedies must be limited. Accordingly, the book outlined the optimal way to do so.

The discussion on adjusting the derivative works right to its underlying justifications shows that basic copyright doctrines should be revisited from time to time even absent an external factor, such as technological advancements or new creative patterns. This is because sometimes the development of a certain doctrine over time, in legislation or case law, removes it from the original purpose and extends or contracts it in a way that contradicts its underlying justifications.

Moreover, the discussion on the adjustment of the derivative works right to incorporate non-legal understandings of creativity is a case study for the interrelations between non-legal fields and the law in general. We saw, for example, that the non-legal understandings of creativity could enrich the normative discussion on copyright. In this context, non-legal fields are useful not only as sources for empirical data for a more accurate economic analysis, rather as a tool for better understanding how other normative approaches, such as right-based theories, should apply to copyright, and provide a broader and richer outlook on the interrelations of different actors in the field of creativity. In addition, we saw that non-legal understandings of creativity could be used to design legal rules, not as an independent normative source, rather as a complementary tool for understanding terms to which copyright applies. At the end of the day, we saw that when the legal doctrine of derivative works is adjusted to fit its normative justifications, the tension with the non-legal understanding of creativity is resolved as well. This does not make a direct normative link between copyright law and non-legal understandings of creativity, but it raises the question whether this is just a happy coincidence or rather a deeper connection between the normative approaches to copyright and non-legal understanding of creativity exists.

Chapter 1 focussed on the interrelations between copyright law and the understanding of the creative process and creativity under cognitive psychology and creativity studies. It argued that although there is a significant match between various copyright doctrines and creativity studies, there is a mismatch as far as derivative works are concerned. The main goal of Chapter 1 was to argue that the distinction between derivative works and original works under copyright law is a legal one that cannot be based on the understanding of the creative process. Therefore, it suggested that there is no qualitative difference between original and derivative works as far as creativity is concerned, and thus the distinction created by law must be reexamined in light of the normative justifications for copyright. To support this argument, various theoretical approaches and empirical and historical researches from the field of creativity studies were discussed. Based on such approaches I suggested that the cognitive process of creativity could be divided into two main stages. The first refers to unfocussed thought in which abstract thought is generated. The second refers to the crystallization of abstract thought to concrete products based on the use of prior domain-relevant knowledge and memory, that include specific expressions and not merely ideas.

Chapter 2 focussed on genre theories and the significance of common building blocks for the development of the creative world. There too, I argued that although several copyright doctrines match genre theories, the derivative works right does not. This is because genre theories qualitatively distinguish between non-creative reproduction and creative derivative works that are closer to original works, in light of the centrality of common building blocks to creativity. This is based on a reading of various approaches to genre theories that focus on the development of artistic texts, according to which common building blocks consist of two main aspects. The first aspect enables creativity within known boundaries, rules and conventions from the viewpoint of the author. The second enables meaning-making for creative products and the creative of social value from the viewpoint of the audience.

Chapter 3 discussed the normative aspects of the derivative works right. It reexamined main normative approaches to copyright to ask whether the current derivative works right fits them. The main argument was that under each of the main approaches to copyright – economic analysis and right-based theories of Locke, Kant and Hegel – the current derivative works right is unjustified, and a more limited derivative works right, which is independent of the reproduction right, could be justified, to the extent that it allows second authors to more freely use preexisting expressions. Aside from the utilitarian use of these approaches to discuss the derivative works right, the discussion suggested refreshed readings of such approaches and showed how non-legal fields could be used to enrich the normative discussion and extend the general viewpoint on the discussion.

Chapter 4 delved into the doctrinal aspects of the derivative works right and outlined the two main aspects of the right that require adjustment to resolve the tension with the normative justifications. The argument was that first the right must be fully separated from the reproduction right and second, the remedies for the derivative works right should be limited. This argument was based both on the normative discussion in Chapter 3 and on a positive review of the derivative works right in current case law. Reviewing its historical development alongside the reproduction right and the way it is reviewed in current case law showed that the two rights almost completely overlap, and that such overlap is unjustified under the normative discussion since it does not allow for an independent existence of the derivative works right, prohibiting the adjustment of its remedies in isolation from the reproduction right.

Chapter 5 followed the main argument in Chapter 4 in the sense that it sought to portray the optimal way to adjust the derivative works right to fit its underlying justifications. The starting point was that the derivative works right must be fully separated from the reproduction right, and that its remedies must be limited. With respect to the first aspect, I suggested a revised definition for the derivative works right that will separate it from reproductions. In short, the right will apply when significant additional creativity is added to existing expressions in an inseparable way, and when such expressions could not be substituted with non-protected expressions without derogating from the purpose of the work. In this context, I suggested five categories of uses that characterize the definition and reviewed its positive implications. As for the second aspect, after reviewing several alternative remedies models suggested in the literature, I argued that the optimal model is compulsory licenses for the making of derivative works, in terms of efficiency, fairness and political plausibility. In short, the model allows second authors to use preexisting expressions to make derivative works subject to paying reasonable royalties from future revenues. If the parties do not consent on a deal, the second author could initiate proceedings to determine the fair royalty rate subject to the payment of a lump sum for the cost of proceedings and the reputation revenues from the first work. The entire model is subject to an initial blocking period allowing first authors to exclusively make derivative works.

On top of the main contribution of this book to the review and redesign of the derivative works right in light of the abovementioned tensions, several discussions in this book offer independent secondary contributions that could be the basis for future research.

The conclusions from creativity studies offer an independent contribution outside of the context of derivative works and even copyright. First, they add to the existing literature on law and psychology generally and the ways in which the law could harness psychological understandings. We saw that such understandings could be utilized within normative approaches such as economic analysis as data to more accurately apply the normative approach. In addition, they could also assist in designing the factual premises of other normative approaches, such as right-based theories, and affect the analysis under such approaches.

Second, in the context of intellectual property, the discussion could make creativity studies more accessible to legal scholars and provide a framework for future research reviewing other doctrines. One example could be the doctrine of improvement patents or a deeper analysis of the originality requirement in copyright law. In general, terms such as originality and creativity could be further reviewed under tools from creativity studies.

Third, from the viewpoint of creativity studies, there is room for future research that will examine how law, and mainly copyright law, affects the creative process and more specifically review how various components of the creative process interrelate to copyright law.

In the context of genre theories too, the conclusions in this book could provide an independent contribution. First, genre theories could be used as an independent normative basis for justifying copyright doctrines. They explain how the creative world develops in the broad context of the field of creativity that includes both authors and the audience, and as we saw, they could well justify the fair use and scènes à faire doctrines.

Second, and more specifically, genre theories could have implications on other copyright doctrines. Copyright law makes categorical distinctions between types of works such as literary, visual, musical and cinematographic works. Genre theories could explain why other distinctions, according to the genre to which the work belongs, might be more useful. Thus, it may be more useful to review a book focussed on the detective character against a television series focussed on a detective story, rather than against academic literature. This is linked to another contribution of genre theories to copyright law – current infringement doctrines. The current legal test to assess whether a work infringes copyright in another work is the substantial similarity test. Additional sub-tests were formed in case law. Genre theories could offer new tools to review alleged copyright infringement claims. For example, instead of asking whether two works are substantially similar under a concept and feel test, it may be more adequate to ask how both works are situated in the genre to which they belong and whether the similar components originate in prohibited copying or in the importance of such components for the specific genre and its development.

The discussion on the normative justifications for copyright, too, could have an independent contribution. As part of this discussion I suggested new readings for some of the main theoretical approaches that better fit the context of intellectual property and copyright in particular. These new readings could be used to reach new conclusions with respect to other copyright doctrines or even to other fields of intellectual property such as patent law.

On top of all, and at the highest level of abstraction, the discussion in this book could be used as a case study for the broader overarching question – to what extent should the law reflect non-legal understandings of behavior and society which it regulates. In the context of the derivative works right, the discussion on the non-legal understandings of creativity was confined to descriptive-critical conclusions and did not attempt to create a necessary normative link between non-legal conclusions and legal outcomes. However, we did see that when a legal doctrine is redesigned to better fit its underlying justifications, it also fits better with non-legal understandings of the regulated field. This may be only a happy coincidence. However, it is possible that such correlation of outcomes implies a deeper normative connection, for example, that to the extent that non-legal understandings of a specific field explain the necessary conditions to achieve the ultimate goal of a legal field, the legal doctrine should reflect such non-legal understandings or at least take them into consideration. This of course extends beyond the scope of this book, but it definitely calls for future research attempting to establish such a link (or refute it).

Bibliography

Legislation

United Kingdom

Copyright Act, 1911
Copyright, Designs and Patents Act, 1988
Dramatic Literary Property Act, 1833
English Copyright Act, 1842
Statute of Anne, 1709

United States

Lanham (Trademark) Act of 1946, codified as 15 U.S.C. § 1051 et seq.
Copyright Act of 1976, codified as 17 U.S.C. § 101 et seq.
Copyright Act of May 31, 1790
Copyright Act of July 8, 1870
Copyright Act of March 4, 1909
House of Representatives Report on Copyright Law Revision, H.R.Rep. No. 94–1476 (1976)
Mechanical and Digital Phonorecord Delivery Rate Determination Proceeding, A Rule by the Copyright Royalty Board on January 26, 2009
U.S. Constitution

Germany

Prussian Statute Book (ALR), Berlin (1794) §§ 996–1036, Primary Sources on Copyright (Lionel Bentley & Martin Kretschmer eds., 1450–1900)
Reprinting Regulation for the Grand Duchy of Baden, Karlsruhe (1806), Primary Sources on Copyright (Lionel Bentley & Martin Kretschmer eds., 1450–1900)
Urheberrechtsgesetz [Copyright Act] Sept. 9, 1965, BGBl. I at 1273, as amended, Oct. 1, 2013, BGBl. I at 3728

France

Code de la Propriété Intellectuelle (C. Prop. Intel.)

International treaties

Agreement on Trade-Related Aspects of Intellectual Property Rights art. 11, 14, Apr. 15, 1994 (TRIPs Agreement)
Berne Convention for the Protection of Literary and Artistic Works art. 12, Nov. 13, 1908
Berne Convention for the Protection of Literary and Artistic Works art. 12, Jun. 26, 1948
Directive on the Harmonisation of Certain Aspects of Copyright and Related Rights in the Information Society 2001/29/EC of the European Parliament and of the Council of 22 May 2001
WIPO Copyright Treaty, Dec. 20, 1996

Case law

United Kingdom

Abraham Moon & Sons Ltd v. Thornber [2012] EWPCC 37
Designers Guild Ltd v. Russell Williams (Textiles) Ltd [2000] 1 W.L.R. 2416
Francis Day & Hunter Ltd. v. Bron [1963] Ch. 587
Hodgson v Isaac [2010] EWPCC 37

United States

Abend v. MCA, Inc., 863 F.2d 1465 (9th Cir. 1988)
Anderson v. Stallone, 1989 U.S. Dist. LEXIS 11109 (C.D. Cal. Apr. 25, 1989)
Authors Guild v. Google, Inc., 2015 U.S. App. LEXIS 17988 (2d Cir. 2015)
Baker v. Selden, 101 U.S. 99 (1879)
Bridgeport Music, Inc. v. UMG Recordings, Inc., 585 F.3d 267 (6th Cir. 2009)
Burnett v. Chetwood, 2 Mer. 441, 35 Eng. Rep. 1008 (Ch. 1720)
Campbell v. Acuff-Rose Music Inc., 510 U.S. 569 (1994)
Castle Rock Ent. v. Carol Pub. Group, Inc., 150 F.3d 132 (2d Cir. 1998)
Copeland v. Bieber, 789 F.3d 484 (4th Cir. 2015)
Daly v. Palmer, 6 F. Cas. 1132 (C.C.S.D.N.Y 1868)
Dastar Corp. v. Twentieth Century Fox Film Corp., 539 U.S. 23 (2003)
Dr. Seuss Enters., L.P. v. Penguin Books USA, Inc., 109 F.3d 1394 (9th Cir. 1997)
eBay Inc. v. MercExchange, L.L.C., 547 U.S. 388 (U.S. 2006)
Elvis Presley Enterprises, Inc. v. Passport Video, 357 F.3d 896 (9th Cir. 2003)
Feist Publications, Inc. v. Rural Telephone Service Company, Inc., 499 U.S. 340 (1991)
Fisher v. Dees, 794 F.2d 432 (9th Cir. 1986)
Galoob Toys, Inc. v. Nintendo of America, Inc., 964 F.2d 965 (9th Cir. 1992)
Gamma Audio & Video, Inc. v. Ean-Chea, 11 F.3d 1106 (1st Cir. 1993)
Gilliam v. American Broadcasting Cos., 538 F.2d 14 (2d Cir. 1976)
Jacobsen v. Desert Book Co., 287 F.3d 936 (10th Cir. 2002)
Kalem Co. v. Harper Bros., 222 U.S. 55 (1911)
King Features Syndicate v. Fleischer, 299 F. 533 (2d Cir. N.Y. 1924)
Kumar v. Inst. of Elec. & Elecs. Eng'rs, 2013 U.S. Dist. LEXIS 140989 (D.N.J. Sept. 30, 2013)
Lee v. A.R.T. Co., 125 F.3d 580 (7th Cir. 1997)
Leibovitz v. Paramount Pictures Corp., 137 F.3d 109 (2d Cir. 1998)
Litchfield v. Spielberg, 736 F.2d 1352 (9th Cir. 1984)
Mayimba Music, Inc. v. Sony Corp. of Am., 2014 U.S. Dist. LEXIS 152051 (S.D.N.Y. Aug. 19, 2014)

Midway Mfg. Co. v. Artic Int'l, Inc., 1981 U.S. Dist. LEXIS 16881, 24 (N.D. Ill. Jun. 2, 1981)
Mirage Editions, Inc. v. Albuquerque A.R.T. Co., 856 F.2d 1341 (9th Cir. 1988)
Mulcahy v. Cheetah Learning LLC, 386 F.3d 849 (8th Cir. 2004)
Muñoz v. Albuquerque A.R.T. Co., 829 F. Supp. 309 (D. Ala. 1993), *aff'd* 38 F.3d 1218 (9th Cir. 1994)
New Line Cinema Corp. v. Bertlesman Music Group, Inc., 693 F. Supp. 1517 (S.D.N.Y. 1988)
Newton v. Diamond, 388 F.3d 1189, 1193 (9th Cir. 2004)
Nichols v. Universal Pictures Corp., 45 F.2d 119 (2d Cir. 1930)
Oracle Am., Inc. v. Google Inc., 750 F.3d 1339 (Fed. Cir. 2014)
Petrella v. MGM, 134 S. Ct. 1962 (U.S. 2014)
Pickett v. Prince, 52 F. Supp. 2d 893 (N.D. Ill. 1999)
Practice Mgmt. Info. Corp. v. AMA, 121 F.3d 516 (9th Cir. 1997)
Ringgold v. Black Entertainment Television, Inc., 126 F.3d 70 (2d Cir. 1997)
Roy Export Co. Establishment v. Columbia Broadcasting Sys., Inc., 503 F. Supp. 1137 (S. D.N.Y. 1980)
Salinger v. Colting, 607 F.3d 68 (2d Cir. 2010)
Salinger v. Random House, Inc., 811 F.2d 90 (2d Cir. 1987)
Sheldon v. Metro-Goldwyn Pictures Corp., 81 F.2d 49 (2d Cir. 1936)
Sherry Mfg. Co. v. Towel King of Fla. Inc., 753 F.2d 1565 (11th Cir. 1985)
Stowe v. Thomas, 23 Fed. Cas. 201 (C.C.E.D. Pa. 1853)
SunTrust Bank v. Houghton Mifflin Co., 268 F.3d 1257 (11th Cir. 2001)
Swirsky v. Carey, 376 F.3d 841 (9th Cir. 2004)
Tempo Music v. Famous Music Corp., 838 F. Supp. 162 (S.D.N.Y. 1993)
TufAmerica Inc. v. Diamond, 968 F. Supp. 2d 588 (S.D.N.Y. 2013)
Twin Peaks Prods. v. Publ'ns Int'l, Ltd., 996 F.2d 1366 (2d Cir. 1993)
Well-Made Toy Mfg. Corp v. Goffa Int'l Corp., 354 F.3d 112 (2nd Cir. 2003)
Williams v. Bridgeport Music, Inc., 2015 U.S. Dist. LEXIS 97262, 121–40 (C.D. Cal. Jul. 14, 2015)

Germany

BVerfG, 1 BvR 1585/13, §§ 66–80, Mai 31, 2016

Literature

Books

Rick Altman, *Film/Genre* (1999)
Teresa M. Amabile, *Creativity in Context* (1996)
Teresa M. Amabile, *The Social Psychology of Creativity* (1983)
Aristotle, *Poetics* (Gerald F.Else trans., 1990)
J. L. Austin, *How to do Things with Words* (1962)
Anis S.Bawarshi & Mary JoReiff, *Genre: An Introduction to History, Theory, Research, and Pedagogy* (2010)
Thomas O. Beebee, *The Ideology of Genre* (1994)
Vijay Bhatia, *Worlds of Written Discourse: A Genre-Based View* (2004)
Ferdinand Brunetiere, *L'Evolution des Genres dans l'Histoire de la Littérature: Leçons Professées à l'Ecole Normale Supérieure* (1914)

Vincent Buranelli, *Edgar Allan Poe* (1961)

Benedetto Croce, *Aesthetic as Science of Expression and General Linguistic* (Douglas Ainslie trans., 1953)

Jonathan Culler, *Structuralist Poetics 5* (1975)

Ferdinandde Saussure, *Course in General Linguistics* (Charles Bally & Albert Sechehayeeds, Wade Baskin trans., 1959)

Peter Drahos, *A Philosophy of Intellectual Property* (1996)

Heather Dubrow, *Genre* (1982)

Graham Duttfield & Uma Suthersanen, *Global Intellectual Property Law* (2008)

Abraham Drassinower, *What's Wrong with Copying?* (2015)

Ronald Dworkin, *Taking Rights Seriously* (1977)

Terry Eagleton, *Literary Theory: An Introduction* (2nd edn1996)

Zohar Efroni, *Access-Right: The Future of Digital Copyright Law* (2010)

Ronald A. Finke, Thomas B. Ward & Steven M. Smith, *Creative Cognition: Theory, Research and Applications* (1992)

William W. Fischer III, *Promises to Keep* (2004)

David Fishelov, *Metaphors of Genre* (1993)

Alastir Fowler, *Kinds of Literature* (1982)

Georg Friedrich Hegel, *Philosophy of Right* (1821) (T.M. Knok trans., 1967)

John Frow, *Genre* (2006)

Northrop Frye, *Anatomy of Criticism* (1957)

Hans-Georg Gadamer, *Truth and Method* (2nd edn, Joel Weinsheimer & Donald G.Marshall trans. & revs., 2004)

Kevin Garnett, Gillian Davies & Gwilym Harbotlle, *Copinger & Skone James on Copyright* (16th edn2011)

Gerard Genette, *The Architext: An Introduction* (Jane E. Lewin trans., 1992)

Daniel Gervais, *The TRIPS Agreement: Drafting History and Analysis* (4th edn 2012)

Jacob W. Getzels & Mihaly Csikszentmihalyi, *The Creative Vision: A Longtitudinal Study of Problem Finding in Art* (1976)

J.P. Guilford, *The Nature of Human Intelligence* (1967)

Howard Haycraft, *Murder for Pleasure: The Life and Times of the Detective Story* (1941)

Georg Wilhelm Friedrich Hegel, 2 *Aesthetics: Lectures on Fine Arts 1038–45* (T.M. Knox trans., 1975)

E.D. Hirsch, Jr., *Validity in Interpretation* (1967)

Victor Hugo, *Odes et Ballades* (1947)

Frederic Jameson, *The Political Unconscious: Narrative as a Socially Symbolic Act* (1981)

Hans Robert Jauss, *Towards an Aesthetic of Reception* (Timothy Bahti trans., 1982)

Benjamin Kaplan, *An Unhurried View of Copyright* (1967)

Stravoula Karapapa, *Private Copying* (2012)

Martin Kretschmer, *Private Copying and Fair Compensation: A Comparative Study of Copyright Levies in Europe* (A Report to the UK Intellectual Property Office, 2011)

Chana Kronfeld, *On the Margins of Modernism: Decentering Literary Dynamics* (1996)

Philippe Lacoue-Labarthe & Jean-Luc Nancy, *The Literary Absolute: The Theory of Literature in German Romanticism* (Philip Barnard & Cheryl Lester trans., 1988)

Hugh Laddie, Peter Prescott & Mary Vitoria, *The Modern Law of Copyright and Designs* (3rd edn 2000)

George Lakoff, *Women, Fire and Dangerous Things: What Categories Reveal about the Mind* (1987)

William M. Landes & Richard A. Posner, *The Economic Structure of Intellectual Property Law* (2003)
John Locke, *Two Treatises of Government* (1689)
Karl Marx & Friedrich Engels, *The Communist Manifesto* (1848) (The Floating Press, 2008)
Kembrew McLeod & Peter Di Cola, *Creative License: The Law and Culture of Digital Sampling* (2011)
Robert P. Merges, *Justifying Intellectual Property* (2011)
A.E. Murch, *The Development of the Detective Novel* (1958)
Melville B. Nimmer & David Nimmer, 2 *Nimmer on Copyright* (2016)
Robert Nozick, Anarchy, *State and Utopia* (1974)
William F. Patry, *Patry on Copyright* (2012)
William Patry, *How to Fix Copyright* (2011)
Plato, *The Republic: Books I-V* (Paul Shorey trans., 1999)
Marie Louise Pratt, *Toward a Speech Act Theory of Literary Discourse* (1977)
Arthur Ripstein, *Force and Freedom: Kant's Legal and Political Philosophy* (2009)
Roberta Rosenthal Kwall, *The Soul of Creativity* (2010)
Adena Rosmarin, *The Power of Genre* (1986)
Friedrich Schlegel, *Literary Notebooks 1797–1801* (Hans Eichner ed., 1957)
Brad Sherman & Lionel Bently, *The Making of Modern Intellectual Property Law: The British Experience, 1760–1911* (1999)
Jessica Silbey, *The Eureka Myth: Creators, Innovators, and Everyday Intellectual Property* (2015)
John Simmons, *The Lockean Theory of Rights* (1992)
Tzvetan Todorov, *Genres in Discourse* (Catherine Porter trans., 1990) (1978)
Jeremy Waldron, *The Right to Private Property* (1988)
Graham Wallas, *The Art of Thought* (1926)
Ernest J. Weinrib, *The Idea of Private Law* (2012)
Ernst J. Weinrib, *Corrective Justice* (2012)
Neil Weinstock Netanel, *Copyright's Paradox* (2008)
Robert W. Weisberg, *Beyond the Myth of Genius* (1993)
Robert W. Weisberg, *Creativity: Understanding Innovation in Problem Solving, Science, Invention, and the Arts* (2006)
Rene Welleck & Austin Warren, *Theory of Literature* (3rd edn 1963)
Georg Wilhelm Friedrich Hegel, *Aesthetics: Lectures on Fine Arts* (T.M. Knoxtrans., 1975)
Ludwig Wittgenstein, *Philosophical Investigations* (G.E.M. Anscombe trans., 3rd edn 1986)

Articles and chapters

Michael Abramowicz, A Theory of Copyright's Derivative Work Right, 90 *Minn. L. Rev.* 317 (2005)
Howard B. Abrams, Copyright's First Compulsory License, 26 *Santa Clara Comp. & High Tech. L.J.* 215 (2010)
Rick Altman, A Semantic/Syntactic Approach to Film Genre, 23 *Cinema J.* 6 (1984)
Kenneth J. Arrow, Economic Welfare and the Allocation of Resources for Invention, in *The Rate and Direction of Inventive Activity: Economic and Social Factors* 609 (The National Bureau of Economic Research ed., 1962)
C. Edwin Baker, First Amendment Limits on Copyright, 55 *Vand. L. Rev.* 891 (2002)

Shyamkrishna Balganesh, Foreseeability and Copyright Incentives, 122 *Harv. L. Rev.* 1569 (2009)
Wayne A. Baughman & Michael D. Mumford, Process-Analytic Models of Creative Capacities: Operations Influencing the Combination-and-Reorganization Process, 8 *Creativity Res. J.* 37 (1995)
Lucian Arye Bebchukm, Litigation and Settlement under Imperfect Information, 15 *Rand J. Econ.* 404 (1984)
Stephan Bechtold, Christopher Buccafusco & Christopher Jon Sprigman, Innovation Heuristics: Experiments on Sequential Creativity in Intellectual Property, *Ind. L. Rev.* (2016)
Lawrence C. Becker, Deserving to Own Intellectual Property, 68 *Chi.-Kent L. Rev.* 609 (1993)
Barton Beebe, An Empirical Study of U.S. Copyright Fair Use Opinions, 1978–2005, 156 *U. Penn. L. Rev. 549* (2008)
Mathias Benedek *et al.*, Alpha Power Increases in Right Parietal Cortex Reflects Focused Internal Attention, 56 *Neuropsychologia* 393 (2014)
Yochai Benkler, Free as the Air to Common Use: First Amendment Constrains on Enclosure of the Public Domain, 74 *NYU L. Rev.* 354 (1999)
Stephen Bertman, Kindered Crimes: Poe's "The Murders in the Rue Morgue" and Doyle's The Sign of Four, 15 *Edgar Allan Poe Rev.* 205 (2014)
Michael Birnhack, The Idea of Progress in Copyright Law, 1 *Buff. IP L.J.* 3 (2001)
Michael Birnhack, Copyright Law and Free Speech After Eldred v. Ashcroft, 76 *S. Cal. L. Rev.* 1275 (2003)
Christina Bohannan, Taming the Derivative Work Right: A Modest Proposal for Reducing Overbreadth and Vagueness in Copyright, 12 *Vand. J. Ent. & Tech. L.* 669 (2010)
Steven S. Boyd, Deriving Originality in Derivative Works: Considering the Quantum of Originality Needed To Attain Copyright Protection in a Derivative Work, 40 *Santa Clara L. Rev.* 325 (2000)
Oren Bracha & Talha Syed, Beyond Efficiency: Consequence-Sensitive Theories of Copyright, 29 *Berkeley Tech. L.J.* 229 (2014)
Oren Bracha, The Ideology of Authorship Revisited: Authors, Markets, and Liberal Values in Early American Copyright, 118 *Yale L.J.* 186 (2008)
Stephen Breyer, The Uneasy Case for Copyright: A Study of Copyright in Books, Photocopies, and Computer Programs, 84 *Harv. L. Rev.* 281(1970)
Annemarie Bridy, Fearless Girl Meets Charging Bull: Copyright and the Regulation of Intertextuality, *UC Irvine L. Rev.* (Forthcoming, 2018)
Ragnhild Brøvig-Hanssen & Paul Harkins, Contextual Incongruity and Musical Congruity: The Aesthetics and Humour of Mash-Ups, 31 *Popular Music* 87 (2012)
Ragnhild Brøvig-Hanssen, Justin Bieber Featuring Slipknot, in *The Oxford Handbook of Music and Virtuality* (Sheila Whiteley & Shara Rambarran eds, 2016)
Ralph S. Brown, The Widening Gyre: Are Derivative Works Getting Out of Hand, 3 *Cardozo Arts & Ent. L.J.* 1 (1984)
Christopher Buccafusco & Christopher Jon Sprigman, The Creativity Effect, 78 *U. Chi. L. Rev.* 31 (2011)
Christopher Buccafusco, Stephan Bechtold & Christopher Jon Sprigman, The Nature of Sequential Innovation, 59 *Wm. & Mary L. Rev.* 1 (2017)
Dana Bullen, The Role of Literary Experts in Plagiarism Trials, 7 *Am. U. L. Rev.* 55 (1958)
Guido Calabresi & A. Douglas Melamed, Property Rules, Liability Rules and Inalienability: One View of the Cathedral, 86 *Harv. L. Rev.* 1089 (1972)
Kelly Casey Mullally, Blocking Copyrights Revisited, 37 *Colum. J.L. & Arts* 57 (2013)

Ivonne Chand & Mark A. Runco, Problem Finding Skills as Components in the Creative Process, 14 *Personality & Individual Differences* 155 (1993)

Bernard Chao, The Infringement Continuum, 35 *Cardozo L. Rev.* 1359(2014)

Julie E. Cohen, Creativity and Culture in Copyright Theory, 40 *U.C. Davis L. Rev.* 1151 (2007)

David Collins, *A Synthesis Process Model of Creative Thinking in Music Composition*, 33 *Psychol. Music* 193 (2005)

Robert Cooter, Stephen Marks & Robert Mnookin, Bargaining in the Shadow of the Law: A Testable Model of Strategic Behavior, 11 *J. Legal Stud.* 225 (1982)

Thomas F. Cotter, Fair Use and Copyright Overenforcement, 93 *Iowa L. Rev.* 1271, 1295 (2008)

Hanoch Dagan, *Property and the Public Domain*, 18 *Yale J.L. & Human.* 84 (2006)

Benjamin G. Damstedt, Note, Limiting Locke: A Natural Law Justification for the Fair Use Doctrine, 112 *Yale L.J.* 1179 (2003)

Nicholas Davis & Ellen Yi-Luen Do, Quantifying the Artistic Experience with Perceptive Sketching Tools: Cognitive Technologies to Support Creativity Researchers Social Process of Creation, 22 *Comunicacao e Sociedade* 76 (2012)

Ronan Deazley, Commentary on Dramatic Literary Property Act 1833, in *Primary Sources on Copyright (1450–1900)* (Lionel Bentley & Martin Kretschmer eds, 2008)

Jacques Derrida, The Law of Genre, 7 *Crit. Inq.* 55 (1980)

Nicholas Diakopoulos, Kurt Luther, Yevgeniy "Eugene" Medynskiy & Irfan Essa, The Evolution of Authorship in a Remix Society, *Proceedings of the Eighteenth Conference on Hypertext and Hypermedia* 133 (Simon Harper *et al.* eds, 2007)

Peter Dicola, An Economic View of Legal Restrictions on Musical Borrowing and Appropriation, in *Making and Unmaking Intellectual Property* 235 (Mario Biagioli, Peter Jaszi & Martha Woodmansee eds, 2011)

Adolf Dietz, Germany, in *International Copyright Law and Practice* (Paul Edward Geller ed., 2014)

Abraham Drassinower, A Rights-Based View of the Idea/Expression Dichotomy in Copyright Law, 16 *Can. J.L. & Juris.* 1 (2003)

Abraham Drassinower, Taking User Rights Seriously, in *In the Public Interest: The Future of Canadian Copyright Law* 462 (2005)

Daralyn J. Durie & Mark A. Lemley, A Structured Approach to Calculating Reasonable Royalties, 14 *Lewis & Clark L. Rev.* 627 (2010)

Ronald Dworkin, Rights as Trumps, in *Theories of Rights* 153 (Jeremy Wadron ed., 1984)

Paul Edward Geller, Copyright in Crisis: Principles for Change, 56 *J. Copyright Soc'y U.S.A.* 165 (2008)

Paul Edward Geller, Hiroshige vs. Van Gogh: Resolving the Dilemma of Copyright Scope in Remedying Infringement, 46 *J. Copyright Soc'y U.S.A.* 39 (1998)

Niva Elkin-Koren, Cyberlaw and Social Change: A Democratic Approach to Copyright Law in Cyberspace, 14 *Cardozo Arts & Ent. L.J.* 215 (1996)

Melissa Ellamil *et al.*, Evaluative and Generative Modes of Thought during the Creative Process, 59 *Neuroimage* 1783 (2012)

Richard H. Fallon, Jr., Daniel J. Meltzer, New Law, Non-Retroactivity, and Constitutional Remedies, 104 *Harv. L. Rev.* 1731 (1990)

Andreas Fink & Mathias Benedek, EEG Alpha Power and Creative Ideation, 44 *Neuroscience & Biobehavioral Rev.* 111 (2014)

William Fisher, Theories of Intellectual Property, in *New Essays in the Legal and Political Theory of Property* 168 (Stephen R. Munzer ed., 2001)

Joseph P. Fishman, Creating Around Copyright, 128 *Harv. L. Rev.* 1333 (2015)
Orit Fishman-Afori, Flexible Remedies as a Means to Counteract Failures in Copyright Law, 29 *Cardozo Arts & Ent. L.J.* 1 (2010)
Owen M. Fiss, Foreword: The Forms of Justice, 93 *Harv. L. Rev.* 1 (1979)
Jeanne C. Fromer, A Psychology of Intellectual Property, 104 *Nw. U. L. Rev.* 1441 (2010)
Daniel Friedman, Rights and Remedies, in *Comparative Remedies for Breach of Contract* 3 (Nili Cohen & Ewan Mckendrick eds 2005)
Liane Gabora, Revenge of the "Neurds": Characterizing Creative Thought in Terms of the Structure and Dynamics of Memory, 22 *Creativity Res. J.* 1 (2010)
Daniel Gervais, The Derivative Right: Or Why Copyright Law Protects Foxes Better Than Hedgehogs, 15 *Van. J. Ent. & Tech. L.* 785 (2013)
Shubha Ghosh, Market Entry and the Proper Scope of Copyright, 12 *Int'l J. Econ. & Bus.* 347, 351 (2005)
James Gibson, Risk Aversion and Rights Accretion in Intellectual Property Law, 116 *Yale L.J.* 882 (2007)
Jane C. Ginsburg, Have Moral Rights Come of (Digital) Age in the United States, 19 *Cardozo Arts & Ent. L.J.* 9 (2001)
Jane C. Ginsburg, Creation and Commercial Value: Copyright Protection of Works of Information, 90 *Colum. L. Rev.* 1865 (1990)
Paul Goldstein, Derivative Rights and Derivative Works in Copyright, 30 *J. Copyright Society U.S.A.* 209 (1983)
Wendy J. Gordon, Toward a Jurisprudence of Benefits: The Norms of Copyright and the Problem of Private Censorship, 57 *U. Chi. L. Rev.* 1009 (1990)
Wendy J. Gordon, A Property Right in Self-Expression: Equality and Individualism in the Natural Law of Intellectual Property, 102 *Yale L.J.* 1533 (1993)
George Grella, Murder and Manners: The Formal Detective Novel, 4 *Novel: A Forum on Fiction* 30 (1970)
Jean Grondin, Gadamer's Basic Understanding of Understanding, in *The Cambridge Companion to Gadamer* 36 (Robert J. Dostal ed., 2002)
Philip A. Gunderson, Danger Mouse's Grey Album, Mash-Ups, and the Age of Composition, 15(1) *Postmodern Culture* (2004)
Orrin G. Hatch, Better Late than Never: Implementation of the 1886 Berne Convention, 22 *Cornell Int'l L.J.* 171(1989)
John R. Hayes. Cognitive Processes in Creativity, in *Handbook of Creativity* 202 (J.A. Glover, R.R. Roning & C.R. Reynolds eds, 1989)
Edwin C. Hettinger, Justifying Intellectual Property, 18 *Phil. & Pub. Affairs* 31 (1989)
Wesley Newcomb Hohfeld, Fundamental Legal Conceptions as Applied in Judicial Reasoning, 26 *Yale L.J.* 710 (1917)
Oliver W. Holmes, The Path of Law, 10 *Harv. L. Rev.* 457 (1897)
A.M. Honorè, Ownership, in *Oxford Essays in Jurisprudence* 370 (A.G. Guest ed., 1961)
A.M. Honorè, Property, Title and Redistribution, in *Philosophy of Law: Classic and Contemporary Readings* 263 (1977) (Larry May & Jeff Brow eds, 2010)
Justin Hughes, The Philosophy of Intellectual Property, 77 *Geo. L.J.* 287 (1988)
Gordon Hull, Clearing the Rubbish: Locke, the Waste Proviso, and the Moral Justification of Intellectual Property, 23 *Pub. Affairs Q.* 67 (2009)
Robert M. Hurt and Robert M. Schuchman, The Economic Rationale of Copyright, 56 *Am. Econ. Rev.* 421 (1966)
Osnat Jacobi & Avi Weiss, *Law Design: Methodology* (working paper 2015)

Peter Jaszi, The Author Effect II, in *The Construction of Authorship* 29 (Martha Woodmansee & Peter Jaszi eds, 1994)

P.N. Johnson-Laird, How Jazz Musicians Improvise, 19 *Music Perception* 415 (2002)

Immanuel Kant, The Metaphysics of Morals, in *Practical Philosophy* (Mary J. Gregor trans. & ed., 1996) (1797)

Immanuel Kant, On the Wrongfulness of Unauthorized Publication of Books, in *Practical Philosophy* (1785) (Mary J. Gregor trans. & ed., 1996)

Matthew A. Kaplan, Rosencrantz and Guildenstern Are Dead, But Are They Copyrightable: Protection of Literary Characters with Respect to Secondary Works, 30 *Rutgers L.J.* 817 (1999)

Aaron Kozbelt, Ronald A. Beghetto & Mark A. Runco, Theories of Creativity, in *The Cambridge Handbook of Creativity* 20 (James C. Kaufman & Robert J. Sternberg eds, 2010)

Daryl J. Levinson, Rights Essentialism and Remedial Equilibration, 99 *Colum. L. Rev.* 857 (1999)

Karl L. Llewellyn, A Realistic Jurisprudence, in *Jurisprudence: Realism in Theory and Practice* 3 (1962)

Karl L. Llewellyn, Some Realism about Realism, in *Jurisprudence: Realism in Theory and Practice* 42 (1962)

William M. Landes & Richard A. Posner, An Economic Analysis of Copyright Law, 18 *J. Legal Stud.* 325 (1989)

Pat Langley & Randolph Jones, A Computational Model of Scientific Insight, in *The Nature of Creativity* 177 (Robert J. Sternberg ed., 1988)

Alan Latman, "Probative Similarity" as Proof of Copying: Toward Dispelling Some Myths in Copyright Infringement, 90 *Colum. L. Rev.* 1187 (1990)

Diane Leenheer Zimmerman, Is There a Right to Have Something to Say – One View of the Public Domain, 73 *Fordham L. Rev.* 297 (2004)

Mark A. Lemley, The Economics of Improvement in Intellectual Property Law, 75 *Tex. L. Rev.* 989 (1997)

Mark A. Lemley, Contracting around Liability Rules, 100 *Cal. L. Rev.* 463 (2012)

Mark A. Lemley, Intellectual Property Rights and Standard-Setting Organizations, 90 *Cal. L. Rev.* 1889 (2002)

Mark A. Lemley & Mark P. Mckenna, Scope, 57 *William & Mary L. Rev.* 2197 (2016)

Mark A. Lemley, Economics of Improvement in Intellectual Property Law, 75 *Tex. L. Rev.* 989 (1997)

Pierre N. Leval, Toward a Fair Use Standard, 103 *Harv. L. Rev.* 1105 (1990)

Yafit Lev-Aretz, The Subtle Incentive Theory of Copyright Licensing, 80 *Brook. L. Rev.* 1357 (2015)

Stan J. Liebowitz & Stephen Margolis, Seventeen Famous Economists Weigh in on Copyright: The Role of Theory, Empirics, and Network Effects, 18 *Harv. J.L. & Tech.* 435 (2005)

Stan J. Liebowitz, Copyright Law, Photocopying, and Price Discrimination, in 8 *Research in Law and Economics: The Economics of Patents and Copyrights* 181 (John Palmer & Richard O. Zerbe, Jr. eds, 1986)

Jessica Litman, The Public Domain, 39 *Emory L.J.* 965 (1990)

Jiarui Liu, Copyright Injunctions after eBay: An Empirical Study, 16 *Lewis & Clark L. Rev.* 215 (2012)

Paul J. Locher, How Does a Visual Artist Create an Artwork, in *The Cambridge Handbook of Creativity* 131 (James C. Kaufman & Robert J. Sternberg eds, 2010)

John Locke, Liberty of the Press (1695), reprinted in *Locke: Political Essays 329* (Mark Goldie ed., 1997)
Todd I. Lubart, Models of the Creative Process: Past, Present and Future, 13 *Creativity Res. J.* 295 (2001)
Todd I. Lubart, Componential Models, in 1 *Encyclopedia of Creativity* 295 (Mark A. Runco & Steven R. Pritzker eds, 1999)
André Lucas & Pascal Kamina, France, in *International Copyright Law and Practice* (Paul Edward Geller ed., 2014)
Glynn S. Lunney, Reexamining Copyright's Incentives-Access Paradigm, 49 *Vand. L. Rev.* 483 (1996)
Mary-Anne Mace & Tony Ward, Modeling the Creative Process: A Grounded Theory Analysis of Creativity in the Domain of Art Making, 14 *Creativity Res. J.* 179 (2002)
Peter S. Menell, Adapting Copyright for the Mashup Generation, 164 *U. Penn. L. Rev.* 441(2016)
Robert P. Merges, A Brief Note on Blocking Patents and Reverse Equivalents: Biotechnology as an Example, 73 *J. Pat. & Trademark Off. Soc'y* 878 (1991)
Robert P. Merges, Intellectual Property Rights and Bargaining Breakdown: The Case of Blocking Patents, 62 *Tenn. L. Rev.* 75 (1994)
Robert P. Merges & Richard R. Nelson, On the Complex Economics of Patent Scope, 90 *Colum. L. Rev.* 839 (1990)
Carolyn R. Miller, Genre as a Social Action, 70 *Q.J. Speech* 151 (1984)
Michele I. Mobley *et al.*, Process Analytic Models of Creative Capacities: Evidence for the Combination and Reorganization Process, 5 *Creativity Res. J.* 125 (1992)
Sandra E. Moriarty& Bruce G. Vandenbergh, Advertising Creatives Look at Creativity, 18 *J. Creative Behav.* 162 (1984)
Robert J. Morrison, Derivers' Licenses: An Argument for Establishing a Statutory License for Derivative Works, 6 *Chi.-Kent J. Intell. Prop.* 87 (2006)
Eduardo Navas, Regressive and Reflexive Mashups in Sampling Culture, in *Mashup Cultures* 157 (Stefan Sonvilla-Weiss ed., 2010)
Neil Netanel, Copyright Alienability Restrictions, 24 *Rutgers L.J.* 374 (1993)
Neil W. Netanel, Copyright and a Democratic Civil Society, 106 *Yale L.J.* 283 (1996)
Allen Newell*et al.*, The Processes of Creative Thinking, in *Contemporary Approaches to Creative Thinking* 62, 78 (Howard E. Gruber, Glenn Terrell & Michael Wertheimer eds, 1962)
Chris Newman, Transformation in Property and Copyright, 56 *Vill. L. Rev.* 251 (2011)
Tyler Ochoa, Copyright, Derivative Works, and Fixation: Is Galoob a Mirage or Does the Form(Gen) of the Alleged Derivative Work Matter?, 20 *Santa Clara Comp. & High Tech. L.J.* 991 (2004)
Patrick W. Ogilvy, Frozen in Time? New Technologies, Fixation, and the Derivative Work Right, 8 *Vand. J. Ent. & Tech. L.* 687 (2006)
Paul W. Orth, The Use of Expert Witnesses in Musical Infringement Cases, 16 *U. Pitt. L. Rev.* 232 (1955)
Lydia Pallas Loren, The Pope's Copyright - Aligning Incentives with Reality by Using Creative Motivation to Shape Copyright Protection, 69 *La. L. Rev.* 1 (2008)
Lydia Pallas Loren, The Changing Nature of Derivative Works in the Face of New Technologies, 4 *J. Small & Emerging Bus. L.* 57 (2000)
Omri Rachum-Twaig & Ohad Somech, The Right-Based View of the Cathedral: Liability Rules and Corrective Justice, 2017 *Pepperdine L. Rev* 463 (2017)
Margaret Jane Radin, Property and Personhood, 34 *Stan. L. Rev.* 957 (1982)

R. Anthony Reese, Transformativeness and the Derivative Work Right, 31 *Colum. J.L. & Arts* 467 (2007)

Jason S. Rooks, Constitutionality of Judicially-Imposed Compulsory Licenses in Copyright Infringement Cases, 3 *J. Intell. Prop. L.* 255 (1995)

Roberta Rosenthal Kwall, Copyright and the Moral Right: Is an American Marriage Possible, 38 *Vand. L. Rev.* 1 (1985)

Jed Rubinfeld, Freedom of Imagination: Copyright's Constitutionality, 112 *Yale L.J.* 1 (2002)

Mark A. Runco & Ivonne Chand, Cognition and Creativity, 7 *Edu. Psych. Rev.* 243 (1995)

M.A. Runco & S. M. Okuda, The Instructional Enhancement of the Flexibility and Originality Scores of Divergent Thinking Tests, 5 *Applied Cognitive Psych.* 435 (1991)

Mark A. Runco, Maximal Performance on Divergent Thinking Tests by Gifted, Talented, and Nongifted Children, 23 *Psych. Schools* 308 (1986)

Matthew Sag, Predicting Fair Use, 73 *Ohio St. L.J.* 47 (2012)

Pamela Samuelson, The Quest for a Sound Conception of Copyright's Derivative Work Right, 101 *Geo. L.J.* 1505 (2013)

Pamela Samuelson, Possible Futures of Fair Use, 90 *Wash. L. Rev.* 815 (2015)

Keith Sawyer, The Cognitive Neuroscience of Creativity: A Critical Review, 23 *Creativity Res. J.* 137 (2011)

Robert C. Schank, Creativity as a Mechanical Process, in *The Nature of Creativity* 220 (R.J. Sternberg ed., 1988)

Molly Shaffer Van Houweling, Distributive Values in Copyright, 83 *Tex. L. Rev.* 1535 (2005)

Seana Shiffrin, Lockean Arguments for Intellectual Property, in *New Essays in the Legal and Political Theory of Property* 139 (Stephen R. Munzer ed., 2001)

John Shiga, Copy-and-Persist: The Logic of Mash-Up Culture, 24 *Critical Stud. Media Comm.* 93 (2007)

Michal Shur-Ofry, The (Copyright) Law of Genre: A Network Perspective on Copyright Protection of Cultural Genres, 2 *Fa. Ent. L. Rev.* 60 (2008)

Michal Shur-Ofry, Popularity as a Factor in Copyright Law, 59 *U. Toronto L.J.* 525 (2009)

Simon Sidney Teiser, Is Doyle a Plagiarist?, 44 *U. Va. Magazine* 468(1901)

Ned Snow, The Regressing Progress Clause: Rethinking Constitutional Indifference to Harmful Content in Copyright, 47 *U.C. Davis L. Rev. 1*, 40 (2013)

Robert L. Solso, Brain Activities in a Skilled versus a Novice Artist: An fMRI Study, 34 *Leonardo* 31 (2001)

Christopher Jon Sprigman, Copyright and Creative Incentives: What We Know (and Don't), 55 *Houston L. Rev.* 451 (2017)

Stewart Sterk, Rhetoric and Reality in Copyright Law, 94 *Mich. L. Rev.* 1197 (1996)

Robert J. Sternberg, A Three-Facet Model of Creativity, in *The Nature of Creativity* 125 (Robert J. Sternberg ed., 1988)

Peter G. Stillman, Property, Contract, and Ethical Life in Hegel's Philosophy of Right, in *Hegel and Legal Theory* 205 (Drucila Cornell, Michel Rosenfeld & David Gray Carlson eds, 1991)

John R. Suler, Primary Process Thinking and Creativity, 88 *Psych. Bulletin* 144 (1980)

John Swales, On Models of Applied Discourse Analysis, in *Research and Practice in Professional Discourse* 61 (C.N. Candlin ed., 2002)

John Tehrainian, Whither Copyright – Transformative Use, Free Speech, and an Intermediate Liability Proposal, 2005 *BYU L. Rev.* 1201 (2005)

Kim Treiger-Bar-Am, Kant on Copyright: Rights on Transformative Authorship, 25 *Cardozo Arts & Ent. L.J.* 1059 (2008)

Rebecca Tushnet, Content, Purpose, or Both, 90 *Wash. L. Rev.* 869 (2015)

Naomi Abe Voegtli, Rethinking Derivative Rights, 63 *Brook. L. Rev.* 1213 (1997)

Sungsoon Wang, Text Types and Dynamism of Genres, in *Discourse, of Course: An Overview of Research in Discourse Studies* 81 (Jan Renkema ed., 2009)

Yingxu Wang & Vincent Chiew, On the Cognitive Process of Human Problem Solving, 11 *Cognitive Sys. Res.* 81 (2010)

Yingxu Wang, On Cognitive Foundations of Creativity and the Cognitive Process of Creation, 3 *Int'l J. Cognitive Informatics & Nat. Intelligence* 1 (2009)

Thomas B. Ward, Structured Imagination: The Role of Category Structure in Exemplar Generation, 27 *Cognitive Psych.* 1 (1994)

Thomas B. Ward, What's Old about New Ideas?, in *The Creative Cognition Approach* 157 (Steven M. Smith, Thomas B. Ward and Ronald A. Finke eds, 1995)

Thomas B. Ward & Yuliya Kolomyts, Cognition and Creativity, in *The Cambridge Handbook of Creativity* 93 (James C. Kaufman & Robert J. Sternberg eds, 2010)

Thomas B. Ward, Steven M. Smith & Ronald A. Finke, Creative Cognition, in *Handbook of Creativity* 189 (Robert J. Sternberg ed., 1999)

Neil Weinstock Netanel, Impose A Noncommercial Use Levy to Allow Free Peer-To-Peer File Sharing, 17 *Harv. J.L. & Tech.* 1 (2003)

Neil Weinstock Netanel, Making Sense of Fair Use, 15 *Lewis & Clark L. Rev.* 715 (2011)

Robert W. Weisberg, Creativity and Knowledge: A Challenge to Theories, in *Handbook of Creativity* 226 (Robert J. Sternberg ed., 1999)

Robert W. Weisberg, Problem Solving and Creativity, in *The Nature of Creativity* 148 (Robert J. Sternberg ed., 1988)

Robert W. Weisberg, Case Studies of Creative Thinking: Reproduction versus Restructuring in the Real World, in The Creative Cognition Approach 53 (Steven M. Smith, Thomas B. Ward & Ronald A. Finke eds, 1995)

Tim Wu, Tolerated Uses, 31 *Colum. J.L. & Arts* 617 (2008)

Alfred C. Yen, Restoring the Natural Law: Copyright as Labor and Possession, 51 *Oh. St. L.J.* 517 (1990)

Sawako Yokochi & Takeshi Okada, Creative Cognitive Process of Art Making: A Field Study of a Traditional Chinese Ink Painter, 17 *Creativity Res. J.* 241 (2005)

Christopher S. Yoo, Copyright and Product Differentiation, 79 *N.Y.U. L. Rev.* 212 (2004)

Sureyya Yoruk & Mark A. Runco, The Neuroscience of Divergent Thinking, 56 *Activitas Nervosa Superior* 1 (2014)

Lior Zemer, The Making of New Copyright Lockean, 29 *Harv. J.L. & Pub. Pol'y* 891 (2006)

Huimin Zheng, Jiayi Luo & Rongjun Yu, From Memory to Prospection: What Are the Overlapping and the Distinct Components between Remembering and Imagining?, 5 *Frontiers Psy.* 1 (2014)

Index

For Product Safety Concerns and Information please contact our EU representative GPSR@taylorandfrancis.com
Taylor & Francis Verlag GmbH, Kaufingerstraße 24, 80331 München, Germany

www.ingramcontent.com/pod-product-compliance
Ingram Content Group UK Ltd.
Pitfield, Milton Keynes, MK11 3LW, UK
UKHW021303190926
475701UK00009B/641
* 9 7 8 0 3 6 7 5 8 3 5 0 7 *